A NEOCLASSICAL ANALYSIS OF MACROECONOMIC POLICY

A neoclassical analysis
of macroeconomic policy

Michael Beenstock

Cambridge University Press
Cambridge
London   New York   New Rochelle
Melbourne   Sydney

Published by the Press Syndicate of the University of Cambridge
The Pitt Building, Trumpington Street, Cambridge CB2 1RP
32 East 57th Street, New York, NY 10022, USA
296 Beaconsfield Parade, Middle Park, Melbourne 3206, Australia

First published 1980

Typeset by ⊞H Charlesworth & Co Ltd, Huddersfield
Printed in Great Britain at the University Press, Cambridge

British Library Cataloguing in Publication Data
Beenstock, Michael
A neoclassical analysis of macroeconomic policy.
1. Economic policy
2. Macroeconomics
I. Title
339   HD82   79-41795

ISBN 0 521 23077 2

CONTENTS

Contents

PREFACE

This book has been written in the belief that the 1970s will mark an important threshold in the history of macroeconomic thought and practice. If 1936, the year Keynes published *The General Theory*, serves as the landmark for the interventionist theory of macroeconomic policy, the 1970s may well be regarded as the decade in which this theory went into decline and a new era was begun. However, instead of a revolutionary change with all the glamor and controversy that this connotes, the 1970s wrought perhaps a more gentle rupture with the past; but a rupture that has as much policy significance as its precursor.

I speak here of the theoretical discovery that expectations and their formation are of major normative significance in policy analysis and in particular of the implications of the rational expectations hypothesis for evaluating macroeconomic policy. I also speak of the practical discovery that 'Keynesian' stabilization policies have been increasingly disappointing and at times even counterproductive. But the intellectual and practical watersheds that appear to have been reached also appear to have laid the ground-rules for their own resolution in a mutually reinforcing way. Perhaps this is no coincidence; the practical men have indeed been influenced by the academic scribblers, but they in turn have distilled and given form to the anxieties of the time.

This essay summarizes and clarifies these new developments and juxtaposes them with the previous conventional wisdom. It integrates them under a unifying framework that is essentially neoclassical so that it is possible to speak of a neoclassical theory of macroeconomic policy. This theory is self-contained and in specifying a static and dynamic form of macroeconomic behavior offers a normative as well as a positive basis for evaluating macroeconomic policy.

During the course of writing this book numerous policy changes have occurred, especially in the UK, which are in the spirit of the analysis that is developed. Not only has there been an abandonment of Keynesian style fine-tuning and a realization of the importance of monetary and financial policy especially in the context of inflation, but the role of expectations has also seen more appreciation by the authorities. Indeed, at the time of writing exchange controls (see Chapter 5) have been abandoned and the government has announced a medium term financial plan.

The detailed exposition requires an understanding of the rudiments of linear algebra and dynamic analysis and therefore does not transcend the mathematics that most undergraduate students are taught nowadays. However, the appendix summarizes the rudiments that are required for the present purposes, and a list of symbols used repeatedly in the text is provided.

In writing this book I have received a great deal of advice (often conflicting) both written and oral from numerous professional colleagues. In this regard I would particularly like to thank Andrew Britton, Alan Budd, Terry Burns, Sean Holly, Patrick Minford, Hyman Minsky and John Williamson. It would have been neither possible nor appropriate to satisfy all the parties concerned and I alone remain responsible for the work as a whole. Finally I would like to thank Roko Morith and Bunty King for their efficiency and forbearance in typing the initial and final drafts respectively.

London Business School
March 1980

LIST OF SYMBOLS AND TERMS

This list includes only those variables to which reference is repeatedly made in Chapters 3 through 7.

B	Stock of bonds (domestic)
B_f	Foreigners' net holdings of domestic bonds
B_w	Residents' net holdings of overseas bonds
C	Domestic credit expansion
DD	Domestic demand
e	Expected value of variable – e.g. S^e is the expected exchange rate
G	Government expenditure at constant prices
I	Import volume
K	Net capital inflow on the balance of payments
L	Employment
M	Money supply
MG	Model consisting of money and goods
MBG	Model consisting of money, bonds and goods
$MGEFB$	Model consisting of money, goods, employment, foreign exchange and bonds
P	General price index
P_d	Price index for non-exportable output
P_m	Price index for imports in foreign currency
P_x	Price index for exportables in domestic currency
P_{xw}	Index for export prices overseas measured in foreign currency
r	Domestic rate of interest
r_w	Overseas rate of interest
R	Borrowing requirement of the government (Occasionally used in Chapter 7 to denote the real rate of interest)
REH	Rational expectations hypothesis
S	Exchange rate index – units of foreign currency per unit of domestic currency
t	Time
T	Income tax rate (Occasionally used to denote current account of

	balance of payments and volume of transactions)
V	Value added tax rate
W	Nominal wage rate
w	Real wage rate
X	Exportable output
X_w^d	Volume of exports
Y	Domestic output
$\bar{Y}$	Full-employment level of output, or level of output consistent with the 'natural' rate of unemployment
Y_w	Index of overseas economic activity
Z	Index of net balance of payments surplus or change in reserves

Unless otherwise stated, these symbols are logarithms

CHAPTER 1

Some recent trends in macroeconomic theory and policy

The basic issue

This book is largely concerned with the theory of macroeconomic policy and especially the case for activist or discretionary policies on the part of the respective authorities with regard to the macroeconomy. Although the degree may vary, activist macroeconomic policies are a standard feature of daily life and it would seem that in one form or another the history of intervention stretches back as far as the historical eye can see. Each day we hear and read how monetary policy has been altered or how fiscal policy might be geared to various economic aggregates such as unemployment or the balance of payments. Or foreign exchange policy may be the focus of attention, and, although it is not generally made public knowledge, the monetary authorities may vary their spot and forward market intervention from one hour to the next.

The instruments of macroeconomic intervention are many. Traditionally, these have included a range of open market operations in relation to various markets such as the markets for bonds, foreign exchange and goods. In addition, the right to tax has conferred an important macroeconomic role on fiscal policy and there are, of course, many different types of fiscal initiative. In this essay our concern is not with the details of these various intervention policies but with the more general question of whether macroeconomic intervention is justified or not. Alternatively, when the authorities actively intervene, what are they in fact doing and what is it likely to achieve? In the case of microeconomic intervention such as a subsidy to ship-building or a grant to New York City the welfare criteria are usually fairly well known in terms of the outputs involved and the beneficiaries that are concerned. Indeed they are usually so well known as to be the cause of political friction. But not so at the macroeconomic level; an open market operation or the purchase of forward exchange does not usually excite sectional political interests and the political interest in fiscal and monetary policy in general is not usually of a sectional nature.

So what are the criteria for assessing whether an open market operation is desirable, whether the public is likely to benefit from a tax cut or whether foreign exchange policies are in the public interest? Our assumption throughout will be that the government as the initiator of the intervention acts in the public interest and, since ultimately it has to finance its operations out of taxation, it is appropriate to ask whether the tax-payer is getting value for money. Or is it the case that the range of intervention weapons are like so many toys to the policy makers who play the various markets with financial immunity because it is the tax-payer who will have to bear the consequences of their poor and even extravagant judgments? Indeed there is an obvious danger that like anything else, discretionary policies can become institutionalized or even a habit; once a precedent has been set for influencing say the exchange rate it is often difficult to dismantle the administrative apparatus upon which such policies are based long after they have become obsolescent. Indeed the sociology of policy formation may perhaps even be carried a stage further in so far as individual officials may identify themselves with particular jobs that are based on intervention in various aspects of the macroeconomy and who feel that they are not earning their salary if they are not seen to be intervening.

Fascinating though it may be, the sociology and political economy of policy formation are beyond the mandate of the present study and would clearly merit a treatment in their own right. In the meanwhile we note the unavoidable political dimension of the task that is in hand and the need to question the legitimacy in terms of social welfare of what at times seems to be accepted as a matter of daily routine – the practice of discretionary macroeconomic intervention. Clearly, the conclusion that there should be no discretionary intervention would raise an array of major political questions in view of the fact that most governments in the mature capitalist economies see themselves as the guardians of 'full-employment', price stability and the balance of payments. To claim that their guardianship was unnecessary or even counter-productive could create an identity or role crisis not only for themselves but for the public servants and institutions that serve as the instruments of this guardianship. On the other hand it may merely be the case that our economic analysis leads us to conclude that some discretionary or activist intervention is desirable, and, even if in practice actual policies have not necessarily been conceived in terms of the principles that will be developed, this is less of a politically embarrassing conclusion than that governments do not have an activist macroeconomic function. However, the main theoretical deductions in this study will lend support to the view that discretionary macroeconomic policies are on the whole undesirable. Alternatively, we seek to identify the set of circumstances under which the opposite and conventional view would be warranted. In principle, it would then be an empirical matter whether or not these circumstances in fact prevailed.

In this essay the subject matter is essentially theoretical, although from time to time, as seems appropriate, empirical instances will be cited to illustrate the plausibility of some of the assumptions, especially in relation to the formation of expectations, which is considered to be a crucial component of the discussion. A set of theoretical propositions that are empirically uncorroborated, it will be rightly agreed, are an inadequate basis for practical action. On the other hand the criteria for corroboration in economics raise a number of conceptual problems in their own right. At what point does the applied econometrician say that his hypothesis has finally been falsified and that there is no point in trying out new proxies for the various unobservables in his model, different polynomials and truncation points on the distributed lags, more complex transformations to circumvent multicollinearity and all the paraphernalia which have earned the sometimes unwarranted but unpleasant collective title of 'data mining'? In practice the lines between falsification and corroboration are difficult to draw in which case (as we have seen from time to time) two competing hypotheses may be both corroborated and falsified in their respective proponent's estimation and the referee who is caught in the middle can do very little methodologically speaking to establish where the balance of the evidence lies.

It is no doubt much to do with this reason that economic policy tends to be such an argumentative subject. Where the physicist on the basis of controlled experiments discards false hypotheses and resumes his search for the truth with methodological confidence and fortitude, the economist is never sure where his ideas stand in relation to the real world. Under such circumstances a priori argumentation assumes a special importance in economic policy formation; our theoretical structures have to be as plausible as possible and it is often the most intuitive and logically conceived of these structures that carries the day.

Consequently, while our subject matter is essentially theoretical, its relevance to the politics of policy formation is immediate enough. Ideally, of course, it would be desirable to test out the hypotheses to be suggested. but this would form the subject matter of a separate study, and for the reasons that have already been stated it would be difficult to discover uncontrovertible econometric evidence. However, our main theoretical conclusion that discretionary macroeconomic policies are on the whole undesirable rests on two crucial propositions, which are:

(i) In the long run excess demands will be eliminated.

(ii) Expectations regarding future macroeconomic aggregates are formed rationally (in the sense defined in Chapter 6).

If either of these assumptions are invalid there will be a strong prima-facie case for activist or discretionary macroeconomic policies of the familiar kind. As we shall see in Chapter 2, Keynes discarded both these assumptions in the *General Theory* and it is most probably no coincidence that, subsequently, activist macroeconomic policies have more or less been the order of the day. In contrast this book is concerned with the demonstration of these two propositions. If indeed the first proposition is accepted and if, as seems reasonable, we assume that all men are rational (or at least form their expectations rationally) until proven otherwise, we may reasonably conclude that discretionary policies may be at best ineffective and at worst disequilibrating. This would throw the burden of proof onto those who claim that discretionary policies are desirable rather than the other way around.

Neoclassical principles

As the title piece of this essay implies, considerable importance is attached to neoclassical principles of economic analysis. In the present context this entails two related considerations which underpin the two crucial propositions just cited and which are necessary for undermining the role of discretionary macroeconomic policies. The first consideration is that macroeconomic markets exist; that is for money, bonds, goods, labour, exports, foreign exchange etc. there is a supply curve, a demand curve and a price which will balance supply and demand in the short and long terms. Naturally all these markets will be interrelated so that factors that bear upon one market will tend to influence other markets via these relationships. Indeed, in Chapter 3 it is shown how macroeconomic models may be considered as a set of such inter-related markets.

An anti-neoclassical position implies that supply and demand do not depend upon price and rejects the market approach to economic analysis. Adjustments are then assumed to occur, if at all, via non-price mechanisms which may or may not be stable and that it is quite possible for imbalances between supply and demand to persist even in the long run. An example of anti-neoclassical economics is the popular view of Keynesian theory that aggregate demand does not depend upon price signals but only on quantity adjustments such as the level of economic activity. According to this view excess supplies of labor and goods may persist even in the long run because price cutting will be ineffective. Clearly, whether the price mechanism works or not has major implications for political economy.

The position taken in this essay is that markets indeed exist; however, quantity adjustments may be influential in the short run but not in the long run. It is in this sense that the analysis is neoclassical – supply and demand are balanced in the long run since price adjustments dominate. In the short run imbalances are allowed to exist but this reflects the functioning of markets under uncertainty and in a world which is essentially stochastic. Thus resources may be unemployed because of unforeseeable random events or because market participants are speculating that by holding resources off the market today they will get a better return tomorrow. It will be argued that such considerations will cause prices and quantities to deviate from their long run equilibrium values.

Malinvaud [1977] has proposed that it makes little sense to speak of these short term developments as disequilibrium situations and that it is merely necessary to distinguish between short term equilibrium on the one hand and long term equilibrium on the other. A short term equilibrium is essentially transient since it is no more than a snapshot of the economy as it tends to its long run solution. In contrast a long run equilibrium is permanent in the sense that once the economy has reached this state it will be at rest. However, in this essay we refer to short run equilibria as disequilibrium states in the sense that they will not persist over time; clearly the issue is merely semantic.

But what is the normative status of such disequilibrium states; is disequilibrium alone a prima facie case for government stabilization? To answer this requires an analysis of the economics of disequilibrium states - which brings us to the second consideration - suggested by neoclassical principles. Optimization is a fundamental neoclassical principle upon which the theory of supply and demand is based. Costs are to be minimized, utility maximized and so on. Under stochastic assumptions the neoclassical principle is recast in terms of expected costs, utility, etc. and it is necessary to specify people's attitudes to risk and uncertainty; see e.g. Tobin [1958]. Although intellectual pedigree as such is obviously unimportant it may be claimed that rational expectations as conceived by Muth [1961] are neoclassical since they are based upon an optimal use of the information that is available. In Chapter 6 it is shown how short term behavior is affected by rational expectations and that this may be used to appraise the normative status of disequilibrium states. This constitutes a new perspective for evaluating the legitimacy of stabilization policies. When these two neoclassical propositions are combined, i.e. when macroeconomic markets are postulated and when individuals are assumed to form their expectations rationally under stochastic assumptions, it is possible to develop a neoclassical theory of macroeconomic policy.

Stabilization intervention and market failure

The principal criterion for government involvement that will be espoused in the present study is the presence of market failure. This too will be recognized as an endorsement of the neoclassical approach to policy formation. If there is no market failure the work of the 'hidden hand' will be optimal and government intervention will be unnecessary. On the other hand if there is market failure, e.g. as in the case of pollution, whale hunting etc., where there is divergence between private and social cost, it is the duty of government to intervene in the interests of society as a whole.

Familiar though this principle may be it is rarely if ever applied to macroeconomic policy formation although in microeconomic contexts it is a respected principle of political economy. In the next chapter it shall be argued that the theory of macroeconomic policy that arose out of Keynes' *General*

Theory was based on an orthodox analysis of market failure which seems to have been forgotten or simply not realized by Keynesian practitioners. An important theme of the present essay will therefore be the restoration of the principle of market failure as the basis for macroeconomic policy evaluation. In this sense macro- and microeconomic policies should be judged upon the same lines.

Market failure, as the previous section suggests, should be judged at two levels; with respect to the short run equilibrium or disequilibrium states and with respect to the long run equilibria. If either of these states are distorted by market failure there is a prima facie case for government involvement. If the former are distorted the disequilibrium behavior of the economy will be suboptimal and stabilization policies will be desirable so that the economy moves back to its optimal path. However, in this case no intervention is required with respect to the long run equilibrium since this does not suffer from any distortions. Conversely, if the latter are distorted it will be necessary for the authorities to intervene so as to equate the long run equilibrium to its socially optimal value while it will be unnecessary to stabilize the disequilibrium path since it is not distorted by market failure. If of course there is market failure with respect to both short and long term equilibria both stabilization and intervention will be required.

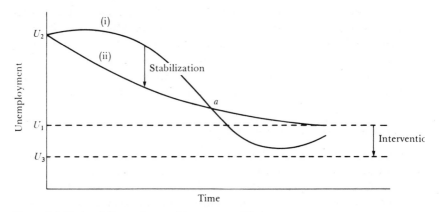

Figure 1-1 Market failure : short and long run equilibria

In fig. 1-1 the long run equilibrium level of unemployment is assumed to be U_1. If initially the economy is out of this equilibrium, say $U = U_2$, we consider two paths of short term equilibria. Curve (i) is assumed to be suboptimal while curve (ii) is assumed to be optimal. The role of the government is then to stabilize U around the path given by curve (ii). Thus, if left to the market, unemployment follows curve (i) and is initially too high and after a it is too low. If the long run equilibrium is optimally U_3 it will be necessary for the government to take measures to stimulate long run employment. In this study our main preoccupation is with stabilization rather than with long term intervention.

Some recent trends in macroeconomic policy

A re-appraisal of macroeconomic policy is timely for a number of reasons. Whereas a decade or so ago various commentators coined the phrase 'we are all Keynesians now', by the second half of the 1970s the confidence in activist macroeconomic policies that lay behind this claim has substantially waned, especially in relation to employment policies. Since 1972 Arthur F. Burns, the influential Chairman of the Board of Governors of the Federal Reserve System campaigned (successfully) for a monetary policy that was not counter-cyclical, a policy which has broadly been maintained by his successors. Likewise in the United Kingdom, Prime Minister Callaghan in an avuncular summary of this new political economy announced an important policy change[1]. 'We used to think that you could just spend your way out of a recession and increase employment by cutting taxes and boosting government spending. I tell you now in all candour that that option no longer exists, and that in so far as it ever did exist, it worked by injecting inflation into the economy.' And in the wake of this pronouncement British economic policy under the Chancellorship of Mr Healey assumed a monetarist complexion which set an entirely new tone to official thinking.

This development has become even more pronounced under Mrs Thatcher's administration and on repeated occasions (such as in the Budget Statements of 12 June 1979 and 26 March 1980) the role of demand management has been declared dead and buried.

In addition, the 'McCracken Report' [1977] which reviewed policies in relation to the international cyclical situation for the OECD countries did not press for vigorous counter-cyclical policies that would push the world economy speedily towards full-employment. On the contrary, the report took a very cautious line in this regard. Apart from macroeconomic policy developments in Britain and the United States, the policy stances in Germany and Japan have been relatively conservative and a cause for political rancor in the politics of international finance.

Thus macroeconomic policy itself, especially as far as domestic economic developments have been concerned, has been at an important cross-roads for some time. During this time there have been various experiments with direct controls on economic aggregates, especially incomes and prices but it has been so far generally accepted that such policies may only be applied temporarily, and any wage and price stability that these policies brought about has on the whole not endured. Indeed, as might be expected (in the light of the discussion in chapter 5) inflation has tended to resurge when the controls were relaxed. There have also been pressures to control the balance of payments by direct means in terms of import quotas but fears of retaliation have so far largely forestalled this tendency (although the developing countries have been confronted with protective barriers, e.g. restrictions on US shoe imports and EEC textile imports).

At this cross-roads, therefore, one of the options has been the 'controlled economy' where activist policies are extended beyond the range of the more traditional open market operations in the various markets that make up the macroeconomy. In the 'controlled economy' wages, prices, the balance of payments, investment and even consumption would ultimately be controlled directly by the authorities and not left to the market forces of even the so-called 'mixed economy'. The political implications that lie behind the concept of the 'controlled economy' have been realized to be very far reaching and inconsistent with the basic political principles of the western democracies. At least this has been the revealed preference so far.

At the same cross-roads in the 1930s the western democracies adopted the principles of activist macroeconomic policies in part because democracy and its preservation necessitated it. It is ironical that forty years on these same principles may have to be abandoned for the same reasons that they were accepted. It would of course, be premature to judge that any clear de facto trend was emerging on macroeconomic policy formation. Most probably the outcome will be to grope pragmatically for a less ambitious degree of activism which will be politically acceptable to those who believe that governments should be seen to govern and those who recognize that such government is unlikely to be in the public interest. Many of the arguments in this book may be regarded as a contribution to some of the intellectual issues that are at stake in this debate.

Apart from the cross-roads in relation to domestic stabilization policies, external stabilization policy has taken on a new dimension with the abandonment of the Bretton Woods System during the first part of the 1970s. The Bretton Woods System necessitated an extensive degree of government activism and intervention in the foreign exchange markets and recent years have witnessed the first tentative steps in floating exchange rates for many of the major currencies. It is common knowledge that most of these floats have been managed and that official intervention in the foreign exchanges has been substantial in many cases. Various attempts (mainly IMF initiatives) to restore a modified version of the Bretton Woods System have been rejected by the monetary authorities and at the present time there seems to be no prospect of such a modification being accepted in the future although from time to time the EEC countries have sought to fix exchange rates among themselves.

This leaves the question of how managed floating ought to be; or how activist this form of macroeconomic intervention should be. The de facto status quo seems to be that activist policies in this area are indeed desirable although, unlike domestic policies, foreign exchange policies tend to be more secretive and the debate consequently tends to be less overtly political than its domestic counterpart.

As with the debate on domestic economic policy, many of the arguments in this essay are concerned with the rationale for managed floating as against 'clean' or free floating. And as before the twin assumptions on page 3 suggest that free floating would be desirable.

Some recent theoretical trends

During the 1950s and the 1960s there were considerable efforts to extend and refine the theory of macroeconomic policy that was implicit in the Keynesian paradigm. A major statement of this theory may be found in Tinbergen [1956] where it was postulated that macroeconomic policy may be conceived as the assignment of a given array of policy instruments such as fiscal policy, monetary policy, etc. to the achievement of a given set of policy goals such as full employment, the balance of payments, etc. A given set of policy targets would require an equal number of policy instruments to be assigned to them; or so the theory went.

The 'assignment' theory of macroeconomic policy was essentially activist; as actual aggregates deviated from their target values the various authorities would change their policy mix to correct the course of the economy. While perhaps the 'assignment' theory has lost some of its sovereignty in academic circles, it is in many respects the conventional wisdom of the day; as part of the status quo it is necessary for its opponents to show where it is wrong while its proponents (so far) as the majority have not had to defend it with comparable fervor, although this may well be changing in a significant way.

With the advent of electronic computers and the age of the econometric model the 'assignment' theory has assumed a particular importance. It is possible to solve for the policy instruments that will satisfy a given set of policy goals in terms of the econometric model. In fact, it has not been quite as simple as this since, as the range of estimation of soft-ware expanded, it was found that dynamic models of economic behavior were more appropriate in which case the 'assignment' had to be solved for dynamically.

Most econometric policy advisors crank their models under different policy assumptions or scenarios and in a fairly ad hoc way juggle with the policy assumptions as best they can to attain a given set of desired values for the target aggregates. A recent but as yet rarely used addition to the soft-ware has been the application of optimal control theory to dynamic econometric models (e.g. Livesey [1971] and Pindyck [1973]) where the instruments are set to minimize the deviations from the target values through time since the lags prevent the simultaneous achievement of all the targets. But optimal control methods are no more than a useful way of doing one's sums in the context of assigning policy instruments and perhaps so far the principal drawback to the application of optimal control theory to large scale nonlinear econometric models is the expensive and difficult numerical methods involved in finding the optimal solutions.

The first major objection to the 'assignment' theory of macroeconomic policy was voiced by Friedman [1959, Chapter 4] who argued that activist or discretionary macroeconomic policy was undesirable since our knowledge about the way in which the economy works is generally too flimsy and that consequently the economy cannot be fine-tuned in the way that the 'assignment' theory implies.[2] Notice that the objection here is not that the 'assignment' approach is inherently harmful but that in practice it is difficult to implement and because we are unsure about the true response patterns of the economy it is considered a dangerous option in practice but presumably not in principle.

Therefore, Friedman advocated a fixed rule for monetary policy[3] – that instead of responding to the deviations from the target values the authorities should sit tight and adhere to a given growth path in money supply. According to Friedman this would guarantee the least deviations from the target values of full employment and price stability. Moreover, he contended that the discretionary policies themselves were to a large extent responsible for rocking the boat and causing the very deviations from the target values that they were designed to rectify.

In reply to this the 'assignment' camp could maintain that with stochastic optimal control theory it is possible to take account of the confidence intervals in their models and that the optimal discretionary policy would in principle reflect the considerations Friedman had in mind. It would only be necessary to eschew activist policies if all that we knew was the long run behavior of the economy and had no confidence at all in its dynamic or short term behavior. But few would accept that short term macroeconomic behavior is a complete enigma.

Consequently Friedman's rebuttal of the 'assignment' theory was certainly not general. It may or may not have been sound practical advice; it certainly was not the deduction of any clearly enunciated set of axioms.

In the last few years the 'assignment' theory has been questioned from a much more fundamental point of view. Indeed there may even be grounds for believing that it has been dealt the coup de grace in the shape of the application of rational expectations to macroeconomic policy discussion.

The rational expectations hypothesis was first suggested by Muth [1961] but for some inexplicable reason it was not until the 1970s that the integration of rational expectations into macroeconomic models was considered.[4] Indeed, prior to this, expectations in economic and econometric models had received a somewhat casual treatment. As it were, to close his model the hard-pressed econometrician would plug in one of the standard expectations hypotheses such as adaptive expectations (after Nerlove [1958]) or extrapolative expectations (e.g. Modigliani and Sutch [1966]) both of which implied that an expected value of a variable depended on its own past. This implied that the dynamic behavior of the model was affected by the precise form of the expectations hypothesis and that the economy could deviate from its target course on account of the influence of expectations. Indeed, an elastic expectations model could even be destabilizing.

This approach to expectations modeling, if anything, enhanced the 'assignment' theory since the authorities would have to offset any counterproductive speculative behavior (in terms of the target values); the market was considered to be taking an arbitrary and wrong view of the future and the social role of government was the familiar one of correcting for market distortions.

According to the rational expectations hypothesis, speculators are assumed to take the correct view of the future, or at least they try to forecast the future in terms of what they consider to be the appropriate model. Indeed, since they have an obvious financial interest in taking the right view of the future the rational expectations hypothesis assumes an almost axiomatic status; any hypothesis that implies that speculators purposefully seek to take an incorrect view of the future sounds implausible. Yet this is precisely what the behavioral theories of expectations[5] imply.

The rational expectations hypothesis might be claimed as the economist's own hypothesis regarding the formation of expectations since it is rooted in economic theory itself. In this way expected values in economic models would no longer be regarded as an after-thought. Instead, expected values are elevated to the fore-front of economic modeling, especially as far as the theory of macroeconomic policy is concerned. For if expectations are formed rationally any decision rule of the authorities regarding optimal stabilization policy would, as an integral part of the model that is used to form the rational expectations, to some extent be reflected in the expectations themselves. If so, the stabilization policy would no longer be optimal. But the same would recur if the authorities drew up a revised optimal stabilization policy.

Drawing on this logic Sargent and Wallace [1975][6] in a seminal paper showed that the optimal monetary policy is a constant rule rather than an activist monetary policy; the limit of the iterative process outlined in the previous paragraph is for all activist monetary policies to be discounted by rational expectations. Once the market realizes that the authorities are going to raise the money supply by a given amount to stem a recession, the market expects prices to rise by a proportionate amount. Monetary policy is fully anticipated, the authorities cannot influence the volume of real balances and stabilization policy is ineffective in relation to the real economy.

In other words Friedman was right after all but for the wrong reasons – a monetary rule is preferable to an activist monetary policy. If indeed expectations are formed rationally the 'assignment' theory would be dead unless the methodology can be determined under which the opposite would be true. The burden of proof would be switched to those who claim that the authorities continue to have a positive role to play in the construction of discretionary macroeconomic policies. In this sense the rational expectations hypothesis may have turned the tide.

However, it seems important to distinguish between two quite separate issues. First is the positive question: under rational expectations, can the authorities influence the real economy? Secondly, even if they can influence the real economy under rational expectations does it automatically follow that they should? Sargent and Wallace [1975, 1976] postulate a model in which the answer to the former question is 'no' so that the second question is hypothetical. But this is merely a consequence of how Sargent and Wallace set up their model and it is easy to devise models where the Sargent and Wallace result breaks down. In contrast Phelps and Taylor [1977], Fischer [1977] and McCallum [1977] have devised models where stabilization policies can be effective even under rational expectations. To achieve a given effect, however, it is necessary for policy makers to take account of the feedback effect from policy to expectations as indeed is the case with some of the models that are explored in Chapters 6 and 7. Of course the answer to the second question depends upon whether the short term equilibria are distorted by market failure, as previously discussed. But this issue has been largely if not completely ignored.

The debate that has been kindled by Sargent and Wallace has been largely concerned with the efficacy of monetary policy as an instrument of demand management. It is equally important to consider the implications of the rational expectations hypothesis for other areas of macroeconomic policy such as fiscal policy and foreign exchange intervention. Can rational expectations frustrate such policies and if so is the degree of frustration total? Attempted answers to these questions form an important component of this book.

The monetarist controversy

During the 1960s the monetarist controversy began in earnest. Our purpose here is not to review this development,[7] but as with the previous sections in this chapter we pick up the threads that are relevant to the main subject matter that will follow. Perhaps the lowest common denominator of monetarism is the view that nominal income is dominated by the money supply and that the stock adjustment theory of financial analysis is more important than the flow theory upon which the 'Keynesian' income–expenditure philosophy is based. It is for this reason that the monetarists hold the view that the effects of a fiscal expansion will be 'crowded out' unless they are accompanied by an expansion in the money stock.

Monetarists do not necessarily hold the view that activist monetary policy cannot work. In other words they do not automatically accept the Sargent and Wallace version of the rational expectations hypothesis or Friedman's 1959 statements on this issue. On the other hand monetarists believe that macroeconomic markets will tend to clear via one adjustment mechanism or another and that in the long run the price level is a monetary phenomenon and the volume of unemployment will tend towards its 'natural' rate. Likewise the rate of interest would tend towards its 'natural' rate too.

This latter aspect is of major importance; if excess demands and supplies will eventually be eliminated the unemployment problem will eventually look after itself. In this context activist macroeconomic policies would be conceived in terms of speeding up the adjustment process – if the unemployment rate is greater than the 'natural' rate why wait for the economy itself to grind its way towards the 'natural' rate?

But what if the economy does not have the equilibrating properties that are imputed to it by the monetarists? Under such circumstances activist policies might be required not just as a short period feature but also as a long term requirement. However, the appropriate policies in this long term context would have to be derived from a model in which long term disequilibrium behavior were possible, and these need not be the same as the policies that have been conventionally practiced. This will be recognized as the principal subject matter of Keynes' *General Theory* and it is for this reason that the *General Theory* is analyzed in detail in Chapter 2.

The monetarist controversy was originally couched by Friedman in the context of a closed economy (as of course was the *General Theory*). The open economy incarnation was developed by Johnson during the 1970s although his seminal statement in Johnson [1972] may be related to some of his earlier contributions.[8] This became known as the monetary approach to the balance of payments and its principal feature was that in small open economies, balance of payments deficits are equal to the excess in the rate of growth of the money supply in relation to the rate of growth in the demand for money. This too was intended as a long term proposition but the rate of unemployment would still tend towards its 'natural' rate and the domestic price level would depend on overseas prices as determined by world monetary conditions.

What then are the implications of the rational expectations hypothesis in a small open economy (which of course is the general case) as far as activist macroeconomic policies are concerned? Can the authorities intervene in the foreign exchange markets as well as the usual domestic markets in order to stabilize the economy when expectations are formed rationally?[9] Or what are the implications if say exchange rate expectations are formed rationally but inflationary expectations are not so formed? These questions too will form part of the subject matter of this book.

The foregoing discussion implies the perhaps surprising judgment that all who hold the view that macroeconomic markets will tend to clear themselves in the long run are monetarists. They are monetarists in the sense that this logic implies all the long run monetarist propositions about inflation, the balance of payments (or exchange rate) and unemployment. Indeed, this proposition is an additional focus of interest in this essay.[10] Perhaps therefore, the terminology of monetarists and non-monetarists is not a useful one as far as economic theory is concerned and we need instead a more meaningful terminology. The previous discussion suggests that the essential distinction is between neoclassicism and Keynesianism – between those who believe markets work and those who hold the opposite view.

The existence of equilibria

A related distinction may be made between those who maintain that market equilibria exist and those who hold the contrary view. Indeed this distinction has tended to become more pronounced during the present decade. The first school holds that it is meaningful to consider monetary equilibrium at the macroeconomic level and Patinkin may be regarded as a principal member of this school of thought. The macroeconomy will have equilibrating tendencies – excess supplies and demands will tend to sort themselves out sooner or later through a mixture of price and quantity adjustments as well as wealth and real balance effects. In other words the concept of the market is applicable in the macroeconomic context too and at this basic level the markets for money, exports, employment and other macroeconomic aggregates are comparable to the markets for apples and oranges. This school, which might be called the 'existentialist' school does not worry unduly about existence problems and the such like, since a glance at the world as it is encourages them to discount such problems as being of any practical importance although they obviously will be of intellectual interest.

The other school of thought contends that the jump between microeconomics and macroeconomics is not so simple and that before it becomes meaningful to talk about practical aspects of macroeconomic policy, and especially monetary policy, it is necessary to articulate the role of money in the economy. In other words it is necessary to demonstrate that a monetary equilibrium can exist as a prerequisite to any recommendations about monetary policy. Important members of this school are Hahn and Grandmont and their work has been usefully reviewed by Weintraub [1977, 1979]. Members of this school are not necessarily claiming that general macroeconomic equilibrium cannot prevail. Rather they are claiming that it has yet to be intellectually articulated how general macroeconomic equilibrium can prevail and that this requires in part-icular an appropriate microeconomic analysis of wage and price determination in a decentralized monetary economy. The set of non-tâtonnement processes has yet to be formulated upon which the existence of equilibrium can be based.

While so far the 'existentialists' have out-competed their 'opponents' in getting their message across outside the academic community, the latter can lay claim to the pedigree of Keynes who also sought to expose the fallacies in the 'existentialist' economics of the classics. Moreover the prevailing view since Keynes in the circles of the policy makers themselves has been largely sceptical of 'existentialism' and it may be largely for this reason that the latter day neoclassical revivalists have been so vociferous outside the confines of the academic community.

The practicing sceptics (i.e. those outside the academic community and especially those charged with policy formulation) broadly believe[11] that, for example, the economy will not tend to full employment unless the authorities set aggregate demand at the appropriate level. They would not wish to rely on the 'hidden hand' and in general they would regard the market as unable to cope with disequilibria in relation to employment, the balance of payments, inflation, etc. These sceptics are necessarily interventionists.

One interpretation of the *General Theory*[12] is that Keynes identified an existence problem in relation to a decentralized monetary economy – he showed how wage flexibility could be destabilizing and how liquidity pre-ference could result in involuntary unemployment. He also outlined the appropriate policies for circumventing the existence problem. Under these circumstances it is necessary to distinguish between short term equilibrium, i.e. when employment settles down below full employment, and long term equilibrium where full employment (appropriately defined) will prevail. 'Existentialists' believe that the latter will eventually prevail.

While certain aspects of macroeconomic disequilibrium will be explored in this essay, the 'existentialist' view-point is assumed to be important. For example, it is considered meaningful to postulate a relationship between the demand for money and income as an index of economic activity without feeling obliged to enumerate all the microeconomic details of optimal transactions behavior in a decentralized economy. Likewise with wage formation, although at each juncture it will be clarified what is being assumed. The so-called 'new microeconomics' need not hold up progress with the 'old macroeconomics'; it is a matter of judgment how explicit and detailed the assumptions need to be, but the hope must be that at some future date the two will converge in a way that is consistent with a seemingly stable world. Just as Sartre's existentialist sets about the practical matter of daily life based on some crude but nonetheless useful view of the world while debating solipsism with his friends over tea, so it is in economics; it might be difficult to prove the existence of equilibrium but it is an empirically useful assumption to proceed with while in the meanwhile we debate its impossibility.[13]

Outline of study

In an essay concerning neoclassical revivalism in relation to the theory of macroeconomic policy it seems appropriate to begin with a statement of what is unsatisfactory about the established theory which is taken to be the economics of the *General Theory*. Chapter 2 is therefore prefaced by a critique of the theoretical underpinning of the IS–LM model. The principal purpose of this critique is to stress the short term nature of the IS–LM equilibria and their limitations as a basis for policy analysis. To provide a satisfactory basis for such analysis it is necessary to extend the IS–LM model in three directions. First it is necessary to derive a more realistic determination of the short term equilibria that are produced by the simple IS–LM specification, especially with regard to the relationship between expenditure and the real stock of financial assets and in terms of specifying an open-economy version of the closed-economy model. An open-economy version should allow for the determination of the current and capital accounts of the balance of payments as well as the exchange rates since it should go without saying that these considerations are critically important for realistic policy analysis.

Secondly, the model should be extended or dynamized so that it affords an analysis of the time path as the economy adjusts from the short term equilibria to its long run steady state. As it were, the IS–LM framework merely provides a snapshot of the economy during this adjustment; the policy maker must be concerned with the expected dynamic relationships which economic analysis indicates are important; his decisions today must reflect their influence on events tomorrow.

Thirdly, as will be stressed repeatedly in this essay, it is vitally important to assess the influence of expectations upon the economy. The simple IS–LM model is devoid of expectational considerations, yet they are crucial for policy assessment. Chapters 3–7 are essentially concerned with extending the IS–LM framework in these three directions and deriving the policy implications that these extensions suggest.

The remainder of Chapter 2 is concerned with two other issues, one historical and the other exegetical. Although it is not essential to the main thesis it is argued that the macroeconomic theories that Keynes expounded in the *General Theory* were not so much an abrupt rupture with the past but a crystallization and integration of a number of ideas that had been around for some time. This does not undermine his enormous achievement but it is never-theless important to see the development of macroeconomic ideas in their appropriate historical perspective. In this context it is argued that Keynes' essential theoretical contributions were the role of quantity adjustments in macroeconomic equilibration, i.e. the theory of effective demand, and the realization that whereas commodity excess demand was expansionary an excess demand for money was recessive. Indeed both of these considerations are incorporated into the models developed in Chapter 3 and in this sense they may be said to have Keynesian characteristics and to integrate Keynesian and neoclassical theories of macroeconomic behavior.

The exegetical focus of Chapter 2 is concerned with what Keynes actually said in the *General Theory* about the existence of macroeconomic equilibria and the associated role of expectations via macroeconomic adjustment. The main argument will be that in both instances Keynes was obscure, perhaps intentionally so, and, as has already been pointed out with respect to the IS–LM model, the inadequate treatment of these issues diminishes the nor-mative basis of the ideas he presents.

The remaining chapters, as already said, are largely concerned with exten-ding the IS–LM model, although the finished product will bear little resem-blance to it. In Chapter 3 the first two extensions are considered while in Chapters 6 and 7 the role of expectations in macroeconomic policy design is elaborated, drawing on the developments of the preceding chapters. Although somewhat artificial, this division of labor is required for expositional pur-poses. The principal ideas of the study are therefore brought together in Chapter 7.

The basic macroeconomic model that we intend to use is described in Chapter 3 and for expositional purposes it is presented in terms of its long run equilibrium format. Two versions of the model are presented; there is the closed economy version and the open economy version. In view of the greater generality of the latter it is the open economy model to which we attach the greater importance. Nevertheless it seems useful in terms of the exposition to consider the closed economy before discussing the open economy.

The model is intended to be eclectic; in other words no new macroecon-omic concepts are suggested. Instead, we mix together a number of old wines and put them into one new bottle.[14] In particular we draw on the Keynesian income–expenditure approach to the theory of effective demand and the portfolio theoretic approach to monetary economics that relates flows of expenditures to stocks of financial assets. Special importance is attached to the role of money as a medium of exchange and to the real balance effect as a major link between the financial and real sectors.

In the open economy version we distinguish between traded and non-traded output as well as transactions in financial assets that will influence the capital account of the balance of payments. These models are cast in the neoclassical mold and it is shown that their long run properties are the same as a number of principal 'monetarist' propositions – that in a closed economy (or when the exchange rate is perfectly flexible) inflation is a domestic monetary phenomenon and the economy will tend to full-employment or the 'natural' rate of unemployment, and that in an open economy inflation will be determined by world price movements and the balance of payments will be a monetary phenomenon.

In Chapters 4 and 5 we explore some static policy implications of the basic model with regard to incomes policy, fiscal policy, monetary policy, etc. We also discuss the theoretical effects of a number of balance of payments policies such as devaluation, import controls, tariffs, export subsidies etc. The main purpose of these chapters is to calculate the long run or general equilibrium responses of the economy to these policy initiatives in contrast to the short term or partial equilibrium responses. For example, if it is granted that an export subsidy will stimulate exports and the balance of payments in partial equilibrium, will the same qualitative results carry over to the general equilibrium situation?

Chapter 4 is prefaced by some empirical illustrations for the UK of the long run macroeconomic relationships that are derived in Chapter 3. Although the focus of this essay is theoretical rather than empirical it seems appropriate to indicate that the ideas developed have prima facie empirical content. However, a detailed empirical investigation is in the advanced stages of preparation. In view of its importance in a number of countries including the UK it is also shown how the results obtained in Chapter 3 are modified when an energy sector is explicitly incorporated into the model. This exercise affords a basis for investigating the effects of energy discoveries on the macroeconomy.

In view of the importance that will be attached to the rational expectations hypothesis, Chapter 6 is devoted to an exposition of the basic ideas that lie behind it. Muth [1961] illustrated the hypothesis in relation to a simple model of a commodities market although it seems to be the case that it is in the sphere of macroeconomics that the rational expectations hypothesis has made its greatest impact. For expositional simplicity, however, we shall also use a very simple model of a commodity market[15] and our objective will be to express how the dynamic behavior of output and price is affected by rational expectations when there is speculation. We shall also compare alternative hypotheses about speculative behavior and the formation of expectations and explore their implications for price behavior.

The simple model is then used to investigate the effects of official intervention in the market, which is the analogue of the activist policies that will be described in relation to macroeconomic policy formation. The main issues here are that if expectations are indeed rational it is unclear how official intervention in the market may stabilize prices in a socially beneficial way. Further-more, if under these circumstances the authorities do intervene it will be necessary for them to take account of the fact that rational expectations may be affected and consequently that the effects of the intervention may be other than intended. As it were, in designing their policies the authorities will have to allow for the feed-back effects of their policies onto speculative behavior.

An additional consideration is that apart from intervention influencing speculative expectations it may also weaken speculative responses in a way that is likely to destabilize price behavior. Heuristic as this model may be it is nevertheless useful to draw a number of practical policy implications from it.

Having elucidated the theory of rational expectations in the very simple setting described in Chapter 6, in Chapter 7 we go back to the models developed in Chapter 3 and reconsider their behavior under the assumption that expectations are formed rationally. The path of the economy under rational expectations provides a benchmark for judging whether macroeconomic stabilization policies are desirable. If the economy is off this path market failure will be present and it will be in the social interest for the government to stabilize economic aggregates around their optimal paths. If, instead, the economy lies on its optimal path, stabilization is not necessary. It is stressed that the criteria for macroeconomic policy design is the orthodox principle that if the market fails there is a prima facie case for corrective action on the part of the auth-orities. Macroeconomic policy design is therefore founded on the same prin-ciples as microeconomic policy design.

The principal random variables that we focus on are the expected rate of inflation and the expected exchange rate. Macroeconomic disequilibrium behavior is explained in terms of the lagged adjustment processes in the basic model and their interaction with the formation of expectations. When expectations are assumed to be formed rationally, disequilibrium behavior is explained in terms of the principles of risk aversion when the economy is subject to unforeseeable random shocks.

Finally, in Chapter 8, we summarize the policy implications of the previous discussion. In particular our attention is focused on whether there is an a priori case for activist macroeconomic policies. This is shown to depend crucially on the assumption of rational expectations. Alternatively our concern is to estab-lish the issues that would have to be clarified before activist or discretionary macroeconomic policies could be legitimately pursued.

CHAPTER 2

A critique of Keynesian macroeconomics

General impressions

Perhaps the most popular view of the Keynesian revolution is that Keynes taught us how in a capitalist economy it was possible for the authorities to devise policies that would cure depressions. Before Keynes' *General Theory*, society had to suffer impotently through the darkness and squalor of protracted years of economic depression, while since then depression, like smallpox, has more or less been abolished.

It was also until fairly recently a view that was respected within the academic community too, although the situation has most probably been changing quite rapidly. No doubt, the vestiges of Keynesianism will continue to thrive in backwaters for some time, but the general impression would seem to be that Keynesian economics has suffered a series of intellectual as well as practical set-backs in recent years. Perhaps the most important of these has been the incidence of 'stagflation' in the industrialized countries which raised serious questions about the application of the traditional Keynesian remedy for depressions of stimulating demand when the rate of inflation was high and accelerating.

If Kuhn's[1] hypothesis regarding the structure of scientific revolutions were correct, out of the 'chaos' that surrounds the 'crisis' in Keynesian economics a new economic 'paradigm' might have been expected to emerge. However, this has not happened, nor are there any signs that Kuhn's predictions are about to be fulfilled. Instead, the profession has responded atavistically in two respects. First, there has been the so-called Keynesian counter-revolution described by Clower (1966) which argues that Keynes merely added to the wisdom of his classical forebears and did not fundamentally replace it. This school, as represented by Patinkin, Friedman and others has tended to synthesize and incorporate Keynesian principles within the neoclassical framework. A major development from this synthesis has been the rise of monetarism. Secondly, there has been a rebuke to the early disciples of Keynes who did much to simplify and popularize the *General Theory*, such as Hicks, Hansen and scores of textbook writers, coupled with the claim that Keynesian economics as popularly understood was not the same thing as the economics of Keynes, whose subtlety and richness went far beyond the popular image. This school, as represented by Leijonhufvud (1968), Minsky (1975) argued that the master had been betrayed by his pupils. A major development from this school has been the attempt to integrate non-market clearing principles (see, e.g., Clower (1966), Barro and Grossman (1976), Malinvaud (1977)) into macroeconomic analysis.

There can be little doubt that the philosophy of macroeconomic policy activism that developed after the Second World War was closely related to the Keynesian revolution and even an integral part of it. In view of our present concern with an appraisal of this philosophy, it is appropriate to probe Keynes' writings regarding the assumptions upon which activism might be based. Therefore, the primary objective of this chapter is to re-appraise the *General Theory* in this light. In particular, we concern ourselves with four main aspects:

   (i) The 'liquidity trap'
   (ii) Expectations theory
   (iii) Existence problems and stability
   (iv) Political economy

The first aspect has often been cited as one of the reasons why in the Keynesian model underemployment equilibrium might exist. However, it seems worth recalling what Keynes himself had to say on this matter. Our greater concern will, however, be with the second and third aspects, as might be inferred from the discussion in the previous chapter, where the rationale for intervention and the nature of economic expectations were shown to be highly interdependent. Furthermore, if the macroeconomy is unstable it might be necessary for the authorities to intervene in order to safeguard macroeconomic stability. Once again, it might be inferred from the previous chapter that the questions of stability, existence and expectations are closely related. Finally, we explore the aspects of political economy in the *General Theory* that might lend themselves to policy activism. In this context we should recall that, especially in the *General Theory*, Keynes teases us by persistently donning and doffing the hats of the theoretician and the practical policy advisor so that he could accept theoretical deductions while rejecting their practical importance or appropriateness.

But before embarking on this discussion we present a brief historical context of the *General Theory* and the Keynesian revolution in economics and economic policy. In particular, it is worth evaluating whether the revolution was so pronounced in the first place. Just how different were economic ideas, both in relation to theory and policy, before and after 1936? Keynes warns us, 'Practical men, who believe themselves to be quite exempt from any intellectual influences, are usually the slaves of some defunct economist. Madmen in authority, who hear voices in the air, are distilling their frenzy from some academic scribbler of a few years back' (1936, p. 383). But cannot this process happen in reverse – with academic scribblers distilling from the air the voices of those practical men who when faced with the abyss have been forced to consider new horizons?

Before the 'revolution'

There can be no doubt that Keynes himself saw the *General Theory* as a revolutionary work that would replace the Ricardian foundations of classical economics: 'To understand my state of mind, however, you have to know that I believe myself to be writing a book on economic theory which will largely revolutionize -- not, I suppose at once but in the course of the next ten years – the way the world thinks about economic problems.'[2] But, in a sense, Keynes too saw his revolution as a forging of links with the writings of the pre-classical economists such as the mercantilists, who had been struggling with the notion of effective demand, but who were overtaken by Ricardian economics:

> Ricardo conquered England as completely as the Holy Inquisition conquered Spain. The great puzzle of Effective Demand with which Malthus had wrestled vanished from the economic literature. You will not find it mentioned even once in the whole works of Marshall, Edgeworth and Professor Pigou, from whose hands the classical theory has received its most mature embodiment. It could only live on furtively, below the surface, in the underworlds of Karl Marx, Silvio Gesell and Major Douglas [1936, p. 32].

Indeed, Chapter 23 of the *General Theory* is virtually a monument to the pre-classical scholars who struggled with the principles of effective demand and who saw that this logic implied an activist and stabilizing role for the authorities.

Therefore, Keynes saw the principal thrust of his revolution in relation to the theory of effective demand. Due to a variety of considerations, in a decentralized monetary economy, it was possible that effective demand could fall short of supply which, in the labor market, for example, could create a situation of involuntary unemployment. The Walrasian assumption that an excess demand in one market for real output would be reflected by an excess supply in another market, or Say's Law that supply creates its own demand, were argued by Keynes to be unrealistic in a decentralized monetary economy. These intellectual constructs could only be applicable in a world where information was costless to obtain or the world of Robinson Crusoe where the right arm of demand was always aware of what the left arm of supply was doing.

Indeed, both Clower and Leijonhufvud adjure to this integration of the theory of effective demand as being the keystone of the Keynesian revolution. 'The conclusion which I draw from all this may be put in the phrase: "either Walras' Law is incompatible with Keynesian Economics or Keynes had nothing fundamentally new to add to orthodox economic theory"' [Clower, 1966, pp. 110–11]. Likewise, with Leijonhufvud:

In its economic reincarnation as Walras' auctioneer, the demon has not yet been exorcised. But this certainly must be what Keynes tried to do. If a single distinction is to be drawn between the economics of Keynes and the economics of our grandfathers, this is it. It is only on this basis that Keynes' claim to having essayed a more 'general theory' can be maintained. If this distinction is not recognized as both valid and important, I believe we must conclude that Keynes' contribution to pure theory was nil [Leijonhufvud, 1968, p. 397].

And as somebody who had lived through the 'revolution', Samuelson [1947] recalls at first hand the impact of the *General Theory*. 'It is quite impossible for modern students to realize the full effect of what has been adversely called the "Keynesian Revolution" upon those of us brought up in the orthodox tradition' [p. 145]. And Samuelson goes on to pin-point the theory of effective demand as the quintessential feature of this 'revolution'.

There can be little doubt that Keynes' theory of effective demand was indeed a revolutionary contribution to economic dynamics; revolutionary in the sense that for over a century economists had been struggling with theories of the trade cycle that were derived largely from classical equilibrium principles, whereas, almost for the first time, effective demand was an essentially disequilibrium principle. Keynes made it possible to consider disequilibrium situations directly rather than viewing disequilibrium states as adjustments in relation to some classical equilibrium state. The guts of the revolution was the opening of the way to a theory of macroeconomic disequilibrium.

Thus the macroeconomics of the pre-classical economists tended to be concerned with what today would be called macroeconomic disequilibrium. Writers such as Petty, Barbon, Quesnay and others never attempted to conceive macroeconomic aggregates as adjusting to a set of equilibrium situations as in the flexi-price models of the classics. Instead, they were generally concerned (in this context) with ensuring that what was supplied would be demanded in a world devoid of price adjustments and where the burden of adjustment was borne by quantity movements.

In the second leg of the dialectic, the classics established clear notions of equilibrium, at first in macroeconomics and later in microeconomics. In retrospect, it seemed almost as if to gain their feet the classics had to expunge the writings of their predecessors. In addition, as Keynes and others have pointed out, the laissez faire political economy that arose out of the writings of Smith, Ricardo and others matched the vested interests of the English establishment of the times. The wretched lot of the working man and the wealth of the landed establishment during the later stages of the industrial revolution could now be justified in terms of the inalienable work of the 'hidden hand'.

The pre-classical scholars were soon forgotten and classical economics came to prevail. But during the second half of the nineteenth century there was a sea-change.

> It was not that there occurred in the seventies any very marked or sudden change in the political attitude of leading economists. But gradually, instead of the free market being held innocent or beneficent until it was proved guilty, while state action was held guilty until proved innocent, the two came to be weighed upon rather more equal terms. In particular, a more systematic attempt came to be made 'to gather together in orderly fashion, and to concentrate more attention on, the cases for state intervention.' [Hutchison, 1953, p. 11]).

In addition attention began to turn to the trade cycle phenomenon, and most of the efforts of macroeconomists in the sixty years preceding the *General Theory* were directed at explaining the trade cycle.

It is curious that these writers related their efforts to the trade cycle rather than to the more general notion of disequilibrium On the other hand the former notion does not necessarily preclude equilibrium states since it is conceivable that equilibrium itself is cyclical. Hutchison [1953, Chapters 22–3] has provided an excellent summary of the various contributions to trade cycle theory during this period. However, a number of observations that relate to our train of thought are made in this connection. First, there was a revival of interest in the issues that had concerned the pre-classics. At the time that Marshall published *Principles* (1890) Foxwell published his study on the *Irregularities of Employment* and Mummery and Hobson published their *Physiology of Industry*. Foxwell was concerned with the stabilization of employment fluctuations as well as price stabilization, i.e. aspects of political economy that would be redundant if Say's Law were true, and Mummery and Hobson were in effect trying to develop their theory of under-consumption into what would later flower as the theory of effective demand. Likewise with other contributors such as Veblen and Davenport. In his *Economics of Enterprise* (1913) Davenport went as far as to consider how in a monetary economy Say's Law could break down since the demand for money as an asset could generate recessive tendencies.

These theoretical developments gave way to some important departures in attitudes to economic policy. As early as 1896 Davenport was recommending public works programs during depressions and the pre-classical revivalists in general considered that price stabilization policies would tend to have beneficial effects during depressions since flexible prices might run the risk of exacerbating any excess supply situations that might arise.

Perhaps the most formidable precursor of Keynes was Johannsen who in 1908 developed what he called the 'Multiplying Principle', which is remarkably similar to the Kahn–Keynes multiplier [Johannsen, 1908, p. 44]. Moreover,

Johannsen was also concerned about the secular stagnation theory[3] that was later to interest Keynes, and Johannsen foresaw some of the policy remedies that were later to feature in the Keynesian revolution in political economy.

A very clear statement about the relationship between employment and public investment policies may be found in J. M. Robertson [1892, pp. 121-2]. Robertson argued that unemployment results when savings exceed investment in wealthy societies and that one of the remedies might be for the state or municipalities to institute public works. Robertson anticipated Keynes in other areas too.

In other words, by the early part of the twentieth century the literature[4] had produced a number of broadly related ideas in theory and policy that had fundamentally broken with the classical tradition. But the opposition was stiff and the pre-classical revivalists[5] failed to gain any significant prestige. In a related context Eshag [1963, p. 93] summarized the situation as follows:

> The real support for a policy of rising prices on the ground of its technical effects on production and employment, however, came from the group of heretics and unorthodox economists. These consisted of members of the Birmingham School, writers like Cliffe-Leslie and Foxwell and the minority members of the Commission on the Depression of Trade and Industry and of the Gold and Silver Commission. These people, who reflected primarily the opinions of bankers, bimetallists, industrialists and merchants, were, however, overwhelmed in public debate by neoclassical economists like Goschen, Giffen and Marshall, who presented the orthodox classical views of Ricardo and Mill.

For a variety of reasons, the so-called heretics failed to make ground, not least of which was the fact that they were concerned with new and particularly difficult areas of economic thought, and so it was relatively easy for their classical critics to fault them. Furthermore, it is possible that in Great Britain at least the times were not politically receptive to their new ideas regardless of whether they were right or wrong. The era of laissez faire was still very much alive and the burden of proof was most probably not fairly distributed on those who argued for policies of macroeconomic intervention. The Labour Party was still on the fringes of political influence, but this was to change rapidly once the century had turned and especially with the socioeconomic changes that followed the Great War.

Nevertheless, even classical orthodoxy was altering in its efforts to provide a theory of cyclical behavior; so much so that it is not easy to judge where orthodoxy ended and heresy began. For example Wicksteed [1910, Vol. I] attempted a theory of macrodynamics based on the relationship between expectations and uncertainty. A disequilibrium situation could reflect unfulfilled expectations, miscalculation or unforeseeable surprises, i.e. notions which

Keynes was to consider and which will be the subject matter in some of our later chapters. Wicksteed [1910, Vol. II, p. 640] also suggested counter-cyclical public works policies as a possible remedy for economic depression

Wicksell's contributions to monetary theory also reflect an important departure from Say's Law. The cumulative process and the relationship between the money and natural rates of interest is essentially a description of disequilibrium behavior, although it does not recognize the principles of effective demand which some of his contemporaries had discerned and which Keynes was later to develop more fully. However, as Eshag [1963, pp. 82–4] documents, Marshall recognized the principle of effective demand and considered the stabilization policies that this principle might imply. Moreover, he attached significance to concepts such as confidence and real balance effects, but he always worked within an equilibrium framework and of course he did not formulate income–expenditure mechanisms.

When he succeeded to Marshall, Pigou in his Inaugural Lecture at Cambridge (1908) embarked by refuting what was later to be identified as the 'Treasury View'. Some years later, Winston Churchill as Chancellor of the Exchequer summarized this view as follows: 'It is orthodox Treasury dogma, steadfastly held, that whatever might be the political or social advantages, very little additional employment can, in fact, and as a general rule, be created by state borrowing and expenditure.'[6] The 'Treasury View' most probably dates back to the times when Ricardo himself was a member of parliament and in the present century Hawtrey was to become the main defender of the faith. Pigou foresaw the principles of the balanced budget multiplier and argued that relief works could stimulate demand.[7]

Indeed, despite Keynes' caricature in the *General Theory*, Pigou was not the classical eminence that is perhaps the popular image. Keynes in the *General Theory* was mainly attacking the Pigou of the *Theory of Unemployment* (1933) rather than Pigou in general. In fact, as Hutchison [1968, appendix] has so ably documented, Pigou and Keynes were not so far apart on the practicality of employment policy as might commonly be thought; Pigou accepted the need for relief works.

Thus, by the time Keynes got round to writing the *General Theory*, and ignoring the degree to which Robertson or Kalecki might have scooped him or not, both in the universities and in the field of policy the ground had been substantially softened. In this connection it should be recalled that the Webbs had already argued in favor of counter-cyclical public works policies in the minority report of the Royal Commission on the Poor Laws (1909) as Beveridge [1909] had done in the same year. In the US, the Report of the President's Conference on Unemployment (1921) endorsed the view that public works should be planned and carried out on a counter-cyclical basis. In the international forum the International Labour Office had been recommending similar policies for some time (as Keynes himself notes in the *General Theory* (p. 349n), and President Hoover had begun to embark on Keynesian type policies, i.e. before Keynes' approach to Roosevelt. In Sweden, Keynesian policies were practiced[8] prior to 1936 and Hitler had already embarked on his employment strategy.[9]

In the even narrower context of the relationship between Keynes and Marshall, Eshag [1963, pp. 108-9] concludes:

> On the basis of the above discussion it would be reasonable to conclude that the fundamental concepts embodied in the General Theory were not as novel and original as they appeared to first sight. They were evolved on the basis of the ideas introduced at Cambridge by Marshall and his pupils, including Keynes himself, prior to the appearance of the *General Theory* in 1936. Marshall's influence on Keynes was not, however, confined to the development of the basic concepts discussed above. Such notions as the predominant role played by 'expectations' on the level of investment and economic activity, the rigidity of wages, salaries and fixed charges, the 'quasi rent' and the equality of the rate of interest and the profit rate in conditions of equilibrium, all these notions embodied in Keynes' *General Theory* were derived directly from Marshall. . . . The real significance of Keynes' work, therefore, lay, not so much in advancing important new concepts in this field, as in constructing a machinery of analysis through which it becomes possible clearly and naturally to determine the volume of effective demand and the level of employment at any given time. The possibility of obtaining an equilibrium below the full employment level, even in normal non-crisis conditions had been partly recognized at Cambridge before the appearance of the *General Theory*. It would seem that looking beyond the confines of Cambridge this conclusion has even greater force and substance.

What then of the Keynesian revolution? Can it be possible that an entire generation can talk of a revolution in economic thought when in fact there was none to speak of? In the broadest of senses there may be nothing new under the sun, and up to a point it serves little purpose to delve into past scriptures so that we can say that such and such a sentiment has already been voiced. Einstein's revolution cannot be belittled by reference to the atomists of Ancient Greece. The same applies to Keynes in relation to his precursors. The keystone of Keynes' revolution was his development of the theory of effective demand as a critical feature of macroeconomic dynamics. With the obvious exception of Hobson, it is most probably true that Keynes was not familiar with the writings of his precursors that have been mentioned here; otherwise he would presumably have made reference to them. But thwarted revolutionaries cannot plead ignorance and it is a testimony to Keynes' originality that despite this ignorance he could eclipse his predecessors and provide a complete intellectual structure where they had trodden so ineffectively.

In this connection it is important to distinguish Keynes the intellectual revolutionary from Keynes the practical revolutionary. In this sense he was like Marx and Lenin rolled into one. Throughout the 1930s he fought to propagate his ideas, even perhaps before they were clearly formulated in his mind.[10] It is of course a hypothetical question, but if Keynes had merely been an intellectual revolutionary and not the wily political economist that he was, the Keynesian revolution as we understand it might never have happened. Like justice, revolutions not only have to be made, but they must also be seen to be made. Keynes saw to that, and this revolutionary aura perhaps owes as much if not more to his personality than it does to his intellect.

In this context, a less generous assessment might have been made. For example Johnson [1975, p. 112] attributes some of the impact of the 'revolution' to the general failure to understand current economic developments.

> Had the policy-makers of the 1930's really understood what was occurring in the international monetary system and their own part in it, or the economists of the time understood it (as they could have done by developing available monetary theory) and explained it effectively, the Great Depression of the 1930's would have been nipped in the bud and the *General Theory* either not been written, or been received as one eccentric English economist's rationalization of his local problems.

While, no doubt there is with hindsight an element of truth to this assertion (Johnson himself forgot to point this out in his review of the *General Theory* after 25 years) it most probably goes too far and ignores the substantive analytical constructions of the *General Theory* as well as the timely challenge to orthodoxy to make its case clear.

Nevertheless, it seems likely that Keynes' revolution has perhaps been over-glorified. In its infancy this may have been understandable, but hopefully the theme that we have been following here will contribute to an appropriate perspective. One of the greatest misfortunes in the history of economic thought was that Keynes never had the chance to refine the *General Theory* and to clear up the many ambiguities that it contains and which have been a source of debate even until today. Thus unlike Freud, Einstein and Marx who had ample years to consolidate their efforts, Keynes through a variety of circumstances was not in so fortunate a position. The main problem, as Minsky [1975] points out, was that Keynes was not a young man when the *General Theory* was published (he was fifty two) and his heart attack in 1937 meant that he could not devote his energies to consolidating the *General Theory*. By the time he had recuperated, the Second World War had broken out and he was heavily involved in HM Treasury as part of the war effort. Within a year of the end of the war he was dead.

Consequently, the *General Theory* has almost a mystical quality in parts, at times it is difficult to know for sure what Keynes really intended, if indeed he knew himself. In the rest of this chapter we focus on the question whether the *General Theory* denies the notion of macroeconomic equilibrium, and, if it does, whether there were sufficient grounds given by Keynes for so doing.

The IS–LM model

But before we press ahead with this matter it is appropriate to take stock of the conventional Keynesian model in relation to these issues. Our concerns may be simply expressed by using the familiar IS–LM framework (which we assume to be so well-known that no explanations are required). In the Keynesian short period wages and prices are assumed to be fixed so that in the face of excess demand resources are rationed rather than prices bid up while in the case of excess supply resources become unemployed rather than prices bid down. The IS–LM model relates to the Keynesian short period and thus assumes that wages and prices are fixed. The burden of adjustment is thus thrown onto quantities although during the short period it is assumed that bond prices may vary.

This immediately brings us to the first criticism – the short period itself is an artificial construct that is either tautologous or meaningless. If time periods are made sufficiently brief it is no doubt true that wages and prices may be taken as fixed, but the same applies to every other variable including interest rates, employment and output. The truth of the matter is that wages, prices and indeed all economic variables are constantly changing in which case the very premises of the IS-LM framework are unreasonable.

As wages and prices fall (rise) the *IS* schedule will tend to move to the right (left) as wealth effects cause an increase (decrease) in expenditure. At the same time as wages and prices fall, the demand for money falls so that the *LM* schedule moves downwards as indicated in fig. 2-1. If, e.g., $\bar{Y}$ represents the full employment level of output while actual output, Y_1 (determined by the intersection of IS_1 and LM_1 at a) is below this level, wages and prices will fall so that over time the *IS* and *LM* schedules will move to determine the trajectory of intersects ab until full-employment is attained at b. Thus to assume the *IS* and *LM* schedules as fixed even in the short run does not seem a fruitful basis for policy discussion.

It might be objected, however, that this argument is asymmetrical; wages and prices might be flexible upwards but rigid downwards. But the growth process largely disposes of this issue since to generate positive wealth effects in a growing economy it is merely necessary that wage inflation be flexible downwards. In any event the asymmetry hypothesis is difficult to test since secular productivity growth implies that nominal wage rates will tend to grow.

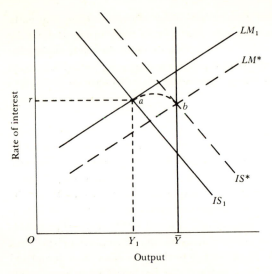

Figure 2-1 Short and long term output equilibria

In the meanwhile it is noted that prices of industrial commodities are flexible downwards, therefore no iron law of asymmetry can be said to exist as a matter of dogma.

The IS–LM framework does not separate out the labor market; it is necessary to distinguish excess supplies of output (where $Y < \bar{Y}$) from excess supplies of labor. Indeed, this distinction forms a central part of Malinvaud's [1977] recent study of unemployment although he takes the Keynesian short period of wage-price fixity as being an acceptable analytical construct. Thus even if $Y = \bar{Y}$, i.e. if the demand and supply of output are in balance, the demand and supply of labor may be unequal in which event real wage rates may be expected to adjust.

Nor does the IS–LM framework recognize the interaction between the *IS* schedule and the *LM* schedule that is implied by the financial operations of the government. For example an increase in government expenditure would push the *IS* schedule out to the right. If, however, the resulting budget deficit is financed by 'printing' money the *LM* schedule would move through time towards the horizontal axis.

A further shortcoming is that the framework is only suitable for a closed economy when in reality no such economy exists. In practice it will be necessary to specify the relationship between the real sector and the world economy that is implied by trade relationships, and between the financial sector and the world economy that is implied by the existence of capital account transactions.

Finally, the framework is devoid of expectational arguments yet it is generally recognized that expectations play an important role in the determination of macroeconomic events. But the introduction of expectations of inflation, etc., further brings into question the usefulness of the Keynesian short term period. For if expectations are rational what is expected today depends on future developments so that what happens today depends upon the future course of the economy. Thus the short period cannot be conceived in isolation from the subsequent periods. It therefore makes more sense to build one's model on firmer ground. In particular it makes sense to specify how prices and wages alter over the short period and to articulate how expectations about future developments influence decision taking in the current period. Indeed, in the remaining chapters an attempt is made to extend the IS–LM framework in all of these directions.

Aspects of the General Theory

The reasons for concentrating on the equilibrium–disequilibrium theme in the *General Theory* seem obvious enough. If for some reason the macroeconomy gets stuck at a point of less than full-employment equilibrium, the authorities might have an active role to play in guiding the economy back to full employment. Indeed, a common conception of the *General Theory* is that it justified the concept of an equilibrium at less than full employment, and that this notion constituted a major advance in the history of economic thought and which had revolutionary implications for macroeconomic policy.

A more dramatic view of the *General Theory* in this context is that Keynes was abandoning the notion of equilibrium altogether, or that he was claiming that full employment equilibrium was inherently unstable. According to this view the *General Theory* is essentially the formulation of an economics of disequilibrium, or, as Minsky [1975, p. 68] has put it, 'Keynesian economics as the economics of disequilibrium is the economics of permanent disequilibrium.'

These views of Keynes are clearly conflicting. Our thesis shall be that Keynes did indeed propose a theory of macroeconomic disequilibrium but that this theory did not necessarily conflict with conventional notions about macroeconomic equilibrium in relation to full employment and price stability. And while at times Keynes might have created the impression that there was such a conflict, a closer scrutiny of texts indicates that this is unlikely to have been the case. Keynes himself never in fact synthesized his disequilibrium economics with the economics of equilibrium and at the practical level during the 1930s there can be no doubt that he considered the factors relating to the economics of disequilibrium to be more important than those relating to the economics of equilibrium. Robinson [1975] recalls that Keynes would disparagingly refer to members of this school as the 'bumists'. Had Keynes adequately demonstrated that this synthesis (or the neoclassical synthesis as it has been called)

was logically impossible, the implications for macroeconomic policy would
have been fundamental to say the least. Our case shall be that Keynes never
did make this demonstration and that he rejected the political economy of
the 'bumists' on practical grounds. But while logical demonstrations have
lasting implications, practical judgments do not. The important issue in the
present context is that among the contributions and insights of the *General
Theory* this logical demonstration will not be found.[11]

The liquidity trap

The so-called liquidity trap is the phenomenon where liquidity preference
prevents the rate of interest from falling below a certain low level and since in
Keynes' model investment (ceteris paribus) is determined by the rate of interest there will be an upper limit to which expansionary monetary policies can
influence the volume of investment. Since employment depends on the volume
of investment, the liquidity trap syndrome has been proposed as a determinant
of under-employment equilibrium in the *General Theory*.

There can be no doubt that Keynes considered this syndrome. At first he
seemed to regard it as a technical or theoretical deduction from his model,
even to the point of precluding it as a practical issue. But later on in the
General Theory he seems to change his mind, even to the point of it being a
factor in the Great Depression.

A. Nevertheless, circumstances can develop in which even a large increase
   in the quantity of money may exert a comparatively small influence on
   the rate of interest. For a large increase in the quantity of money may
   cause so much uncertainty about the future that liquidity-preferences
   due to the security-motive may be strengthened [p. 172].
B. [In reference to the rate of interest] But it may fluctuate for decades
   about a level which is chronically too high for full employment (p. 204).
C. . . . after the rate of interest has fallen to a certain level, liquidity-pre-
   ference may become virtually absolute . . . But whilst this case might
   become practically important in the future, I know of no example of
   it hitherto. Indeed, owing to the unwillingness of most monetary authorities to deal boldly in debts of long term, there has not been much
   opportunity for a test [p. 207].
D. It seems, then, that the rate of interest on money plays a peculiar part
   in setting a limit to the level of employment, since it sets a standard to
   which the marginal efficiency of a capital-asset must attain if it is to be
   newly produced [p. 222].
E. For, in certain circumstances such as will often occur, these will cause
   the rate of interest to be insensitive, particularly below a certain figure
   [p. 233].

F. That the world after several millenia of steady individual saving is so poor as it is in accumulated capital-assets, is to be explained, in my opinion, neither by the improvident propensities of mankind, nor even by the destruction of war, but by the high liquidity premiums formerly attaching to the ownership of land and now attaching to money [p. 242].

G. The acuteness and the peculiarity of our contemporary problem arises, therefore, out of the possibility that the average rate of interest which will allow a reasonable average level of employment is one so unacceptable to wealth-owners that it cannot be readily established by manipulating the quantity of money [pp. 308–9].

These seven references indicate that Keynes changed his mind dramatically while writing the *General Theory*.[12] A and B are taken from essentially theoretical contexts and in C Keynes underlines that the liquidity trap has not been an issue in the past. However, the context of D seems to imply a practical relevance of the liquidity trap, while F and G testify to its historical and contemporaneous relevances respectively. If final words represent final opinions, we must conclude that Keynes attached considerable importance to the liquidity trap. But this leads us into the enigma of why Keynes apparently discounted the possibility of real balance effects which could have circumvented the liquidity trap.

But before we turn to this, was Keynes correct in attributing the apparent inefficiency of monetary expansions to the liquidity trap; especially since this also happens to be a deduction of the neoclassical model (that Keynes was supposed to be deposing) when inflationary expectations are formed rationally, as Sargent and Wallace [1976] have argued. Indeed, Keynes recognizes that the trap need not be associated with a unique rate of interest [p. 203]. If the trap was allowed to move, Keynes' theory would run the risk of becoming a tautology. The crucial issue in this context that differentiates the liquidity trap from the neoclassical result is the implication that people are prepared to accumulate real balances as well as nominal money balances while they are in the trap.

Real balance effect

For some inexplicable reason Keynes had a highly restricted view of the transmission mechanism of monetary policy. Monetary aggregates could influence the real economy only via the relationship between the rate of interest and investment. An increase in the supply of money would have to lower the rate of interest before Keynes would agree that real demand would be stimulated. In other words he persistently precluded the real balance effect and without providing any justification for so doing.[13]

However, Keynes went out of his way to discuss how real balances could be altered by wage–price movements on at least two instances in the *General Theory*.

A. . . . as money-values fall, the stock of money will have a higher proportion to the total wealth of the community.

It is not possible to dispute on theoretical grounds that this reaction might be capable of allowing an adequate decline in the rate of interest [p. 232].

B. It is, therefore, on the effect of a falling wage- and price-level on the demand for money that those who believe in the self-adjusting quality of the economic system must rest the weight of their argument; though I am not aware that they have done so. If the quantity of money is itself a function of the wage- and price-level, there is indeed, nothing to hope in this direction. But if the quantity is virtually fixed, it is evident that its quantity in terms of wage-units can be indefinitely increased by a sufficient reduction in money-wages . . . We can, therefore, theoretically at least, produce precisely the same effects on the rate of interest by reducing wages, whilst leaving the quantity of money unchanged, that we can produce by increasing the quantity of money whilst leaving the level of wages unchanged [p. 266].

Both these quotations draw attention to Keynes' exclusion of the real balance effect; changes in real balances can only affect the real economy via the rate of interest. The implication of B would seem to be that the real balance effect could clinch the argument and much of what Keynes had to say about macroeconomic disequilibrium would have to be severely modified if indeed it was not entirely discredited.

While Keynes precludes the real balance effect he does not preclude wealth effects in general. He will not agree that changes in real money balances may directly influence real expenditure but he accepts that changes in the value of wealth in general may directly influence aggregate demand.

C. The consumption of the wealth-owning class may be extremely susceptible to unforeseen changes in the money-value of its wealth. This should be classified amongst the major factors capable of causing short-period changes in the propensity to consume [pp. 92–3].

D. Perhaps the most important influence, operating through changes in the rate of interest, on the readiness to spend out of a given income, depends on the effect of these changes on the appreciation or depreciation in the price of securities and other assets . . . Apart from this, the main conclusion suggested by experience is, I think, that the short-period influence of the rate of interest on individual spending out of a given income is secondary and unimportant, except, perhaps, where unusually large changes are in question [p. 94].

E. Indeed if the fall of wages and prices goes far, the embarrassment of those entrepreneurs who are heavily indebted may soon reach the point of insolvency – with severely adverse effects on investment [p. 264].

D is a clear statement of the interest-induced wealth effect, but Keynes seems to be arguing that in the short period it is unimportant. This would appear to conflict with C unless we say that Keynes had another kind of wealth effect in mind or that he was referring to large changes in interest rates. Pesek and Saving [1967, pp. 18–19] try to argue that Keynes indeed had the price-induced wealth effect in mind. Whatever the case, E is a clear enough reference to the price-induced wealth effect.

Several issues are unclear at this point.

(i) Why did Keynes preclude real balance effects when he was prepared to admit wealth effects?

(ii) In particular, how could he accept a price-induced wealth effect yet reject real balance effects?

(iii) What are the implications of aggregate balance sheet analysis for the wealth effect, i.e. at the level of abstraction in the *General Theory* won't debtors' gains equal creditors' losses?

We could say that although he did not mention it Keynes was referring to an economy where all wealth was of the inside variety and that this was the reason for his eventual ignoring of wealth effects.[14] Alternatively, on all these questions we could admit that Keynes was simply wrong and that the implications of the *General Theory* require modification. However, on this and related issues we reserve judgment until the next section.

Leijonhufvud has argued in this context that Keynes' transmission mechanism (or the 'Keynes effect') has been generally misunderstood since Keynes disaggregated between consumer goods, money and non-money assets whereas his neoclassical critics implied that he disaggregated between output, money and bonds. Thus the real balance effect that concerns the aggregate price level was not a major issue for Keynes who was concerned with disequilibrium in relative price levels. The 'Keynes effect' was aimed therefore at the relative price between investment and consumption goods. From this it follows that while Keynes may have been technically at fault for underplaying the analytical substance of wealth and real balance effects, in the context of his own model this constituted justifiable neglect. As Leijonhufvud [1968, p. 330] argues, 'No participant in the debate has argued that the Pigou-effect proper is of major magnitude "within the normal range" of price-level variation. Still, Keynes' critics insist that his theory is *fatally* flawed by his lack of concern for this effect. Clearly, it appears fatal only because the Neoclassicists refuse to take the Keynes-effect seriously.' And later in relation to the Pigou-effect he states, 'In retrospect, it is hard to see that this point deserved much more ink than Keynes spilt on it (in dismissing it), though a veritable torrent has been forthcoming' [p. 342].

We shall not indulge here in the textual issue of the disaggregation in Keynes' model. But even assuming that Leijonhufvud's judgment is correct, the main thrust of the neoclassical criticism would still remain, but perhaps with a slightly modified emphasis: real balance effects would still be activated in the wage–price deflation syndrome that Keynes describes, although there could be the additional issue of relative price disequilibrium. Moreover, we should not be over-concerned with what constitutes fair game in Keynes' model. The real issue is the appropriate reaction to the real balance effect in an appropriate model; not Keynes' reaction in relation to the aggregative structure of his own particular model. Therefore, the flaw still remains.[15]

Expectations

The *General Theory* lays paramount emphasis on expectations despite the fact that Keynesian economics as it was taught failed adequately to mention the general area of macroeconomic expectations and their implications for disequilibrium behavior and policy. Keynes repeatedly refers to the potentially destabilizing effects of speculation and expectations, yet he does so in an ad hoc fashion and without providing any satisfactory integration between expectations and macroeconomic disequilibrium.

Leijonhufvud [1968, p. 178] acknowledges that 'Keynes' theory of expectations was sketchy at best and this he was certainly aware of', while Samuelson [1946, p. 192] concludes, 'As for expectations, the General Theory is brilliant in calling attention to their importance and in suggesting many of the central features of uncertainty and speculation. It paves the way for a theory of expectations but it hardly provides one.'

The discussion in the previous chapter has already drawn attention to the crucial relationship between expectations, their formation, disequilibrium behavior and stability. Therefore, the absence of an adequate theory of expectations in the *General Theory* is a major omission in the context of the issues Keynes was seeking to cover. In this case, the missing link is like Hamlet without the Prince. As we shall see in the next section, Keynes' discussions of macroeconomic stability in the *General Theory* are obscured if not marred by an inadequate integration of expectations into the analysis. In this section, we summarize what Keynes had to say about expectations and related matters. In particular, we focus on the relationship between these views and the rational expectations hypothesis. It is important to determine whether Keynes rejected this hypothesis in favor of one that implied that the macroeconomy had a potentially unstable propensity.

Rutledge [1974, pp. 9-10] points out that in the *Treatise on Money*

Keynes was in effect arguing that inflationary expectations are formed along the lines of the rational expectations hypothesis where the 'appropriate model' was based on the quantity theory of money. However, since Keynes changed his mind on so many intellectual issues between 1931 and 1936, it would be unfair to draw distinctions between the treatment of expectations in the *General Theory* and their treatment in the *Treatise* or the *Tract on Monetary Reform*.[16] Therefore, we mainly limit ourselves to the *General Theory*.

Keynes distinguishes between short and long term expectations [1936, pp. 46–7] depending on whether or not capital equipment is fixed. Since long term expectations influence investment and employment via the marginal efficiency of capital, Keynes focuses his attention on the motive and determinants of long term expectations. However, before we turn to how Keynes considered these expectations to be determined we discuss what Keynes had to say in the *General Theory* about the formation of short term expectations.

In a variety of contexts, e.g. as in Chapter 19 where he discusses the implications of wage-price flexibility and in Chapter 22 where he discusses the trade cycle, Keynes seems to support the extrapolative hypothesis of expectations as considered in the previous chapter. While he could have been more explicit, he allows for the possibility that changes in economic aggregates could induce expectations of further changes in the same direction. On at least two occasions however, he was quite explicit about this prospect.

A. . . . in practice the process of revision of short term expectations is a gradual and continuous one, carried on largely in the light of realized results; so that expected and realized results run into and overlap one another in their influence . . . the most recent results usually play a predominant part in determining what these expectations are. It would be too complicated to work out the expectations *de novo* whenever a productive process was being started; and it would, moreover, be a waste of time since a large part of the circumstances usually continue substantially unchanged from one day to the next. Accordingly it is sensible for producers to base their expectations on the assumption that the most recently realized results will continue, except in so far as there are definite reasons for expecting a change [pp. 50–1].

B. Moreover, the expectation of future consumption is so largely based on current experience of present consumption that a reduction in the latter is likely to depress the former [p. 210].

While B is clearly supportive of the extrapolative model, the hypothesis in A is more complex. Keynes seems to be explicit enough in supporting the extrapolative model but in a characteristically tantalizing way he throws in notions which also cover the costs of information gathering, rational expectations as well as adaptive expectations. On the other hand, it could be the case that Keynes simply had not thought through what he had in mind. The complicating factor is that Keynes does not clarify the underlying determinants of the expectations in A, but only the proximate determinants of the most recently realized results.

On long term expectations Keynes was much more forthcoming, if not overwhelmingly so, dedicating an entire chapter to this subject [Chapter 12]. Since long term expectations are the major determinant of the marginal efficiency of capital and since the marginal efficiency of capital is in turn seen by Keynes to be the major determinant of macroeconomic activity, the importance of the role of long term expectations in the *General Theory* cannot be sufficiently emphasized. Yet Chapter 12 seems to be little more than the exuberant utterances of the polemicist in political economy rather than the detached scientific and logical analyst that might be expected for so crucial a part of his thesis. What we seem to have here is Keynes of the *Essays in Persuasion* rather than the Keynes of the *Treatise*. It is perhaps significant that while Keynes did not bother to reply to most of his critics in the wake of the publication of the *General Theory*, he saw it necessary to rebut Viner's review[17] by emphasizing the interactions between speculation, expectations, uncertainty, etc. Rightly, he saw this as a critical set of issues, but did he also see them as a possible Achilles heel in his model? If the published letters are anything to go by,[18] Keynes does not seem to show any particular qualms in this area. On the other hand, this issue was not apparently raised by his correspondents, with the exception of Viner's review.

We shall first attempt to summarize, in so far as it is possible, what Keynes was trying to say in Chapter 12. Keynes believed that business expectations were highly volatile and whimsical and that the stock market in particular was like a casino where what mattered was not reasoned economic assessment but the short term outguessing of what the market was going to do next regardless of underlying economic considerations. In other words he regarded the equity market as monumentally imperfect in the sense that it was highly unlikely that equity prices would reflect the true values of the earnings stream that the equity represented. If equity prices were 'wrong', inappropriate decisions would be induced about capital formation since the decision to invest in capital and the decision to invest in equities are substitutes as well as complements.

Keynes draws a scarcely veiled distinction between the nature of entrepreneurial expectations, i.e. the expectations of those responsible for capital formation, and speculative expectations, i.e. in relation to equity prices. Entrepreneurial expectations are conceived by Keynes in very loose terms, indeed he eschewed the notion that entrepreneurs based their investment decisions on clear notions of expected returns. On the contrary – 'if animal spirits are dimmed and the spontaneous optimism falters, leaving us to depend on nothing but a mathematical expectation, enterprise will fade and die' [p. 162]. Rather it was Keynes' opinion, perhaps a reflection of his privileged victorian heritage, that the investing class did so out of animal spirits and the thrill of taking on the unknown: 'Most, probably, of our decisions to do something positive, the full consequences of which will be drawn out over many days to come, can only be taken as a result of animal spirits – of a spontaneous urge to action rather than inaction, and not as the outcome of a weighted average of quantitative benefits multiplied by quantitative probabilities' [p. 161].[19]

In other words entrepreneurial expectations, at least in the mathematical sense, are discounted 'since the basis for making such calculations does not exist' [p. 163]. Instead, 'Businessmen play a mixed game of skill and chance, the average results of which to the players are not known by those who take a hand' [p. 150]. Keynes seems to imply that the distribution about the expectation is undefined so that instead of a risky situation we have an uncertain situation. On a later occasion he developed this theme in greater detail [Keynes, 1937, pp. 213-4].

> By 'uncertain' knowledge, let me explain, I do not mean merely to distinguish what is known for certain from what is only probable. The game of roulette is not subject, in this sense, to uncertainty; nor is the prospect of a Victory Bond being drawn. Or, again, the expectation of life is only slightly uncertain. Even the weather is only moderately uncertain. The sense in which I am using the term is that in which the prospect of a European war is uncertain, or the price of copper and the rate of interest twenty years hence, or the obsolescence of a new invention, or the position of private wealth-owners in the social system in 1970. About these matters there is no scientific basis to form any calculable probability whatever.

Keynes would therefore deny that entrepreneurs can form rational expectations of their future profits and that it is possible to derive expected values of future prices based on the serial dependence of the appropriate model. The fact remains that, behaviorally, firms do make projections about future market developments and form their best estimates of costs and prices. Currently the price of energy twenty years hence is being seriously studied by exploring the set of appropriate models and in principle future outcomes such as the price of tuna fish in 1990 have expected values, although the variance might increase the more we peer into the future. Otherwise, it is tautological to discuss mathematical expectations on the grounds that there is no scientific basis for accepting the contrary view. Yet Keynes does no more than this. In any event the rate of discount would reduce the importance of the more remote expectations while the nearer-term expectations might be more likely to have an expected value. Had Keynes addressed himself to these more appropriate expectations, his argument might have become more transparent. As it was, he left the way in which long term entrepreneurial expectations alter in extremely vague terms despite the major role they are attributed in determining the variance of the marginal efficiency of capital. It is one thing to claim that entrepreneurial expected values cannot exist; it is quite another to go on to deliberate how 'the delicate balance of spontaneous optimism' relates 'to the nerves and hysteria and even the digestions and reactions to the weather of those upon whose spontaneous activities it [investment] largely depends.' [p. 162] and to treat the result as a key-stone of a theory about macrodynamics.

As unsatisfactory and confusing as his 'theory' of entrepreneurial expectations may be, Keynes' analysis of speculative expectations is hardly less exasperating. To some extent this analysis hinges upon his conclusions about entrepreneurial expectations, since he argues [pp. 152–3] that an investor can avoid the need to form long term entrepreneurial expectations by holding stock so that 'the only risk he runs is that of a genuine change in the news *over the near future*, as to the likelihood of which he can attempt to form his own judgement, and which is unlikely to be very large'. In other words Keynes concedes that over the near future expected values exist. But he goes on to argue that speculators (i.e. stock holders) ignore the long term and react irresponsibly to short term developments. (But how can they take a reasoned long term view when Keynes himself has just told us that this is impossible?!) His contempt is exuberant:

> This battle of wits to anticipate the basis of conventional valuation a few months hence, rather than the prospective yield of an investment over a long term of years, does not even require gulls amongst the public to feed the maws of the professional; – it can be played by professionals amongst themselves. Nor is it necessary that anyone should keep his simple faith in the conventional basis of valuation having any genuine long-term validity. For it is, so to speak, a game of Snap, of Old Maid, of Musical Chairs – a pastime in which he is victor who says Snap neither too soon nor too late, who passes the Old Maid to his neighbour before the game is over, who secures a chair for himself when the music stops. These games can be played with zest and enjoyment, though all the players know that it is the Old Maid which is circulating, or that when the music stops some of the players will find themselves unseated.
>
> Or, to change the metaphor slightly, professional investment may be likened to those newspaper competitions in which the competitors have to pick out the six prettiest faces from a hundred photographs, the prize being awarded to the competitor whose choice most nearly corresponds to the average preferences of the competitors as a whole; so that each competitor has to pick, not those faces which he himself finds prettiest, but those which he thinks likeliest to catch the fancy of the other competitors, all of

whom are looking at the problem from the same point of view. It is not a case of choosing those which, to the best of one's judgement, are really the prettiest, nor even those which average opinion genuinely thinks the prettiest. We have reached the third degree where we devote our intelligences to anticipating what average opinion expects the average opinion to be. And there are some, I believe, who practise the fourth, fifth and higher degrees [pp. 155-6].

As evidence for this view, Keynes cites [p. 154] the fact that the stock market does not discount seasonal influences on share prices, e.g. higher ice sales in the summer. But is he drawing the correct conclusions from such observations? In a world of perfect certainty, where investors know for sure what the seasonal demand will be, there should be no seasonal variation in share prices in an efficient market. But in practice it is difficult to unscramble seasonal effects from systematic influences on demand in which event the uncertainty that is implied may result in some seasonal variation. Since Keynes draws attention to the role of uncertainty in speculative behavior it is odd that he should have ignored its implications in this instance.

It is also clear that Keynes' arguments were heavily influenced by the Great Crash:

As the organization of investment markets improves, the risk of the pre-dominance of speculation does, however, increase. In one of the greatest investment markets in the world, namely, New York, the influence of spec-ulation is enormous. Even outside the field of finance, Americans are apt to be unduly interested in discovering what average opinion believes average opinion to be; and this national weakness finds its nemesis in the stock market [pp. 158-9].

However, his interpretation of the average opinion syndrome is unnecessarily exclusive, since the rational expectations hypothesis also requires investors to take a view of average opinion. In this case, however (as described in Chapter 6), average opinion is based upon underlying market forces and exerts a stabilizing influence on price movements and economic activity. It is rational enough for speculators to guess what the market will do tomorrow and it is also the case that these speculators are the market. The insight of the rational expectations hypothesis is that the expectation for tomorrow is not independent of the expectation for the day after tomorrow or the day after that, etc., etc. In this way, short term expectations are linked to longer term expectations and since the latter are likely to depend on long term equilibrium consider-ations the average opinion syndrome is constrained by the boundary conditions that this observation implies. The mere existence of short term speculative holding periods is no more an indication of the irrationality of speculators than is the observation that, at any moment in time on their long distance journeys, truck-drivers focus on the next half mile or so an indication of the irrationality of truck-drivers. In a journey from Washington DC to San Francisco the next half mile depends critically on the destination itself; a similar relationship exists between short term speculation and long term equilibrium.

Perhaps to Keynes, speculation is regarded as a will-of-the-wisp because he rules out the concept of long term expected values; as it were, our truck-driver has no clear destination when he leaves Washington DC. Nevertheless, Keynes stops to consider the role of the long term view.

If the reader interjects that there must surely be large profits to be gained from the other players in the long run by a skilled individual who, unperturbed by the prevailing pastime, continues to purchase investments on the best genuine long-term expectations he can frame, he must be answered, first of all, that there are, indeed, such serious-minded individuals and that it makes a vast difference to an investment market whether or not they predominate in their influence over the game-players. But we must also add that there are several factors which jeopardise the predominance of such individuals in modern investment markets. Investment based on genuine long-term expectation is so difficult today as to be scarcely practicable. He who attempts it must surely lead much more laborious days and run greater risks than he who tries to guess better than the crowd how the crowd will behave; and, given equal intelligence, he may make more disastrous mistakes. There is no clear evidence from experience that the investment policy which is socially advantageous coincides with that which is most profitable. It needs more intelligence to defeat the forces of time and our ignorance of the future than to beat the gun. Moreover, life is not long enough; – human nature desires quick results, there is a peculiar zest in making money quickly, and remoter gains are discounted by the average man at a very high rate. The game of professional investment is intolerably boring and overexacting to anyone who is entirely exempt from the gambling instinct; whilst he who has it must pay to this propensity the appropriate toll. Furthermore, an investor who proposes to ignore near-term market fluctuations needs greater resources for safety and must not operate on so large a scale, if at all, with borrowed money – a further reason for the higher return from the pastime to a given stock of intelligence and resources. Finally it is the long-term investor, he who most promotes the public interest, who will in practice come in for most criticism, wherever investment funds are managed by committees or boards or banks. For it is in the essence of his behaviour that he should be eccentric, unconventional and rash in the eyes of average opinion. If he is successful, that will only confirm the general belief in his rashness; and if in the short run he is unsuccessful, which is very likely, he will not receive much mercy. Worldly wisdom teaches that it is better for reputation to fail conventionally than to succeed unconventionally [pp. 156–8].

But is brilliant invective enough here? Or is the diatribe a reflection of his own personal life? We know that in his earlier days (up to 1920) Keynes found it difficult to resist the temptation of the gaming-table. But once he turned to professional speculation the gaming-tables became less seductive and from 1919 through 1937 he ran a highly active speculative account in foreign exchange, commodities and stocks for himself and in 1924 he became First Bursar of King's College in which capacity he accumulated substantial speculative profits. Harrod [1951] tells us that Keynes' market tactic was to take the long view and to stick with it through the vicissitudes of the market. However, in May 1924 he was 'ruined' when the German mark suddenly appreciated for a three month period and he had to sell. Could Keynes possibly be referring to himself when he talks about the 'skilled individual' and 'the investor who proposes to ignore near-term market fluctuations'. Also, as Harrod [1951, pp. 351 and 354] tells us, Keynes had considerable disagreement with his colleagues on the various investment trusts of which he was a member about his refusal to deviate from his long term view. Perhaps this is what Keynes had in mind in the closing sentence of the previous quotation. All this is by way of hypothesis, but there is a genuine possibility that Keynes is extrapolating from his own experiences. Certainly, he provides no logical basis for his claims; a reversal of his conclusions would have been equally plausible.

An interesting aside is that Keynes experimented with trade cycle theory to forecast stock movements but Harrod [1951, p. 352] records, 'In due course he himself became sceptical of the practical value of business-cycle theory for the purpose of private gain, and concentrated on the careful choice of particular investments, mainly with a view to their long term prospects.' Taking the long view is a form of rational expectations in itself, but Keynes the professional speculator seemed to discount the practicability of fully rational expectations in rejecting the cyclical information conveyed by the appropriate model. We therefore have an interesting dichotomy between Keynes the professional speculator and Keynes the academic writing about speculation.

All this led Keynes to the conclusion that 'The spectacle of modern investment markets has sometimes moved me towards the conclusion that to make the purchase of an investment permanent and indissoluble, like marriage except by reason of death or other grave cause, might be a useful remedy for our contemporary evils' [p. 160]. On the same basis he advised high capital transfer taxes to reduce the liquidity of equities. On the other hand, if expectations are formed rationally the conclusions that Keynes draws in Chapter

12 of the *General Theory* fall away. Our case is that Keynes never successfully
repudiated the principles that lie behind the rational expectations hypothesis
although it is evident that he attempted to do so. Of course, we should recall
that the rational expectations hypothesis was not formalized until well after
Keynes had died.

Stability

As discussed in the previous chapter, and further clarified in Chapter 6 below,
it is difficult to conduct a meaningful discussion about stability in the absence
of a satisfactory theory of expectations. In view of our conclusions in the previous section it follows that much of what Keynes had to say about stability
in the *General Theory* is spoilt by the unsatisfactory treatment of expectations.
Nevertheless, a number of issues seem worth discussing, especially in relation
to what Keynes had to say about stability and wage flexibility.

His main thesis was that a fall in money wages in the face of unemployment
could exacerbate a depression since effective demand would be lowered. However, once wages had fallen so low that they were expected to rise again
(Keynes never gave a reason for this) the marginal efficiency of capital would
be raised and the economy would recover. Keynes is therefore suggesting
global stability but local instability in the labor market and consequently
rejects money-wage flexibility on purely practical grounds: 'it would be much
better that wages should be rigidly fixed and deemed incapable of material
changes, than that depressions should be accompanied by a gradual downward
tendency of money wages' [p. 265]. This conclusion is repeated on page 270;
as it were, the cure of downward wage flexibility is worse than the disease.

To his comfort, Keynes hypothesized that money wages would in any event
tend to be rigid, especially in a downward direction. He argued that workers
and their trade unions attempt to maintain wage relativities rather than absolute
real wage levels. Thus a rise in prices that reduces all workers' real wages is
more acceptable than a decentralized unilateral series of nominal wage reductions that would have the same effect. It would be a different matter if
the labor market were centralized and prices could be coordinated with wages;
at this level of abstraction Keynes would accept the nostrums of the classics
regarding real wage flexibility. But in the real world he is forced to reject
them. He notes that 'it is fortunate that the workers, though unconsciously,
are instinctively more reasonable than the classical school, inasmuch as they
resist reductions in money-wages' [p. 14]. In other words, trade union practice unwittingly has a stabilizing effect on the economy. But the important
thing to notice is that Keynes' main arguments about wage rigidity are normative rather than positive; the economy is likely to run more smoothly if
money wages are rigid than if they are not. Also, if money wages are flexible,

prices would be flexible and, as we shall see, Keynes thought that flexibility and volatility would go together. Wage flexibility would therefore undermine the role of money in the economy. 'The normal expectation that the value of output will be more stable in terms of money than in terms of any other commodity, depends of course, not on wages being arranged in terms of money, but on wages being relatively *sticky* in terms of money' [p. 237]. And, 'It is because of money's other characteristics – those, especially, which make it *liquid* – that wages where fixed in terms of it, tend to be sticky' [p. 233]. By 'tend', Keynes seems to mean 'ought'. In other words, Keynes' thesis about the local instability of money wage rates led him to conclude that not only would wage flexibility be disruptive in the labor market, it would also undermine the role of money in the economy. Indeed, vestiges of his view that wage and price stability are desirable may be found in the *Tract*, where the idea was first pioneered. At the best of times, Keynes' references to wage-price instability are obscure. We cite some examples.

A. If, indeed, some attempt were made to stabilize real wages by fixing wages in terms of wage goods, the effect could only be to cause a violent oscillation of money prices. For every small fluctuation in the propensity to consume and the inducement to invest would cause money-prices to rush violently between zero and infinity. That money wages should be more stable than real wages is a condition of the system possessing inherent stability [p. 239].

B. For if competition between unemployed workers always led to a very great reduction of the money-wage, there would be a violent instability of the price level. Moreover, there might be no position of stable equilibrium except in conditions consistent with full employment; since the wage-unit might have to fall without limit until it reached a point where the effect of the abundance of money in terms of the wage-unit on the rate of interest was sufficient to restore a level of full employment [p. 253].

C. It follows therefore, that if labour were to respond to conditions of gradually diminishing employment by offering its services at a gradually diminishing money-wage, this would not, as a rule, have the effect of reducing real wages and might even have the effect of increasing them, through its adverse influence on the volume of output. The chief result of this policy would be to cause a great instability of prices, so violent perhaps as to make business calculations futile in an economic society functioning after the manner of that in which we live. To suppose that a flexible wage policy is a right and proper adjunct of a system which on the whole is one of laissez faire, is the opposite of the truth. It is only in a highly authoritarian society, where sudden substantial, all-round

changes could be decreed that a flexible wage-policy could function
with success. One can imagine it in operation in Italy, Germany or
Russia, but not in France, the United States or Great Britain [p. 269].

D. If, on the contrary, money-wages were to fall without limit whenever
there was a tendency for less than full employment . . . there would be
no resting place below full employment until either the rate of interest
was incapable of falling further or wages were zero. In fact we must
have *some* factor, the values of which in terms of money is, if not fixed,
at least sticky, to give us any stability of values in a monetary system
[pp. 303-4].

Why did Keynes believe so strongly that the labor market was inherently
unstable? B suggests that the instability is a general equilibrium rather than a
partial equilibrium phenomenon, i.e. as wages fall effective demand is increased
indirectly via the additional investment induced by the fall in the rate of
interest when prices fall, but this feed-back is insufficiently strong to generate
local stability. The same applies to C. Since, as already discussed, Keynes chose
to discount the real balance effect he has ignored a stabilizing factor in the
situation.[20] On the other hand, A seems to conform to conventional notions
about partial equilibrium responses. If real wages are fixed, an excess supply
of labor will cause a downward wage–price spiral and the converse if there is
an excess demand. But the relationship with the market for money is unclear
in this context. Finally, D should be interpreted in the light of B and C, i.e.
the instability is not due to unstable roots in the labor market but unstable
roots in the general equilibrium model that Keynes poses, i.e. the effect of
falling interest rates on investment is judged to be insufficiently strong to
guarantee stability.

It should be pointed out that even in Keynes' model there is no inherent
reason why these roots should be unstable since, if the reactions in the investment and money markets were strong enough, the feed-back from the stimulus
to effective demand when wages fall would stabilize the situation. We must
conclude, therefore, that Keynes considered the instability to be an empirical
matter rather than an issue of principle and Keynes no more than surmises
about this important matter.

At this juncture it is worth commenting on the familiar notion of 'under
full-employment equilibrium'. This issue first arises on page 30 of the *General
Theory:* 'the economic system may find itself in stable equilibrium with N
[employment] at a level below full employment'. But the context here is the
ceteris paribus or partial equilibrium one of constant wages and prices. Once
Keynes endogenizes wages and prices the concept of 'under full-employment
equilibrium' vanishes and in this general equilibrium context the real issue that
emerges in the *General Theory* is that of local instability, as we have seen.[21]

However, the logical flaw of the 'liquidity trap' syndrome would still remain, subject of course to the criticisms that have already been proposed. Thus, apart from his failure to consider the possibility of rational expectations in his treatment of stability as well as his ignoring the role of the real balance effect, Keynes' own model would not seem to be necessarily unstable. Keynes merely assumed that the parameter sizes were such as to render it unstable and even then Keynes seemed to discount global instability although at times even this was unclear. However, Minsky's claim that 'Keynesian economics as the economics of disequilibrium is the economics of permanent disequilibrium' (Minsky [1975, p. 68]) and his related argument that 'Each state nurtures forces that lead to its own destruction' [p. 128] would seem to be an unacceptably imaginative interpretation of the General Theory. For in abandoning the notion of local stability it does not automatically follow that Keynes also abandoned the notion of the equilibrium about which the solution was locally unstable. Indeed, as we have seen, the contrary is explicit in the General Theory itself.[22]

In this context the real component of the Keynesian revolution would seem to be, as Clower [1966] pointed out, in terms of the departure from conventional Walrasian notions in a decentralized monetary economy. Apart from the dichotomy that a decision to save today did not reappear in the Walrasian system as a vector of future consumption in the various goods markets, there was another equally important dichotomy. An excess demand for money, unlike an excess demand for bananas, would have deflationary tendencies. In the real world, fiat money acts as yet another slip twixt cup and lip of one real market and another; and so unemployment may result during the ensuing adjustment process. Or, as Keynes puts it:

> Unemployment develops, that is to say, because people want the moon; – men cannot be employed when the object of desire (i.e. money) is something which cannot be produced and the demand for which cannot be readily choked off. There is no remedy but to persuade the public that green cheese is practically the same thing and to have a green cheese factory (i.e. central bank) under public control [p. 235].

This and the investment–saving dichotomy were the essential revolutionary insights of the General Theory rather than Keynes' personal views about local and global instability.

Political economy

We have already remarked that part of the popular imagery of the Keynesian revolution is that Keynes paved the way for a strategy of activism in macroeconomic policy. Oddly enough, Keynes did not devote too much time to policy matters in the *General Theory* although where he does his position is clear enough and the popular imagery is indeed appropriate. We have to bear in mind that the *General Theory* is the product of a brilliant academic who at the same time was a compulsive commentator on current issues, and the economic issues of 1933–35 (while he was writing the *General Theory*) must have been provoking indeed. In the next section we shall delve further into what some of Keynes' motivations might have been, but it is difficult to judge how far Keynes intended the *General Theory* to be a scientific contribution and how far he was writing political economy, while it is clear enough that he was writing some mixture of the two. We cannot rule out the possibility that at times he might have sacrificed science for political economy and that under less pressing circumstances his scientific standpoint might have been different. For example Johnson [1975, p. 115–16] has speculated that Keynes was propagating second best policies since the authorities had ruled out the first best options. If so, the applied economics in the *General Theory* would be of a transient value, and unless the forthcoming Keynes Papers unearth any inner thoughts of Keynes on this issue we shall never be able to resolve it.

On the basis of the arguments considered in the previous section Keynes decided that wage deflation was an anti-social adjustment mechanism in relation to unemployment. As Leijonhufvud [1968, p. 335] has put it, 'to him the "classical" cure smacked of leeches and bloodletting – primitive and disrespectable methods which were likely, as often as not, so to weaken the patient as to kill him'. The wage deflation cure was considered to be worse than the disease. The alternative was to expand demand through monetary policy – as it were, to pull the economy up to a new equilibrium rather than to force it back into an old equilibrium. 'Having regard to human nature and our institutions, it can only be a foolish person who would prefer a flexible wage policy to a flexible money policy, unless he can point to advantages from the former which are not obtainable from the latter' [p. 268]. But the question has been begged and there are reasons why there may be disadvantages to Keynes' prescription although it might have been too much to have expected this insight in the 1930s. The problem is that if society grows to realize that the authorities will do their best to guarantee full employment via demand management policies, we are crossing the Rubicon from a money standard to a labor standard. In the first instance wage demands will tend to become undisciplined since the full employment policy will ensure that unrequited wage increases will be costless to those who press for them. In the aggregate, the worst that can happen to the labor market is that full employment will be eventually restored by the authorities, in which case nothing can be lost by excessive wage settlements. But there is a divergence between the individual worker or trade union and the economy as a whole, and eventually the individual loses confidence in the value of money since the pursuit of full employment policies makes monetary growth endemic, given undisciplined wage settlements, and an accelerationist model of inflationary expectations results. The lid is off, the sky is the limit and the money standard, which is the bulwark of the exchange economy, is lost. The logical result is not full employment, but barter. Thus rather than 'leeches and bloodletting' the Keynesian remedy is like the drug that ultimately can never satisfy; although in the short term it may be effective, in the long term it may destroy.

Keynes argued for the socialization of investment on two quite separate accounts, the short term and the long term. The short term argument follows from his analysis of the irrationality of expectations in relation to the stock market and investment. 'I expect to see the State, which is in a position to calculate the marginal efficiency of capital goods on long views and on the basis of the general social advantage, taking an even greater responsibility for directly organizing investment' [p. 164; see also p. 320]. But if expectations are formed irrationally, what guarantee is there that the views of officials who are not even risking their own capital will take a more responsible view? The political economist has to balance the prospect of market failure against the equally plausible prospect of government failure, and it is hardly necessary to list the instances of the latter in countries where investment has been socialized. However, we have already queried Keynes' premise about the inefficiency of capital markets upon which this important result is based.

Keynes' argument for the long term socialization of investment was based on the fear that as consumer demand ultimately became satiated, then, along with the euthanasia of the rentier, the marginal efficiency of capital would approach zero and private investment would cease in face of the 'liquidity trap'. Thus capitalism under *laissez-faire* was subject to secular depression, especially in the mature capitalist economies. 'I conceive, therefore, that a somewhat comprehensive socialization of investment will prove the only means of securing an approximation to full employment; though this need not exclude all manner of compromises and of devices by which public authority will cooperate with private initiative' [p. 378]. It might of course be asked why under such idealized circumstances full employment should be desirable. If we all have to work half-time to meet our wants then so be it; in the limit we should be as Adam and Eve before the Fall in the Garden of Eden. More fundamentally, however, it would seem that Keynes' case is like Malthus in reverse since the richest societies even after the one or two generations that Keynes allowed for show no indication of any secular satiety of consumer desires. On the contrary, there seem to be no practical limits to what man can think of consuming and that the only limits to growth are social and physical.[23]

Concluding remarks

No attempt will be made to summarize the foregoing discussion. Instead, it may be useful to place what has been said in an appropriate perspective. Hopefully the impression has not been that Keynes had been pre-empted by some of his predecessors and that many if not most of the main ideas in the *General Theory* were ill considered. Far from it. Nevertheless, our objective has been to scrutinize a number of important sacred cows at fairly close range, especially those that are germane to the general subject matter of this essay on the principle of macroeconomic intervention and policy. The main thesis has been that the normative economics in the *General Theory* rest on weak and questionable foundations and to an obvious extent this judgment implicates some of the positive economics too.

What has been said is consistent with Clower's interpretation of the Keynesian revolution, although not necessarily the interpretations of Leijonhufvud and Minsky. We refer here to the intellectual revolution in relation to Keynes' departure from Walrasiana to a world of decentralized money systems where an excess supply in one real market does not necessarily translate into an excess demand in another on account of the savings–investment dichotomy, the dichotomy generated through the market for money where money is not a commodity, and the false trading generated by imperfect information. While his predecessors had grappled with these issues, as has been pointed out, it was Keynes who managed to forge them into a plausible intellectual framework on the basis of which others might proceed.

The implication of this intellectual revolution (which may sound commonplace now) is that 'Keynesian economics brings current transactions into price theory whereas traditional analysis explicitly leaves them out' (Clower [1966]). The result of this is that 'when income appears as an independent variable in the market excess-demand functions – more generally, where transactions quantities enter into the definition of these functions – traditional price theory ceases to shed any light on the dynamic stability of a market economy'. This last statement is also true, but what seems questionable is whether Keynes adequately showed in the *General Theory* that the macroeconomy based on this model was locally unstable, especially since almost all of his main policy prescriptions were based on this deduction.

Was Keynes aware of this weakness? Patinkin [1976, page 115] in a related context suspects that he was. We have already commented on the balance between Keynes, the intellectual and Keynes, the political economist. Also, we have commented on some possible personal motivations that Keynes might have had when writing about macroeconomic expectations. Casual psychoanalysis of scientific expression seems an unfair occupation. Nevertheless, it would seem that an appreciation of Keynes, the economist, without a consideration of Keynes, the stylist, would be an incomplete one.

We begin by considering why Keynes eschewed a mathematical presentation of his ideas in the *General Theory*. His feelings on this matter are clear:

> It is a great fault of symbolic pseudo-mathematical methods of formalizing a system of economic analysis . . . that they expressly assume strict independence between the factors involved and lose all their cogency and authority if this hypothesis is disallowed; whereas, in ordinary discourse, where we are not blindly manipulating but know all the time what we are doing and what the words mean, we can keep 'at the back of our head' the necessary reserves and qualifications and the adjustments which we shall have to make later on, in a way in which we cannot keep complicated partial differentials 'at the back' of several pages of algebra which assume they all vanish. Too large a proportion of recent 'mathematical' economics are mere concoctions, as imprecise as the initial assumptions they rest on, which allow the author to lose sight of the complexities and interdependencies of the real world in a maze of pretentious and unhelpful symbols. [pp. 297-8].

As may be realized by glancing at page 275 of the *General Theory*, it would seem that this out-burst is aimed at Pigou's *Theory of Unemployment* rather than mathematical economics in general.[24] Indeed, the *General Theory* itself occasionally adopts a mathematical presentation, and some would say that this representation violated precisely what Keynes had in mind. Moreover, it should be recalled that by the standards of the day the *General Theory* must have looked forbidding enough in view of its departure from a strict literary style. For Keynes apparently only set-down a partial equilibrium presentation of his model; he never made a serious effort to formalize his entire model (as others have attempted to do since) and to show how and where his macro-economics departed from those of his predecessors. Instead he too assumed, in his presentation, that partial differentials would vanish. Had Keynes been more mathematically precise it is arguable that the *General Theory* would have been less ambiguous, clearer and not the subject matter for exegetical discourse about what the master himself really meant. Perhaps this would have torn away some of the mystique that Keynes intended. To have been too precise might have revealed too much of a proximity between the *General Theory* and the economics of his predecessors. It might have established the 'neoclassical synthesis' even before the dichotomy had been satisfactorily established.

Therefore, it is possible that in 1936 mathematical clarity would not have served his revolutionary purposes. On the other hand it is possible that he genuinely believed that his model was not mathematically tractable, especially in view of the conceptual difficulties associated with the treatment of expectations. A hint of this comes in a letter he wrote to Gerald Shove[25] shortly after the *General Theory* was published.

But you ought not to feel inhibited by a difficulty in making the solution precise. It may be that a part of the error in the classical analysis is due to that attempt. As soon as one is dealing with the influence of expectations and of transitory experience, one is, in the nature of things, outside the realm of the formally exact.

Keynes seems to be implying here that stochastic processes are not amenable to formal presentation, or that the subject matter required a different mathematical technique such as that of dynamic stochastic processes. It would have been useful to know whether Keynes thought these alternative techniques were inappropriate too or whether he was simply unaware of them.[26] On the other hand, it has taken virtually forty years since the *General Theory* was published for the profession to realize that the subject matter of macroeconomics requires such techniques as is illustrated by the mode of presentation of the rational expectations hypothesis during recent years.

In his *Treatise on Probability* he wrote, 'In writing a book of this kind, the author must, if he is to put his point of view clearly, pretend sometimes to a little more conviction than he feels. He must give his own argument a chance, so to speak, nor be too ready to depress its vitality with a wet cloud of doubt.' This could just as easily have been written in relation to the *General Theory*. Indeed, Harrod was most concerned about Keynes' style in this context, except he thought Keynes was exaggerating the differences between himself and the 'classics'. In August 1935 he wrote to Keynes:[27]

> What I think is important from the point of view of the effect and influence of the work is that you should minimize and not maximize the amount of generally accepted doctrine that your view entails scrapping of. A general holocaust is more exciting. But anything you write now has such immense relevance that you no longer require these artificial stimulants to secure attention. Everyone will be all attention in any case. Don't go out of your way to provoke dogged resistance on the part of professional economists.[28]

Elizabeth Johnson [1977] has drawn attention to Keynes' bombastic writing style and that Keynes believed that 'Words should be a little wild for they are the assault of thoughts upon the unthinking.' His tendency was to exaggerate rather than to integrate, and there can be little doubt that Keynes was at his most characteristic in this regard in writing the *General Theory*. With the benefit of hindsight it seems more like the case that Keynes' style was a source of confusion in this context than help to his own cause. Just a few days before this correspondence with Harrod began we find Keynes himself in a somewhat apprehensive frame of mind in a letter to Kahn who was Keynes' closest intellectual confidante while writing the *General Theory*. He wrote,[29] 'I am in the stage of not liking my book very much. It all seems very angry

and much ado about a matter much simpler than I make it appear.' Nevertheless his reply to Harrod was perhaps characteristic:[30]

> But the general effect of your reaction, apart from making me realize that
> I must re-write all this drastically if I am to make myself clear, is to make
> me feel that my assault on the classical school ought to be intensified rather
> than abated. My motive is, of course, not in order to get read. But it may
> be needed in order to get understood. I am frightfully afraid of the ten-
> dency, of which I see some signs in you, to appear to accept my constructive
> part and to find some accommodation between this and deeply cherished
> views which would in fact only be possible if my constructive part has been
> partially misunderstood. That is to say, I expect a great deal of what I write
> to be water off a duck's back. I am certain that it will be water off a duck's
> back unless I am sufficiently strong in my criticism to force the classicals
> to make rejoinders. I *want*, so to speak, to raise a dust; because it is only out
> of the controversy that will arise that what I am saying will get understood.

This line of thought has already been noted by Patinkin [1976, p. 115]. We
cannot rule out the possibility that Keynes overstated his case or obscured it
where it was weak in order to raise the dust. It is also possible that he chose
to ignore the neoclassical synthesis which was perhaps the ultimate rejoinder
of the classicals or neoclassicals. To have presented this in the *General Theory*
could have been counter-productive.

Patinkin's thesis is perhaps supported by two further observations. First,
in the preface to the *General Theory* we still find Keynes in a state of appre-
hension: 'My controversial passages are aimed at providing some material for
an answer; and I must ask forgiveness if, in the pursuit of sharp distinctions,
my controversy is itself too keen.' And, shortly after the publication of the
General Theory, Hawtrey prepared a memorandum for circulation within HM
Treasury which was supposed to be a critical clarification of the *General
Theory*. Keynes objected in the strongest terms to the contents of this memorandum and replied arguing to Hawtrey,[31] 'it seems to me clear that at least
half my book has been for you like water off a duck's back, and the other
half, which you have attended to very closely, you have tried to interpret in
the light of ideas which were not mine'.

So, we find Keynes still troubled by the prospect of the *General Theory*
'falling like water off a duck's back'. It was obviously on his mind, rightly or
wrongly, and it is likely that these fears introduced an unscientific element
into the *General Theory* which in the short term may or may not have had
the intended effect. In the longer term the wood can be seen for the trees.

CHAPTER 3

The basic neoclassical model

In this and the remaining chapters of the book, we explore a number of theoretical issues in macroeconomic modeling where the main purpose of the discussion is to shape a view about the appropriate form of macroeconomic stabilization. The present chapter is concerned with setting out the basic analytical tools that will be used and the presentation will proceed from highly aggregated and simplified models of a closed economy to disaggregated and more sophisticated models of an open economy. The presentation will also be static in two respects. First, throughout this book we shall abstract from secular economic growth in terms of wealth, labor force, output, etc., since an analysis of growth will not be germane to the main discussion. Secondly, we shall assume that all the behavioral relationships and adjustment processes are instantaneous, i.e. they have no lags. Since this assumption is germane to the discussion it shall be relaxed in Chapter 7. However, for expositional purposes it seemed advantageous to explore the long-run version of the model first.

The basic conception of the models to be discussed is neoclassical in the sense discussed in Chapter 1. In other words a series of aggregated markets are postulated for money, bonds, goods, etc., which are assumed to clear simultaneously and in the present context more or less instantaneously. An excess supply of any particular product or asset will generate price changes for the asset which in turn will repercuss onto other assets and their prices. In other words, the macroeconomy can be conceived as a series of related markets where everything affects everything else.

A non-neoclassical view of macroeconomic behavior would be based on the assumption that the macroeconomy cannot be conceived of as a series of connected markets which have clearing tendencies *even in the long term.* At least two possible justifications for this spring to mind. First, prices might be rigid so that, by assumption, markets are prevented from clearing in the normal way. Nevertheless, nature abhors a vacuum and so they might clear in an abnormal and inefficient way. An example of this is the clearing process described by Harris & Todaro [1970] where rigid wages in the context of a dual labor market may lead to urban unemployment as an equilibrating phenomenon. Price 'stickiness' on the other hand would merely slow down the clearing process rather than distort it or prevent it completely. The implications of price 'stickiness' will be taken on board in Chapter 7. Secondly, the markets might be affected by existence problems, which in this context might have two versions. First, the roots of the model might be considered unstable, in which case for all practical purposes equilibrium prices are unlikely to emerge. Secondly, in a decentralized economy where information is difficult to obtain and where false trading cannot generally be revoked the economy might be physically unable to eliminate all involuntary excess demand and supply. Clearly, the breakdown of markets would undermine the neoclassical theory that is to be developed in this essay.

The possible instability of roots will be discussed in Chapter 6. The second version of the existence problem is much more fundamental since it may amount to the argument that we do not as yet have a satisfactory theory of the transmission of information, search, etc., in which case market analysis has yet to be defined satisfactorily and a theory of supply and demand is premature. A related criticism is that the role of money in the economy has yet to be demonstrated,[1] in which case there would as yet be no basis for specifying demand functions for money. While sympathizing with the need for stronger microeconomic foundations to macro-theory, the assumption made in this book is that it is reasonable to proceed at the aggregative level despite allegations of microeconomic infirmity.[2] Alternatively the assumption is to proceed as if the structural macroeconomic relationships to be postulated are plausible. Keynes was anti-neoclassical under both of the above assumptions although it is difficult to be too clear about this, as we have seen in the previous chapter. However, we should take care to discount the phony sceptics who, because of mis-specification or incomplete specification mistake partial equilibrium solutions for the truth about the long run and who then seek out policy solutions for essentially imaginary problems.

We begin by discussing the case of the closed economy. Thereafter the analysis is extended to the 'small' open economy case.

I The closed economy

The objective in this section is to explore a series of related analytical issues in a closed-economy setting which takes up the objections to the conventional IS–LM framework that were raised in Chapter 2. Although in the interests of realism the model that is developed eventually becomes quite complicated we begin with simple models which stand in their own right and which afford an opportunity to familiarize with the basic concepts which serve as building-blocks in the more sophisticated models. It is stressed that all these models are specific versions of the general neoclassical idea and that while they inevitably differ on points of detail they cohere in terms of basic economic principles. They cohere in the sense that in each case the basic processes are based upon market analysis; that excess supply or demand generate price responses which eventually equilibrate the markets which are considered.

It is therefore the processes rather than the details of the models that are important. Moreover, in developing these models we shall draw on well-established ideas and principles of macroeconomic analysis, yet in every case it will be shown that the basic results are similar and are robust to a broad spectrum of alternative specifications. Indeed, this is a crucial theme to this and Chapters 4 and 5.

The particular issues explored in this section are

   (i) the relationship between money and output or the simple quantity theory of money,

  (ii) the real balance effect,

 (iii) the income–expenditure analysis of Keynesian economics,

 (iv) the role of bonds and 'crowding out',

  (v) the introduction of employment into the model, and

 (vi) a review of the Keynesian model.

Money and goods

The technology of exchange. The simplest conceivable model of macroeconomic behavior is also most probably the oldest, namely a model consisting of goods or homogeneous output on the one hand and money on the other. This will also be recognized as the simple quantity theory of money where money (M) and the price level (P) are proportionate, i.e. where

$$MV = PT \tag{3-1}$$

assuming as usual that velocity (V) is a constant and that the number of transactions (T) is also fixed. The quantity theory emphasizes the role of money as a medium of exchange for a given transactions technology. This technology refers to the way in which society has organized its trading in terms of shopping, inventories, payment periods, etc. For example, each individual has the choice of going to the supermarket less often and of holding larger inventories of food and other household goods instead. With deep-freezers and a large enough larder the individual could buy in bulk and make perhaps only one very large transaction a year. His decision will depend on the costs of storage, the costs of the trips to the supermarket, the discounts he can get on bulk-buying, etc. The same principles will apply to firms, who will have to balance the costs of larger inventories against the benefits of a larger transactions period and lower transactions and exchange costs.

We may assume that households and firms will seek to minimize their exchange costs along the lines described in fig. 3-1. The curve II' illustrates the positive relationship between storage or inventory costs (physical as well as financial), while TT' indicates the inverse relationship between the transactions period and marketing costs in terms of fewer trips to the shop, etc. Adding these two curves together implies the total cost curve of CC'. Transactions costs as a whole are minimized at a, in which case TP^* is the optimal transactions period and C^* is the minimum transactions cost.[3]

Each household and firm will tend to determine its own optimal transactions behavior and for society as a whole the volume of transactions (T) will reflect the technology of exchange that emerges from this optimization process. Clearly a society which selects relatively long transactions periods will require fewer services of money as a medium of exchange since there will be fewer exchanges to make. Also, the medium of exchange requirement will tend to depend on the relationship between purchases and salary receipts. If we were all paid on the same day that we needed to make our purchases, i.e. if there were no lag between our receipts and expenditures, there would be scarcely any need to hold inventories of money at all. On the other hand if we get paid monthly and we need to make purchases on a daily basis, we should have to hold cash inventories between one pay-day and the next to tide us over between transactions. Up to a point the individual might wish to relate his transactions period to his pay period since part of his transactions costs will consist of inventories of cash balances. This possibility is outlined in fig. 3-2.

Curve CC' is taken from fig. 3-1, while MM' is the cash balance cost relation-

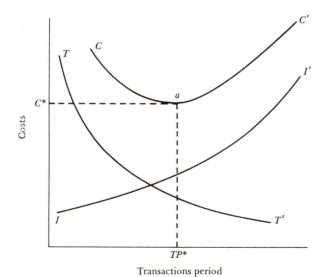

Figure 3-1 The optimal transactions period

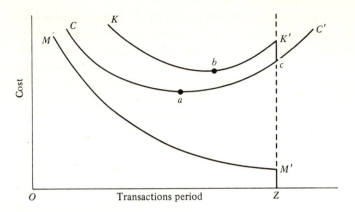

Figure 3-2 Transactions and payment periods

ship reflecting the length of the transactions period; the shorter the transactions period the longer the average volume of cash balances that are required, and/or the more frequent the trips that have to be made to the bank to economize on these balances. However, the basic costs to holding cash balances is the rate of interest that is forgone as well as the greater exposure to risk of robbery or loss. The higher the rate of interest, the higher will be MM'. OZ is the length of the payment period. If the individual is paid monthly OZ will be a month. Notice that if the individual can synchronize his transactions period with his payment period his cash balance costs will be virtually zero, hence the cash balance cost relationship is in effect given by $MM'Z$. If $MM'Z$ is now added to CC', the result is $KK'c$. Whereas previously the optimal transactions period was given by a along CC', the minimum cost point is now at b along $KK'c$. In other words, when the costs of cash balances are taken into consideration it pays to lengthen the transactions period in order to reduce the need for costly inventories of cash balances – assuming that the payment period is longer than the optimal transactions period given by a.

It might happen that at c total exchange costs are less than at b. If this happens the individual will seek to wait until pay-day to make his purchases. However, this is unlikely to serve as a general solution, especially in societies where payment periods are longer than a week.

In this study we assume away the important microeconomic issues associated with real phenomena such as payments and transactions periods and how actual exchange technologies emerge. The previous comments merely reflect on awareness about a general problem area which merits a detailed study in its own right. This study might also cover the role of credit cards, changing work patterns (especially in relation to women), etc. It would also have to develop a theory of how optimal transactions periods derived at the microeconomic level would relate at the macro level since individuals' transactions periods must ultimately relate to each other if any actual transactions are to take place. We therefore assume that T is given as well as the relationship between the demand for money balances and the volume of transactions as determined by the relationship between the payments technology and the exchange technology for society as a whole.

We also assume a fixed relationship between the gross domestic product (Y) and the volume of transactions. In other words, if output increases, the volume of transactions increases proportionately. This assumption seems more plausible in relation to increases in the price level where, say, a 10% increase in the price level is likely to raise the money value of transactions by 10% too, than it does in relation to changes in real output where the volume of transactions might not have a simple relationship with the volume of output. If this is so the income elasticity of demand for money with respect to real output might be significantly different from unity while the elasticity with respect to the price level would not be.

Clearly, what is needed is a theory about the relationship between Y and T, or we ideally require data on T rather than Y. In the meanwhile we shall have to be content with the crude assumption that $T = aY$.

At least these relations lie behind the Cambridge version of the quantity theory

$$\frac{M}{P} = kY \tag{3-2}$$

where the coefficient, k, reflects two factors. First it reflects the relationship between the payments and transactions periods. The more that they coincide the smaller will be the value of k since cash balance requirements will be lower. Secondly, it will reflect the implicit relationship between T and Y. If as Y rises T rises less than proportionately, k will tend to be smaller since a marginal increase in Y will generate a smaller increase in the volume of transactions.

The real balance effect. If Y in equation (3-2) is fixed, an increase in the quantity of money will bring about a proportionate increase in the price level. This of course is the basic postulate of the quantity theory. This process takes place through the real balance effect that is implicit in equation (3-2). Consider a situation where the actual supply of real balances is greater than the desired volume of real balances as determined by equation (3-2). The demand for goods will tend to rise as each individual attempts to restore a balanced portfolio by switching out of money and into goods. Of course society as a whole cannot hold more goods since their volume is determined by the productive capacity of the economy. Consequently, we have a situation where too much money is chasing too few goods and the general price level begins to rise. It will continue to rise until the volume of real balances has been reduced to a level which is consistent with capacity output.

In equilibrium the demand for real output will equal $\bar{Y}$ which is capacity output. Generally, i.e. allowing for disequilibrium situations, the demand for real output will depend on the underlying demand plus the net demand generated by the real balance effect. Thus the generalized demand schedule may be written as

$$Y = \bar{Y} + b(M - P - kY) \qquad (3\text{-}3)$$

where Y, M and P are logarithms.[4] If the demand for real balances, kY, equals the supply of real balances, $M - P$, the demand for output will be at its capacity level, $\bar{Y}$. The coefficient b indicates the rate at which society attempts to divest itself of its surplus real balances.

In equation (3-4) we assume that the rate of inflation depends on the pressure of demand, which is measured by the percentage difference between demand, Y, and potential supply, $\bar{Y}$. Alternatively, $\bar{Y}$ is defined as the level of aggregate demand at which prices are stable, i.e. $\dot{P} = 0$, so that supply and demand are in balance. In general we assume that price inflation depends in the short term on the pressure of demand - as indicated in equation (3-4), i.e. that prices do not adjust instantaneously to equate Y with $\bar{Y}$. This is a common enough assumption and is the basis of much of Phillips Curve theory. Nevertheless it requires some justification since it has to be explained why prices do not adjust fully and instantaneously. This happens because people are assumed to proceed cautiously in the face of market signals. As they perceive a sellers' market they adjust prices upwards but not necessarily by an amount to equate Y and $\bar{Y}$. Thus short term market imbalances reflect the innate cautiousness of man. We shall return to the normative significance of such behavior in Chapters 6 and 7. We therefore postulate that

$$\dot{P} = c(Y - \bar{Y}) \qquad (3\text{-}4)$$

If we now substitute equation (3-3) into equation (3-4) we obtain a first order differential equation in the price level whose general solution is given in equation (3-5).

$$P(t) = Ae^{-dt} + M - k\bar{Y} \qquad (3\text{-}5)$$

where

$$d = cb/(1 + bk)$$

In other words, since the term Ae^{-dt} will tend to approach zero over time the price level in equilibrium will depend on capacity output and it will vary proportionately with the quantity of money. Also, this very simple model implies that the economy will tend to capacity output in the long run since for $\dot{P} = 0$ it is necessary that $Y = \bar{Y}$.

The rate of adjustment of the economy will depend on the parameters c, b and k. The greater the value of d the faster will be the speed of adjustment and d will vary directly with c and b and inversely with k. As b and c increase an excess real balance position will translate more rapidly into price increases as people divest themselves more rapidly of their excess balances and as traders raise their prices more rapidly as a consequence. The greater is k the less rapid the adjustment since the demand for money will tend to rise at a faster rate when Y increases and the real balance effect will consequently be milder.

These possibilities are illustrated in fig. 3-3, where initially the economy is at 'full-employment' at $\bar{Y}$ and the price level is initially P_0. We assume, however, that a bank failure or some other factor reduces the supply of money so that unemployment is generated and output falls to Y_1. The equilibrium price level that corresponds to this decline in the money supply is assumed to be P_1. Curves (i) and (ii) are implied by equation (3-5), i.e. as the price level gradually approaches its equilibrium value at b along curve (ii), full employment[5] is gradually restored at b along curve (i). If d is some larger number, curves (iii) and (iv) would be applicable and the adjustment would be faster and the volume of unemployment during the adjustment period would be less. In this case the new equilibrium is restored at a along curve (iii).

In other words the model that has been proposed is self correcting and has the properties of the quantity theory. It also provides for unemployment as an aspect of monetary disequilibrium, with the real balance effect acting as the main link between the real and monetary sectors. Notice that it makes no difference whether the money in the model is of the 'inside' or 'outside'

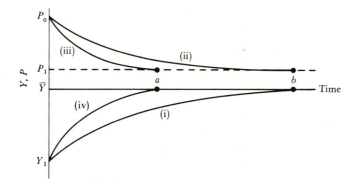

Figure 3-3 The real balance effect and unemployment

variety along the lines discussed by Gurley and Shaw [1960]. Wealth effects and real balance effects are conceptually quite different. If the price of bonds rises, creditors' gains will be matched by debtors' losses if they are 'inside' assets, and apart from a possible redistributive impact the wealth effect should net out to zero. The story, of course, would be different in the case of 'outside' assets. But the real balance effect is no more a wealth effect than is the peanut effect when the supply of peanuts is greater than their demand. For the supply of pecuniary services from money balances is a real phenomenon which does not disappear over the balance sheets any more than would the supply of television sets disappear over the balance sheet when TV sets are exchanged for financial assets. If society is oversupplied with monetary services it will attempt to divest itself of surplus balances whatever the origins of the money itself.

If money is of the 'outside' variety there may be wealth effects as well as real balance effects. Thus a price fall will raise the volume of real balances and this will generate real balance effects. But society as a whole will be richer since the real value of its wealth will have risen and a portfolio decision will have to be taken about how the new wealth shall be held. However, in this study, we do not concern ourselves with wealth effects in general but the real balance effect in particular. This view of the relationship between 'inside' money and the real balance effect has much in common with the view proposed originally by Pesek and Saving [1967].

The model encapsulated in equations (3-2)-(3-4) has significant dynamic elements in the sense that the general solution for the endogenous variables was dynamic. However, our intention in this chapter was to preoccupy ourselves with macro-statics rather than macro-dynamics. The Phillips Curve relationship implicit in equation (3-4) and the real balance effect in equation (3-3) combine to form a dynamic model of the economy reflecting the underlying assumptions of partial adjustment. Nevertheless, both of these relationships are instantaneous; they do not operate via distributed lags and it is in this special sense that the model is considered to be static. Also, we have abstracted from the role of expectations, which is considered in Chapters 6 and 7. It might therefore be more accurate to refer to the model as quasi-equilibrium or quasi-static since this will recognize that while each structural equation does not include any lagged effects, the general solutions for the endogenous variables are dynamic.

The income-expenditure effect. So far the model has incorporated monetary adjustments of the stock–flow type. When the stock of real balances was out of equilibrium flows of real expenditures were generated. Henceforth we shall refer to this as the stock–flow logic. As we have already noted in the previous chapter, the essence of the Keynesian revolution (following the thesis in Clower [1966]) was the insight that income should appear as an independent variable in market excess demand functions. This was necessary in view of the fact that in the real world expenditure is likely to be income-constrained. We shall henceforth refer to the relationship which follows from this as the income-expenditure logic.

The income-expenditure logic induces further dynamic aspects to macroeconomic behavior. We may demonstrate this by introducing the income-expenditure logic into the simple model that we have used so far. Equation (3-3) may be rewritten as

$$Y = (1 - h)\bar{Y} + b(M - P - kY) + hY \tag{3-6}$$

where the term hY acknowledges the role of the income-expenditure mechanism that Keynes developed. (It is necessary to multiply $\bar{Y}$ by $1 - h$ since if $M - P = kY$ and $Y = \bar{Y}$ the equation would not hold otherwise.) Equation (3-6) therefore incorporates real balance and income-expenditure effects and is consequently a generalized expenditure function as far as the simple model is concerned. Substituting equation (3-6) into equation (3-4) implies the following general solution for the price level

$$P(t) = Be^{-gt} + M - k\bar{Y} \tag{3-7}$$

where

$$g = cb/(1 + bk - h)$$

Notice that the particular integral in equation (3-7) is exactly the same as its counterpart in equation (3-5), in which case the income-expenditure mechanism does not change the long run properties of the model. The price level varies directly with the money supply and capacity output adjusted for the income elasticity of the demand for money, i.e. in accordance with the quantity theory. The only difference is that the root in equation (3-7) is larger in absolute terms than its counterpart in equation (3-5) since $g > d$. Also notice that, since the marginal propensity to consume is assumed to be less than the average propensity, $h < 1$ and $g > 0$. Thus the introduction of the income-expenditure logic merely alters the speed of adjustment without upsetting the long run implications of the underlying monetary mechanisms. In fact since $g > d$ the adjustment process will be faster since stabilizing changes in income will have the tendency to reinforce themselves. For example, a 10% increase in money supply will eventually cause prices to rise by 10%. The speed at which this is achieved depends upon the path of output. According to equation (3-6) positive real balance effects will generate multiplier effects which cause output to attain a higher level. Consequently demand pressure is higher and P reaches its new equilibrium more rapidly.

Money, goods and bonds

We next introduce a bond into the model so far developed. Once more, we do not stop seriously to consider the role of this innovation in the real economy but presumably the role of financial assets in society is to provide its members with a wider choice regarding their wealth holdings and it will ease the process of financial intermediation, bringing borrowers and lenders into more efficient contact with each other. If so, then, apart from psychic income being enhanced, real output is likely to be higher. However, we take the financial technology as a parameter as we did the technology of exchange in the previous section and once more take $\bar{Y}$ to be a parameter unaffected by changes in the supply of bonds.

The demand for money must now reflect the fact that the opportunity cost on holdings of money is the rate of interest on bonds (r). Hence the demand for money may be written as

$$M^d = kY + P - jr \tag{3-8}$$

i.e. it varies inversely with the rate of interest. The expenditure function in equation (3-6) must now be modified to reflect two related aspects. First, the real balance effect must take account of the variable velocity of circulation of money implied by equation (3-8). Secondly, as interest rates rise the demand for goods might fall since financial accumulation would be more attractive at the margin than expenditure. Therefore, we rewrite equation (3-6) as

$$Y = (1 - h)\bar{Y} + b(M - P - kY + jr) + hY - ur \tag{3-9}$$

Notice that the rate of interest appears twice in this equation. The first appearance reflects the fact that as the rate of interest rises the demand for money will fall and as money balances are reduced the demand for output will rise. The second appearance reflects substitution effects between bonds and expenditure, and for the usual negative effect of the rate of interest on expenditure it would be necessary to restrict the model so that $u > bj$.

Equation (3-4) will still apply. To close the model it is necessary to equate the demand for money with its (exogenous) supply

$$M^d = M \tag{3-10}$$

The conditions for equilibrium in the bond market are

$$B^d = B^s \tag{3-11}$$

but if the money and goods markets are in equilibrium, the bond market will be in equilibrium by Walras' Law. Consequently, in what follows we 'drop' equation (3-11).

The model now stands as equations (3-4), (3-8), (3-9) and (3-10) which solves for P, M^d, Y and r, and can be rewritten as

$$\begin{bmatrix} k & 1 & -j \\ -c & D & 0 \\ 1+bk-h & b & u-bj \end{bmatrix} \begin{bmatrix} Y \\ P \\ r \end{bmatrix} = \begin{bmatrix} M \\ -c\bar{Y} \\ (1-h)\bar{Y}+bM \end{bmatrix} \tag{3-12}$$

where D is the differential operator d/dt. The determinant of the system is

$$det = (uk + j(1-h))D + cu \tag{3-13}$$

which implies a single stable root:

$$m = -cu/(uk + j(1-h)) \tag{3-14}$$

The general solutions for the endogenous variables in equation (3-12) are:

$$\left. \begin{array}{ll} Y = A_1 e^{mt} + \bar{Y} & \text{(i)} \\ P = A_2 e^{mt} + M - k\bar{Y} & \text{(ii)} \\ r = A_3 e^{mt} + \text{constant} & \text{(iii)} \end{array} \right\} \tag{3-15}$$

Since e^{mt} approaches zero over time the particular integrals are the long run determinants of the endogenous variables. The first equation implies that 'full employment' is eventually restored. The price equation is once more as it was in equations (3-7) and (3-5), i.e. in accordance with the postulates of the quantity theory. Finally, the rate of interest is equal to a constant (not shown in the model) which is represented by the 'natural' rate of interest.

In other words when bonds are introduced into the model the only analytical difference is that the adjustment path is altered, but the equilibrium or long term properties of the model remain unchanged. However, notice in this presentation that m does not depend on b, for the following reason. To determine the rate of interest it is necessary to equate the demand and supply of money. But when this is done there cannot be an excess supply of real balances. Instead, the rate of interest acts as the principal direct link between the financial and real markets. Thus, when a bond is introduced into the model the rate of interest maintains equilibrium in the financial markets and the real balance effect is replaced by the interest rate effect as the principal transmission mechanism between the money and real sectors. Previously, of course, the only conceivable transmission mechanism was the real balance effect itself. We shall be returning to this observation and its implications later.

'Crowding out' and government finance[6]

The previous analysis implies that in the long term the price level depends upon the quantity of money and capacity output, $\bar{Y}$. It also implies that the price level does not depend upon the stock of bonds outstanding, B. This important result implies that, given the specification in equations (3-8)–(3-11), governments may finance their budget deficits through bond sales without generating any inflation. If instead budget deficits are financed through increases in the money supply the result will be inflationary.

Thus an open market sale of bonds has the effect of reducing the money supply. Initially this raises interest rates but eventually, as has just been shown, these bond sales have the effect of 'crowding out' private sector expenditure so that the price level falls. Prices continue to fall until the percentage fall in the money supply and the percentage fall in the price level are equal. According to equation (3-8) this implies that interest rates must revert to their erstwhile level. At this new equilibrium society is holding the same quantity of money in real terms as it was before, but it is also holding more bonds. These bonds are held in return for the resources released by the private sector to the public sector during the periods that the 'crowding out' took place.

The 'crowding out' of private sector expenditure by bond sales at higher interest rates seems intuitive enough but once the bond sales cease it is necessary to consider more carefully how the economy might react to a higher proportion of bonds in portfolios. The model so far described only attaches importance to the flow of bond sales rather than the stock and assumes that the private sector savings ratio varies directly with the rate of interest. This enables a given flow of bond sales to continue indefinitely at a given level of the rate of interest. However, it does not seem reasonable to assume that portfolio holders are indifferent about the stock of financial assets. If they are not, the simple quantity theory postulates which so far have been robust with respect to a variety of model specifications break down or at least must be modified.

To show this we specify a demand function for bonds of the following form

$$B^d = P + (v_1 + 1)r + v_2 V \tag{3-17}$$

where V represents the real wealth of the private sector defined as

$$V = w_1(M - P) + w_2(B - r - P) + (1 - w_1 - w_2)\delta \bar{Y} \tag{3-18}$$

The term $\delta \bar{Y}$ represents the stock of physical capital which is assumed to be proportional to $\bar{Y}$ so that δ is the capital–output ratio when output is equal to its 'natural' rate. Thus the private sector holds its wealth in money balances, bonds and capital. Equation (3-17) states that the real demand for bonds in market value terms $(B - r - P)$ varies directly with their rate of return and wealth. Bond holdings expressed as a proportion of wealth will only increase if their rate of return is raised. This specification implies a stock demand for bonds in contrast to the flow demand implied in the previous model.

Next we may either take the demand for money as given by equation (3-8) or we may add a wealth term

$$M^d = kY + P - jr + j_1 V \tag{3-19}$$

In this case it is assumed that real balances are demanded not merely for transactions purposes, although it is difficult to see why an inferior asset (because it bears no interest) such as money should be related to wealth. However, since it is not crucial to our analysis we continue with this more general specification.

In full equilibrium $Y = \overline{Y}$, in which case equations (3-17)-(3-19) will solve for P and r for given values of M and B. The equilibrium solution for P is (ignoring terms in $\overline{Y}$)

$$P = \alpha M + (1 - \alpha)B \qquad 0 < \alpha < 1 \tag{3-20}$$

where

$$\alpha = \frac{(1 + v_1 - v_2 w_2)(1 - j_1 w_1) - (j + j_1 w_2) v_2 w_1}{(1 - j_1 w_1 - j_1 w_2)(1 + v_1 - v_2 w_2) + (1 - v_2 w_1 - v_2 w_2)(j + j_1 w_2)}$$

Thus the price level is not only affected by the quantity of money, but it is also affected by the quantity of bonds. In general P will vary in less than strict proportions with both M and B while the homogeneity condition now applies to the total of M and B. However, when $j = j_1 = 0$, $\alpha = 1$, i.e. when the demand for money is not affected by the rate of interest or wealth the market for money totally determines the price level. In general, the money and bond markets are interdependent, so that B affects P via portfolio considerations which affect the demand for money.

The equilibrium solution for the rate of interest is

$$r = \beta_1 B - \beta_2 M \tag{3-21}$$

where

$$\beta_1 = \frac{(1 - j_1 w_1 - j_1 w_2)(1 - v_2 w_2) + (1 + v_1 - v_2 w_2) j_1 w_2}{(1 - j_1 w_1 - j_1 w_2)(1 + v_1 - v_2 w_2) + (1 - v_2 w_1 - v_2 w_2)(j + j_1 w_2)}$$

$$\beta_2 = \frac{(1 - j_1 w_1 - j_1 w_2) v_2 w_1 + (1 + v_1 - v_2 w_2)(1 - j_1 w_1)}{(1 - j_1 w_1 - j_1 w_2)(1 + v_2 - v_2 w_2) + (1 - v_2 w_1 - v_2 w_2)(j + j_1 w_2)}$$

Equation (3-21) states that the rate of interest rises with the supply of bonds since society will only accept more bonds at a higher rate of interest. It also states that the rate of interest varies inversely with the supply of money since the latter raises the demand for bonds.

It should be stressed that these results are only valid for the case where the capital stock, and thence $\bar{Y}$, is assumed to be fixed. However, $\bar{Y}$ may be endogenized in terms of r since the rate of interest should equal the marginal product of capital in equilibrium. In this case an increase in B would raise the price level for two reasons. First, P would rise via equation (3-20). Secondly, since r is increased $\bar{Y}$ will fall and the price level will tend to rise. Nevertheless, equation (3-20) continues to apply.

Since budget deficits must be financed via money creation or bond sales to the private sector the above specification suggests that both fiscal and monetary policy are likely to determine the pace of inflation, and not just monetary policy alone.

In the rest of this study we proceed under the assumption that non-inflationary 'crowding out' is feasible, i.e. we do not adopt equations (3-17) and (3-18). This choice does not reflect any strong convictions about the matter but the need for a modus operandi for presenting the analysis. Nevertheless, it should be recalled at all stages that such 'crowding out' may in fact be impossible and the zealous reader should feel free to rework the analysis under such assumptions. In the meanwhile we note the important policy implications raised by these issues. Whereas equation (3-15 (ii)) implies that monetary policy alone determines the price level and the rate of inflation while fiscal policy does not play an independent role, equation (3-20) attributes an independent importance to fiscal policy. Since budget deficits must be financed through credit creation or through sales of debt to the private sector both fiscal and monetary policy are likely to determine the pace of inflation.

Money, goods and employment

Next, we introduce employment into the model. However, we suppress the bond market in the interest of expositional simplicity. At the end of the chapter we will activate the model with all the markets that will have been discussed in simultaneous operation. In a sense all these partial equilibrium or incomplete models are unreasonable since for example it is inconceivable that production can take place at all without labor or capital. In the simple money-goods model it was therefore implicit that there is a fixed volume of renewable output $(\bar{Y})$ which society had to hold. It was also implicit that at any moment in time the demand for those goods could diverge from this fixed supply because of imperfect information and other trading imperfections.

With the introduction of employment into the model we may postulate a production function where output depends on employment and where capacity output depends on full employment. By full employment (which so far we have used somewhat loosely) we refer to the volume of employment at which real wage inflation is zero. Alternatively we may use the term, the 'natural' rate of unemployment as discussed previously by Friedman [1968].

Those concepts are illustrated on Fig. 3-4. The demand for labor in this presentation (L^d) is assumed to depend on the neoclassical relationship between the real wage rate and the marginal productivity of labor. In the long run, and assuming the economy to be competitive, firms will only be able to afford to pay labor no more and no less than its marginal product. Hence, the lower the real wage the greater the longer term demand for labor by firms. The labor demand schedule is drawn for a given capital stock. In this neoclassical presentation an increase in the capital stock would tend to raise labor productivity and the labor demand schedule would tend to rise. For the present we assume that the capital stock is given.

The supply of employment (L^s) will tend to diverge from the supply of labor (L^s_T) since at any moment in time a number of workers equal to $L^s_T - L^s$ will be involved in job search as the natural labor market turnover proceeds. The factors that might determine the divergence between L^s and L^s_T are many and primarily institutional. If employment information is difficult to obtain, e.g. because of the absence of labor exchanges, poor communications, etc., the divergence will tend to be wider. Similarly if the private opportunity cost of unemployment is low, e.g. because of unemployment benefit,[7] workers will tend to spend more time between jobs. This possibility is illustrated on fig. 3-5.

On the diagram, OS is the wage that the individual would obtain if he took the first job that came along. However, if he takes his time in searching the labor market he might be able to improve his wage prospects. The curve SS^1 is drawn under the assumption that the more he searches, the higher the earnings he will be able to obtain; however, there may be diminishing returns to search. At least this is the assumption in fig. 3-5. Using a different scale on the vertical

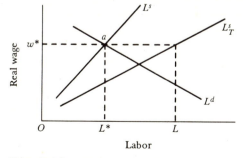

Figure 3-4 Employment equilibrium

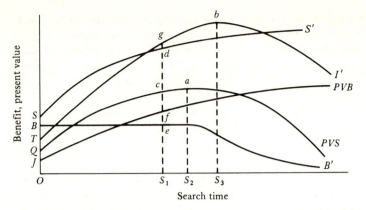

Figure 3-5 Optimal job search

axis the curve $QPVS$ plots the relationship between the present value of the earnings stream that is eventually obtained and the search time. Say for example that OS_1 of search time is expended so that a wage S_1d is obtained. The earnings stream that this implies when discounted back to the present (i.e. when search time is zero) is (using a different scale) equal to S_1c. This present value will reflect the fact that the individual earns nothing over the period OS_1 and earns a wage of S_1d thereafter.

If the individual searches in order to maximize the (expected) present value of his future earnings he will spend OS_2 of search time since the present value becomes a maximum at a along $QPVS$. The unemployment implied by this investment in search time will be part of the 'natural' rate of unemployment $L_T^s - L^s$ in fig. 3-4. If the discount rate is lower or if diminishing returns to search set in more slowly the optimum search time will be longer since the point a will lie further to the right, and the 'natural' rate of unemployment will be greater.

In modern economies most unemployed receive unemployment benefit in one form or another. Usually the benefit is related to the duration of unemployment so that it is graduated downward the longer the period of unemployment. This is the assumption behind the BB^1 schedule that plots unemployment benefit against the period of unemployment or search time. The curve $JPVB$ bears the same relationship to BB^1 that $QPVS$ bears to SS^1 - i.e. it is the present value of the benefits received. Thus if the individual takes a job after searching for OS_1, the present value of the unemployment benefit received up to that time is S_1f. The sum of the present value of the unemployment benefit and the present value of the earnings stream will give the total present value of a given investment in search time. Curve TT^1 is the sum of $QPVS$ and $JPVB$. If the individual takes a job after searching OS_1 the total present value will be S_1g. If, as before, the individual is assumed to search until the present value of this investment is maximized he will choose OS_3 as his optimal investment in search since b is a maximum along TT^1. The point b is bound to be north-east of the point a in which event unemployment benefit will tend to raise the optimal search time and consequently the 'natural' rate of unemployment.

Our purpose here has not been to spell out a detailed theory of the microeconomics of the labor market.[8] Our concern has been to show how even in equilibrium at a on fig. 3-4 some unemployment will be observed and that social policies are likely to affect the volume of unemployment at the structural level. In fig. 3-4, it is assumed that the 'naturally' unemployed bear a roughly proportionate relationship to the volume of actual employment. The equilibrium real wage will be w^* and the 'natural' rate of unemployment at this equilibrium will be L^*L/OL.

When out of this equilibrium, wages are hypothesized to adjust via a Phillips Curve relationship analogous to equation (3-4) and, for analogous reasons

$$\dot{W} = n(L - L^*) \tag{3-22}$$

i.e. the various components of the labor market can only respond by changing nominal wage rates (W) since they cannot negotiate real wages directly. Notice that equation (3-22) omits the expected rate of inflation since it is out of bounds in our present quasi static context. However, we shall return to this issue in Chapter 7.[9] Since Y and $\bar{Y}$ depend exclusively on L and L^* in this model we may rewrite equation (3-22) as

$$\dot{W} = n(Y - \bar{Y}) \tag{3-23}$$

and we may also assume that

$$P = W + \text{constant} \tag{3-24}$$

since wages are the only variable factor input and therefore the only cost item upon which prices might depend. This leaves us with a model which is almost identical to the one described by equations (3-4) and (3-6). In fact we may continue with equation (3-6) as the expenditure function and a price equation which is

$$\dot{P} = n(Y - \bar{Y}) \tag{3-25}$$

As before (in equation (3-23)) the general solution for the price level is

$$P(t) = B_1 e^{-qt} + M - k\bar{Y} \tag{3-26}$$

where

$$q = nb/(1 + bk - h)$$

In other words, the postulates of the quantity theory continue to hold in the long run. In the short run, however, unrequited wage claims could cause inflation even though, in the model, wages cannot cause inflation in the long run. Consider, for example, what happens when say trade unions raise wages by 10% when previously the volume of unemployment had been at its 'natural' rate. Note that we also assume that the authorities hold the money supply fixed and that capacity output has not changed (i.e. $\overline{Y}$ is unchanged). Via equation (3-24) prices will rise by 10%, but this price increase will reduce the volume of real balances and the real balance effect will reduce effective demand via equation (3-6). As a result, Y will fall below $\overline{Y}$ and the recession will generate wage deflation via equation (3-23) and price deflation via equation (3-24). Since M and $\overline{Y}$ are assumed fixed this deflationary process will continue until the original values for P and W are restored. It may therefore be concluded that as long as the money supply is constant, autonomous nominal wage increases such as might be induced by trade union activity

(i) can only have a short term inflationary effect

(ii) will tend to induce deflation and unemployment in the medium term, and

(iii) will not have a long term inflationary effect.

If, however, the authorities raise the money supply by 10% when wages rise by 10%, prices will rise by 10% in equilibrium.[10] But the fundamental determinant of the price rise is not the wage increase, as we have seen, but the validation of the wage increase by the monetary expansion.

The influence of trade unions

In the preceding paragraphs it was argued that in the neoclassical model trade unions cannot influence inflation in the long run. In certain countries (such as the United Kingdom) it is a popularly held view that trade unions cause inflation and their influence upon the economy is very serious. What influence, if any, do trade unions have in the light of neoclassical economic analysis? To answer this question it is sensible to identify two distinct cases. In the first case it is assumed that all economic activities are unionized and that closed shop agreements are in operation. In the second case we assume a dual model in which some activities are unionized while others are not.

Case 1 – If all activities are unionized then unions are in a position to determine the total volume of employment by enforcing closed shop agreements and thereby prevent people from working. By restricting the supply of labor they force up the real wage for those employed while those debarred from work by the closed shop agreement become unemployed, indeed unemployable. This possibility is illustrated on fig. 3-6 where, as on fig. 3-4, L^s represents the neoclassical supply schedule for labor while L^d represents the neoclassical downward sloping demand curve for labor. Competitive equilibrium is determined at a so that the equilibrium real wage is w_1 and equilibrium employment is L_1. For simplicity we omit the 'naturally' unemployed since they were incorporated into fig. 3-4.

In the presence of total unionization and closed shop agreements it is legally possible for trade unions to debar people from working by excluding them from the union. (We shall not discuss the dubious morality that lies behind such agreements and practices.) Thus in fig. 3-6, if L_2L_1 of potential workers are excluded from trade unions the effective supply of employment falls from L_1 to L_2. This in turn allows trade unions, through the processes of collective-bargaining, to force real wage settlements on their employers so that wages rates rise from w_1 to w_2.

The excluded workers join the ranks of the unemployed. In fact, at the higher real wage additional people will be tempted into signing on the employment register without any hope, of course, of finding a job. Thus unemployment will increase by L_2L_3 of which L_2L_1 are excluded workers and L_1L_3 are people who previously chose not to participate in the labor force. As it were, we may call L_2L_1 'unnatural' unemployment since these are the workers who have lost their jobs through the restrictive practices of trade union monopsony of employment.

This suggests that monopsony power can only be deployed at the expense of kindred workers. Those lucky enough to be left with a job are better off, the others are forced out onto social security. It is also likely that as unions

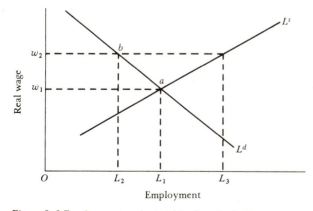

Figure 3-6 Employment under total trade unionization

deploy their monopsony power prices will rise. In the neoclassical model they
do not rise because of wage increases since, if wage increases are passed on in
higher prices, portfolio imbalance would be generated for a given supply of
money and a short term recession would follow. Prices rise because output $(\bar{Y})$
falls and for a given quantity of money this implies an increase in the price
level. In fig. 3–6 the output loss is represented by the area L_2baL_1.

Case 2 – The assumption of total unionization is an interesting limiting case
but it is hardly realistic since in most societies there is also a large non-unionized
employment sector. Thus the workers excluded from union membership by
closed-shop agreements may always seek employment in the free sector. This
case is illustrated on fig. 3–7 where the left hand diagram refers to the unionized
sector and the right hand diagram to the free sector. In competitive equilibrium,
wage rates will be equated between the two sectors at w_1 and employment
will be respectively L_1 and L_2. As before we next assume that in the unionized
sector L_1L_3 of workers are excluded from unions so that real wage rates of
trade union members rise to w_2 from w_1.

Whereas in Case 1 the excluded workers joined the ranks of the unemployed
in the present case a proportion of them will seek employment in the free
sector. If the supply of labor is perfectly inelastic with respect to real wage
rates $L_2L_4 = L_3L_1$. More generally, however, $L_2L_4 < L_3L_1$ since the supply of
labor will be elastic to some degree. In the free sector wage rates will be
reduced to w_3 in which case union workers benefit at the expense of non-union
workers. Therefore in the partially unionized case the effect of trade unions
on real wage rates as a whole is unlikely to be large – some wages are increased
while others are reduced.

However, total output will fall and as before this will tend to raise the price
level if the money supply is unchanged. In fig. 3–7 (and assuming that L_3L_1
$= L_2L_4$) the output loss will be $bca + efd$ which is generated by allocative
inefficiency with regard to labor use. If $L_2L_4 < L_1L_3$ the output loss will be
greater.

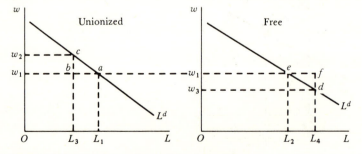

Figure 3–7 Employment under partial unionization

It follows then that trade unions and the legislation that gives them monopsony power have two main effects. First, social injustice is generated since the distribution of wage rates becomes arbitrarily distorted. Secondly, economic inefficiency is generated since output will fall.

In the remainder of this study the labor market will be treated as a simple aggregate as in the case of equations (3-22) and (3-23) although we should bear in mind that in reality the labor market is dualistic as in case 2. Thus $\bar{Y}$ may be distorted because of trade union restrictive practices and w and L will be indices of the two sets of wage rates and employment levels. At the disaggregated level it is assumed that the equilibrium employment rate in the unionized sector is L_3 and in the free sector L_4 and that these are achieved when output is equal to $\bar{Y}$.

The Keynesian model

In the discussion so far the models have been stable with respect to the price level, the 'natural' rate of interest and the 'natural' rate of unemployment. In other words they have conformed to the neoclassical conception of macroeconomic behavior. On the other hand, the model comprising money, bonds and goods (MBG) is not very different at least from popularized versions of the Keynesian system. For example the demand function for money in equation (3-8) is Keynesian and the expenditure function in equation (3-9) is Keynesian too. The former function requires no explanation but perhaps the latter function does. The term hY will be recognized as the marginal propensity to consume and the term $-ur$ is the relationship between investment and the rate of interest which in the Keynesian system may be written as

$$I = u(MEC - r) \tag{3-27}$$

where MEC is the marginal efficiency of capital, which in this present static context may be assumed to be predetermined.

In other words, the MBG model is an extended version of the IS-LM framework. It is extended in the sense that not only are savings and investment assumed to be equated and that the demand for money is equated with its supply but also the demand for output must equal its supply. It is this last component that endogenizes the price level. In the IS-LM framework the real markets are left in a state of disequilibrium and the price level is assumed to be fixed. Alternatively the IS-LM framework is a partial equilibrium or short term model. Completing the model by endogenizing prices induces equilibrating mechanisms in the IS-LM version of the Keynesian model.

If, however, a 'liquidity trap' is assumed to exist in the MBG model, and the demand for money becomes infinitely elastic at some low rate of interest, successive price falls may not raise effective demand since the rate of interest would not be able to fall and stimulate investment. Under these (non-linear) circumstances the *MBG* model would go into an endless deflationary spiral which will be recognized as the existence problem that was discussed in Chapter 2. Eventually the economy would be flooded with real balances which the specification will prevent from influencing the real economy.

It seems entirely implausible that, even in such a pathological case as the 'liquidity trap', households and firms may be presumed endlessly to accumulate real balances on the assumption that the risks incurred by holding other financial assets will be prohibitive. The expected marginal utility of money as a store of value in terms of financial assets might remain constant, but the marginal utility of real balances as a medium of exchange will tend to decline as the volume of real balances grows. It may be the case that, at relatively high rates of interest, increases in the money supply have a relatively larger impact on the bond market and a smaller one on effective demand (the real balance effect) in view of the high opportunity cost of money as a store of value, while at relatively low interest rates the impact on effective demand is relatively large since the marginal utility of money as a means of exchange is low.

For practical purposes, then, it seems desirable to specify the volume of real balances directly in the expenditure function. In equation (3-9) $b(M - P - kY + jr)$ is redundant since by virtue of equation (3-8) it is equal to zero. If equation (3-9) is rewritten in terms of the volume of real balances rather than the difference between the demand and supply of money, we may express it as

$$Y = \text{constant} + b(M - P) + hY - ur \qquad (3\text{-}28)$$

so that even if r remains constant via equation (3-8) as M increases or as P falls effective demand will rise. The implications of this specification are illustrated on fig. 3–8.

The *ED* schedules are the effective demand relationships in terms of the rate of interest. The lower the rate of interest, the greater the effective demand. r_T denotes the rate of interest implied by the 'liquidity trap' in which event the segment aD_1 of E_1D_1 will be unattainable. In fact let us assume that the economy is initially caught in the 'liquidity trap' at a along E_1D_1. If the rate of interest could fall to b, effective demand would be increased to $\overline{Y}$ from Y_1 and full employment and price stability would be restored. But the rate of interest cannot fall in this way by assumption. Since Y_1 is less than $\overline{Y}$ the resultant price deflation will increase the volume of real balances and via equation (3-28) effective demand will rise in the direction of the arrows. The *ED* schedule will continue to expand as long as $\overline{Y}$ is greater than Y. The expansion will cease when the *ED* schedule becomes E^*D^*, and a full-employment equilibrium will be reached at c.

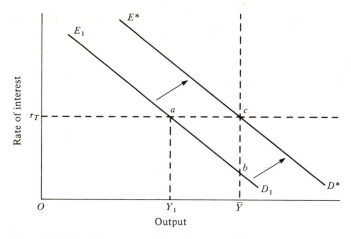

Figure 3-8 'Liquidity trap' and the real balance effect

The 'liquidity trap' seems to be beyond the purview of practical economic policy and as we saw in the previous chapter even Keynes was not too sure how much significance to attach to it as an explanation for persistent depression. Our purpose here is the more technical one of indicating that the Keynesian model when augmented by the real balance effect generates a unique equilibrium even in the special case of the 'liquidity trap'.

Disaggregation

The models that have been discussed are highly aggregative and intentionally simple. But the general nature of the solutions does not depend on the order of aggregation. It would not make any substantive difference if the goods market were disaggregated into a multiplicity of different outputs and the markets for bonds were disaggregated into a range of different financial assets. For example, if there were G different outputs and F different financial assets (apart from money) the *MBG* model could be extended along the following lines. The demand function for money (equation (3-8)) would be rewritten as

$$M^d = \sum_{g=1}^{G} (k_g Y_g + v_g P_g) - \sum_{f=1}^{F} j_f r_f \qquad (3\text{-}29)$$

i.e. we assume that real balances are required in each real sector while every financial asset is in competition with money in individuals' portfolios. For the homogeneity postulate it would be necessary that $\sum_g v_g = 1$.

If the monetary sector is composed of a rich spectrum of non-bank financial intermediaries F will be relatively large since there will generally be a market

in the liabilities of those intermediaries and some competitive deposit rate
(assuming the absence of government controls or restrictive practices). There
will also be other financial assets to consider, e.g. equities, government debt
of different maturities, etc.

Whereas previously in the MBG model the bond market was 'eliminated' by
Walras' Law, in the present situation we may 'eliminate' the Fth bond market
and there will be F-1 clearing conditions in the financial markets

$$B_f^d = B_f^s \qquad f = 1,2,...,F\text{-}1 \tag{3-30}$$

Assuming the stock of bonds is fixed, the set of demand functions for financial assets may be written as

$$B_f^d = q_{ff}r_f - \sum_{i \neq f}^{F} q_{it}r_i - yY - zP \qquad f = 1,2,...,F\text{-}1 \tag{3-31}$$

i.e. competing rates of return reduce the stock demand for the financial asset.
As Y and P rise, the demand for money rises and the demand for bonds falls.

There will be G different expenditure functions and we may disaggregate
equation (3–28) as:

$$Y_g = \text{constant}_g + b_g(M - P) + h_g Y - \sum_{f=1}^{F} u_{gf}r_f - e_g P_g + \sum_{i \neq g}^{G} e_{ig}P_i$$

$$g = 1,2,...,G \tag{3-32}$$

i.e. the real balance effect influences each real market as does every rate of
interest, although in practice some of the u_{gf} coefficients might be zero. Also,
there may be relative price effects; if P_g rises the relative demand for the gth
output might fall, while the converse might happen if competing prices were
to rise.

The disaggregated model is closed by assuming that in each real market
prices adjust along the lines already discussed.

$$\dot{P}_g = n_g(Y_g - \bar{Y}_g) \qquad g = 1,2,...,G \tag{3-33}$$

The model contains G prices and F interest rates and there are $G + F$ independent equations. Substituting for Y_g into equation (3–33) yields G independent
equations and substituting for B_f^d into equation (3–30) yields F-1 equations.
The final equation is the assumption that $M^d = M^s$.

The disaggregated MBG model is analytically the same as its aggregated
counterpart. If M rises, a range of interest rates will fall, triggering increases in
desired real expenditure. Also, the real balance effect will have an expansionary

influence. Initially the distribution of the impact on the real and financial markets might be uneven in which case a spectrum of relative price effects will be triggered. In general, prices will begin to rise although it may happen that some prices fall for a while, depending on the complexity of the cross elasticity structure in the real and financial markets. In equilibrium, Y_g will equal $\bar{Y}_g$ and since $\bar{Y}_g$ has remained unchanged relative prices will be unchanged too. Similarly, relative interest rates will be unchanged. In view of the homogeneity postulate all prices will have risen in proportion to the increase in the money supply.

II The open economy

Money, goods, employment and foreign exchange (MGEF)

In discussing the open economy case it becomes essential to disaggregate goods in terms of exportables, imports, import substitutes and non-traded output. We may depict these sectors in terms of a series of underlying supply and demand functions. We also postulate a homogeneous labor market, i.e. we do not differentiate between different kinds of labor. We begin by considering the underlying determinants of the production of non-traded output.

Non-traded output. The basic assumption is that the proportion of output in each sector to total output depends on the relative profitability of production in that sector. Unit profits will equal price minus unit labor and import costs. In the non-traded goods sector unit profits may be approximated (in logarithms) as

$$\Pi_n \simeq \text{constant} + P_n - w_{n_1}W - w_{n_2}(P_m - S) \tag{3-34}$$

where

P_n: price index of non-traded goods
P_m: price index of imports in foreign currency
S: exchange rate – units of foreign currency per unit of domestic currency
W: wage index
w_{n_1}: share of wages in costs
w_{n_2}: share of imports in costs

This relationship could have been generalized in terms of the input–output matrix where the production of traded goods requires all the other goods as inputs. However, equation (3-34) provides sufficient complications as it stands.

The supply of non-traded goods depends proportionately on the resource constraint and relative profitability.

$$N^s = \text{constant} + \bar{Y} + a_1 \Pi_n - a_2 \Pi_x - a_3 \Pi_{ms} \qquad (3\text{-}35)$$

where subscripts x and ms refer to exportables and import substitutes respectively. The demand for non-traded goods in the $MGEF$ model will depend on relative prices, income and the effects of portfolio imbalance

$$N^d = \text{constant} - b_1 P_n + b_2 P_{ms} + b_3 (P_m - S) + b_4 P_x + b_5 Y$$
$$+ b_6 (M - P - kY) \qquad (3\text{-}36)$$

It may be the case that some of the price elasticities will be very small since, e.g. there is likely to be little substitution in demand between non-traded goods and imports. In equilibrium the supply and demand for non-traded goods must be equal

$$N^s = N^d \qquad (3\text{-}37)$$

Exportables. Analogously to equation (3–35) we may write

$$X^s = \text{constant} + \bar{Y} + c_1 \Pi_x - c_2 \Pi_n - c_3 \Pi_{ms} \qquad (3\text{-}38)$$

and the analogue of equation (3–36) will be

$$X^d = \text{constant} - d_1 P_x + d_2 P_{ms} + d_3 (P_m - S) + d_4 P_m + d_5 Y$$
$$+ d_6 (M - P - kY) \qquad (3\text{-}39)$$

It will also be necessary to take into consideration the overseas demand for exportables

$$X^d_w = \text{constant} - e_1 (P_x + S - P_{xw}) + e_2 Y_w \qquad (3\text{-}40)$$

where Y_w is an index of overseas economic activity and P_{xw} is an index of equation (3–41) implies[13] that export prices are a weighted average of domestic and competing export prices overseas in addition to depending on overseas demand:

$$X^s = \text{constant} + v X^d_w + (1 - v) X^d \qquad (3\text{-}41)$$

where v is the share of exports in the total demand for exportables.

A graphical presentation of the model for exportables is illustrated in fig. 3-9.

The supply schedule for exportables has been drawn for given assumptions about Π in competing sectors and $\bar{Y}$. For example, if competing values of Π were to rise, the X^s schedule would shift to the left. The domestic demand

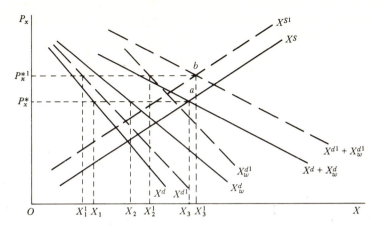

Figure 3–9 The market for exportables

schedule for exportables is drawn for given assumptions about competing prices and income, and likewise for the foreign demand for exports. The total demand for exportables is represented by the schedule $X^d + X^d_w$ and the equilibrium will be at a. At the equilibrium price of P^*_x, the total production of exportables will be X_3 of which X_2 will be exports and X_1 will be consumed at home. A devaluation will raise the overseas demand for exports to X^{d1}_w. In addition, and to the extent that imports are a substitute for exportables in domestic expenditure the domestic demand for exportables may rise to X^{d1}. Even in this partial equilibrium setting it is difficult to judge the effects of the devaluation on the supply schedule for exportables. On the one hand the increase in costs will cause the schedule to contract. But on the other hand profitability will have fallen in the competing sectors. The assumption in fig. 3–9 is that relative profitability deteriorates in the exportable sector, i.e. because exportables are assumed to be relatively import-intensive. The new equilibrium will be at b; the production of exportables will now be X^1_3 while the volume of exports will have risen to X^1_2.

Imports. Since we are dealing with the 'small country' case we assume that import prices are exogenous when measured in foreign currency terms. The demand for imports will depend on relative prices, the level of economic activity and the real balance effect:

$$I = \text{constant} - f_1(P_m - S) + f_2 P_n + f_3 P_{ms} + f_4 P_x + f_5 Y$$
$$+ f_6(M - P - kY) \tag{3-42}$$

where f_1 is the familiar price elasticity of demand for imports and f_5 is the income elasticity of demand for imports. Likewise the demand for import substitutes may be specified as

$$MS^d = \text{constant} - g_1 P_{ms} + g_2(P_m - S) + g_3 P_n + g_4 P_x + g_5 Y \\ + g_6(M - P - kY) \tag{3-43}$$

and the supply of import substitutes may be written as

$$MS^s = \text{constant} + \bar{Y} + h_1 \Pi_{ms} - h_2 \Pi_x - h_3 \Pi_n \tag{3-44}$$

In equilibrium, supply and demand will be equal

$$MS^d = MS^s \tag{3-45}$$

To close the model it is necessary to specify the price and output identities

$$P = \text{constant} + u_1 P_n + u_2 P_x + u_3(P_m - S) + u_4 P_{ms} \tag{3-46}$$

$$Y = \text{constant} + h_1 N^s + h_2 X^s + h_3 MS^s \tag{3-47}$$

where $\Sigma_{i=1}^{4} u_i = 1$, $\Sigma_{i=1}^{3} h_i = 1$ and where the weights reflect the importance of the various outputs in total output. Finally, wages are assumed to be determined via a Phillips Curve relationship

$$\dot{W} = j_0(Y - \bar{Y}) \tag{3-48}$$

as in equations (3-22) and (3-23).

Foreign exchange. At least, this almost closes the model. The only remaining consideration is the determination of the money supply itself which in the economy context will depend on the balance of payments (Z) and the domestic credit policies of the authorities. A balance of payments improvement will add to the domestic money supply since the additional receipts of foreign exchange will be held by the authorities in return for domestic currency. If exporters receive 100 units of foreign exchange they may exchange this for $100/S$ units of domestic currency with the monetary authorities. Or if exports are invoiced in domestic currency, overseas customers will have to exchange 100 units of foreign currency directly with the authorities, assuming the exchange rate to be perfectly fixed. Either way the reserves will increase by 100 and the domestic money supply by $100/S$.

The authorities may change the money supply even in the absence of a balance of payments improvement or they may offset the monetary effects of changes in the balance of payments by changing their domestic credit policies.

However, in what follows it is useful to distinguish between the balance of payments effects and the effects of domestic credit policies on the money supply. Since in our model M is the logarithm of the money stock we may write this index of the money stock as a first derivative with respect to time

$$\dot{M} \simeq \text{constant} + Z + C \qquad (3\text{-}49)$$

where C is an index of domestic credit expansion. C is an exogenous variable since it is assumed to be under the control of the authorities while Z is endogenous since it will depend on the diverse components of the balance of payments considered in equation (3-50) and which are determined by the model. From equation (3-49) it is possible to derive the domestic credit policies (C) that will (ceteris paribus) set monetary growth to zero or any other target value. The balance of payments in the $MGEF$ model is the sum of export receipts minus import payments, or

$$Z \simeq \text{constant} + (X_w^d + P_x) - (I + P_m - S) \qquad (3\text{-}50)$$

If the exchange rate S is fixed the authorities will be obliged to respond to any non-zero value of Z by intervening in the foreign exchange market. If Z is positive the official reserves of foreign exchange will increase as the authorities cream off the excess demand for domestic exchange, while if Z is negative the authorities will be obliged to dip into their reserves if the exchange rate is to be protected. If Z is positive monetary growth will be higher than otherwise via equation (3-49) while if there is a balance of payments deficit the converse will be true.

If the exchange rate is perfectly flexible, i.e. where the authorities do not accommodate even in part any excess demand for ($Z < 0$) or excess supply ($Z > 0$) of foreign exchange, Z must be zero for otherwise the authorities would be required to intervene. Thus equation (3-50) acts as a clearing equation for the market in foreign exchange. If Z is constrained to equal zero the system will solve for S. If S is fixed the system will solve for Z. There will always be these two main cases to consider.

Money, goods, employment, foreign exchange and bonds (MGEFB)

Rather than solve the $MGEF$ model that has been described we proceed directly to include bonds as a representative non-money financial asset in the open economy model. The $MGEFB$ model constitutes the most sophisticated and general model that shall be considered in this volume. In solving the $MGEFB$ model we shall automatically have to take into consideration the contributions to its solution of all the previous generations of closed and open economy model so far described including of course the $MGEF$ model.

In the open economy context the introduction of bonds focuses attention on the capital account of the balance of payments since foreigners may invest in domestic bonds or residents may invest in overseas bonds. In principle foreigners may also hold part of the domestic money stock but they would forgo interest in the process; therefore we assume that foreign holdings of domestic bonds (B_f) are motivated by the desire to earn income from interest as well as capital gains in terms of foreign exchange in the light of prospective exchange rate movements. According to portfolio theory B_f will depend on the expected return on domestic bond holdings in terms of foreign exchange.[11] We may write this relationship as

$$B_f = q_1(r - r_w) + q_2(S^e - S) + \text{constant} \tag{3-51}$$

where r_w is the overseas rate of interest and S^e is the expected future spot rate, while the equilibrium volume of foreign bonds which residents wish to hold will depend on the same general influences, except with signs reversed.

$$B_w = q_3(r_w - r) + q_4(S - S^e) + \text{constant} \tag{3-52}$$

The constant terms reflect wealth and other scale effects which in this presentation are assumed to be fixed parameters. Capital flows in the balance of payments (K) are the difference between changes in net foreign holdings of domestic bonds and changes in net holdings of foreign bonds by residents

$$K = (q_1 + q_3)(\dot{r} - \dot{r}_w) + (q_2 + q_4)(\dot{S}^e - \dot{S}) \tag{3-53}$$

and the balance of payments identity in equation (3-50) has to be expanded to take account of capital flows[12]

$$Z \eqsim \text{constant} + (X_w^d + P_x) - (I + P_m - S) + K \tag{3-54}$$

In the *MGEFB* model it will also be necessary to introduce interest rate effects into expenditure relationships and the demand for money. In the next section we simplify the *MGEFB* model that has been developed in this and the previous section in order to explore the general equilibrium relationships that the model implies.

The MGEFB model simplified

The simplified version of the model is presented in the equations below and is based on the analytical notions that have already been introduced. Equation (3-47) is modified to

$$Y \eqsim \text{constant} + DD + X_w^d - I \tag{3-55}$$

i.e. in consolidating non-traded goods, import substitutes and domestically consumed exportables we introduce the familiar notion of domestic demand (DD) which is hypothesized to depend on an interest rate effect, a real balance effect and an income–expenditure effect

$$DD = \text{constant} - a_1 r + a_2(M - P) + a_3 Y \tag{3-56}$$

Equation (3–46) is appropriately modified so that the aggregate price level becomes

$$P = \text{constant} + b_1 P_d + b_2 P_x + b_3(P_m - S) \tag{3-57}$$

where P_d is the price of non-exportables. There will, however, be a relationship between P_x and P_d as equations (3–38)–(3–41) imply. Assuming that the supply of and domestic demand for exportables depends on the relative export price, $P_x - P_d$ [i.e., where

$$\left. \begin{aligned} X^s &= \text{constant} + c(P_x - P_d) \\ X^d &= \text{constant} - d(P_x - P_d)], \end{aligned} \right\} \tag{3-58}$$

equation (3–41) implies[13] that export prices are a weighted average of domestic and competing export prices overseas in addition to depending on overseas demand:

$$P_x = \text{constant} + \alpha_1 P_d + (1 - \alpha_1)(P_{xw} - S) + \alpha_2 Y_w \tag{3-59}$$

where

$$\left. \begin{aligned} \alpha_1 &= \frac{c + (1 - v)d}{c + (1 - v)d + ve_1} \quad \text{(i)} \\ \alpha_2 &= \frac{ve_2}{c + (1 - v)d + ve_1} \quad \text{(ii)} \end{aligned} \right\} \tag{3-60}$$

This formulation implies that costs do not affect the relative supply of exportables, although the price of exportables will be affected via the influence of costs on P_d. The rate of domestic price inflation is assumed to depend on the pressure of demand (demand pull) and the cost push of wage and import cost inflation

$$\dot{P}_d = \text{constant} + j_1(Y - \bar{Y}) + j_2 \dot{W} + j_3(\dot{P}_m - \dot{S}) \tag{3-61}$$

which when combined with equation (3–48) implies

$$\dot{P}_d = \text{constant} + j_4(Y - \bar{Y}) + j_3(\dot{P}_m - \dot{S}) \tag{3-62}$$

where

$$j_4 = j_1 + j_2 j_0 \tag{3-63}$$

The only equation that requires simplification is equation (3-42) where the volume of imports is assumed to be determined by relative prices and income:

$$I = \text{constant} - f_1(P_m - S - P_d) - f_2(P_m - S - P_x) + f_s Y \tag{3-64}$$

i.e. we assume that imports depend indirectly on the real balance effect and the rate of interest via equations (3-55) and (3-56). The equations that do not require modification are equations (3-8), (3-10), (3-49), (3-53) and (3-54). As before, the market for bonds is 'excluded' by Walras' Law.

On the basis of repeated substitution the model may be reduced to the following equation system[14] when the exchange rate is assumed to be fixed

$$
\begin{bmatrix}
1 & f_s & \beta_1 & -\beta_2 D \\
0 & \gamma_1 & \gamma_2 & \gamma_3 \\
0 & -j_4 & D & 0 \\
-1 & -kD & -\delta_1 D & jD
\end{bmatrix}
\begin{bmatrix}
Z \\
Y \\
P_d \\
r
\end{bmatrix}
=
\begin{bmatrix}
\beta_3 & 0 & (\beta_4 - \beta_5 D) & \beta_5 & \beta_6 & \beta_7 & -\beta_2 & 0 \\
\gamma_4 & 0 & \gamma_5 & 0 & \gamma_6 & \gamma_7 & 0 & 0 \\
0 & 0 & -j_3 D & 0 & 0 & j_3 D & 0 & -j_4 \\
\delta_2 D & -1 & -\delta_3 D & 0 & b_2 \alpha_2 D & b_3 D & 0 & 0
\end{bmatrix}
\begin{bmatrix}
P_{xw} \\
C \\
S \\
S^e \\
Y_w \\
P_m \\
\dot{r}_w \\
Y
\end{bmatrix}
\tag{3-65}
$$

so that Z appears as an endogenous variable since a fixed exchange rate implies that the balance of payments will be endogenous while S appears as an exogenous variable. The parametric abbreviations are given in equations (3-66).

$$
\left.
\begin{aligned}
\beta_1 &= f_1 + \alpha_1(f_2 - (1 - e_1)) & \text{(i)} \\
\beta_2 &= (q_1 + q_3) & \text{(ii)} \\
\beta_3 &= (1 - \alpha_1)((1 - e_1) - f_2) + e_1 & \text{(iii)} \\
\beta_4 &= (1 - f_1 - f_2) - \beta_3 & \text{(iv)} \\
\beta_5 &= (q_2 + q_4) & \text{(v)} \\
\beta_6 &= \alpha_2((1 - e_1) - f_2) + e_2 & \text{(vi)} \\
\beta_7 &= (f_2 + f_1 - 1) & \text{(vii)} \\
\gamma_1 &= 1 - (a_2 k + a_3) & \text{(viii)} \\
\gamma_2 &= f_1 - \alpha_1(f_2 - e_1) & \text{(ix)} \\
\gamma_3 &= (a_1 + a_2 j) & \text{(x)} \\
\gamma_4 &= (1 - \alpha_1)(f_2 - e_1) + e_1 & \text{(xi)} \\
\gamma_5 &= -(f_1 + f_2) - \gamma_4 & \text{(xii)}
\end{aligned}
\right\}
\tag{3-66}
$$

$$\gamma_6 = \alpha_2(f_2 - e_1) + e_2 \qquad\qquad \text{(xiii)}$$
$$\gamma_7 = (f_1 + f_2) \qquad\qquad\qquad\quad \text{(xiv)}$$
$$\delta_1 = b_1 + b_2\alpha_1 \qquad\qquad\qquad\; \text{(xv)}$$
$$\delta_2 = b_2(1 - \alpha_1) \qquad\qquad\quad\; \text{(xvi)}$$
$$\delta_3 = b_3 + \delta_3 \qquad\qquad\qquad\;\; \text{(xvii)}$$
$$D = d/dt \;\text{(differential operator)} \qquad \text{(xviii)}$$

in which case the determinant of the system is

$$(\gamma_1 j + \gamma_3 k + \gamma_1\beta_2)D^2 + (j_4(\gamma_2 j + \gamma_3\delta_1 + \beta_2\gamma_2) + f_5\gamma_3)D + j_4\beta_1\gamma_3 = 0 \qquad (3\text{-}67)$$

When the exchange rate is assumed to be flexible, i.e. when $Z = 0$, the exchange rate becomes an endogenous variable and the $MGEFB$ model condenses to

$$\begin{bmatrix} (\beta_5 D - \beta_4)\, f_5 & \beta_1 & -\beta_2 D \\ -\gamma_5 & \gamma_1 & \gamma_2 & \gamma_3 \\ j_3 D & -j_4 & D & 0 \\ \delta_3 & -k & -\delta_1 & j \end{bmatrix}\begin{bmatrix} S \\ Y \\ P_d \\ r \end{bmatrix} = \begin{bmatrix} \beta_3 & 0 & \beta_5 & \beta_6 & \beta_7 & -\beta_2 & 0 \\ \gamma_4 & 0 & 0 & \gamma_6 & \gamma_7 & 0 & 0 \\ 0 & 0 & 0 & 0 & j_3 D & 0 & -j_4 \\ \delta_2 & -1 & 0 & b_2\alpha_2 & b_3 & 0 & 0 \end{bmatrix}\begin{bmatrix} P_{xw} \\ C^* \\ S^e \\ Y_w \\ P_m \\ r_w \\ \bar{Y} \end{bmatrix}$$

$$(3\text{-}68)$$

where C^* is the accumulation of domestic credit expansion (C).

The determinant of this system is

$$[\gamma_1(\beta_5 j + j_3\delta_1\beta_2 + \delta_3\beta_2) + k(\beta_5\gamma_3 - \gamma_5\beta_2 - j_3\gamma_2\beta_2)]D^2 + [\beta_4\gamma_1 j + \beta_4 k\gamma_3$$
$$+ j_4(\gamma_2 j + \delta_1\gamma_3)\beta_5 + \gamma_5(f_5 - j_4\delta_1\beta_2) + j_3 f_5(\gamma_2 j + \delta_1\gamma_3) - j_3(\gamma_1\beta_1 j + k\gamma_3)$$
$$+ \delta_3(f_5\gamma_3 + j_4\gamma_2\beta_2]D + j_4[-\beta_4(\gamma_2 j + \delta_1\gamma_3) + \beta_1(\gamma_5 j + \gamma_3\delta_3)] = 0 \qquad (3\text{-}69)$$

Since all the coefficients of D^2, D and the constant term in equation (3-67) are positive the fixed exchange rate model will be stable, while the stability picture is less clear in the case of equation (3-69). A detailed discussion of the stability issue is reserved for Chapter 6 where it shall be argued that an analysis of expectations and their formation is indispensable.

For the present our concern is to derive the long run properties of the MGEFB model and it is assumed in the meanwhile that both of the roots are stable. Notice that in 'opening' the model we have gained an additional root. This may be attributed to the stock–flow logic in the model of the balance of payments and the monetary sector since the domestic price level generates flows of current account transactions which changes the stock of domestic financial assets. This triggers a series of domestic stock-adjustments which change prices and so the process is repeated. While in the closed economy model the root was attributed to the Phillips Curve assumption, in the case of the open economy one root is attributed to the Phillips Curve while the second is attributed to the stock–flow specification of the balance of payments in its relation to the monetary sector. Thus even if we assume that the structural relationships do not incorporate any distributed lags, macroeconomic behavior, according to the specification that has been presented, is unavoidably dynamic.

Rather than to present the general solutions for the endogenous variables in equations (3–64) and (3–68), only the particular integrals (long term solutions) are supplied. However, whereas in fig. 3–3 the adjustment process was geometric and therefore monotonic, in the open-economy case the set of possible adjustment paths is richer. If the roots are complex an oscillatory adjustment profile would be implied, with successive over-shooting of the long run equilibrium of the system. Alternatively, the adjustment path might not be monotonic although there may not be any over-shooting. We shall return to these issues in Chapter 7.

As complicated as the model might seem, the set of particular integrals are extremely simple, especially when the exchange rate is fixed. In this case they are

$$
\begin{aligned}
&Z = -C && \text{(i)} \\
&Y = \bar{Y} && \text{(ii)} \\
&P_d = [-f_s \bar{Y} + C + \beta_3 P_{xw} - \beta_4 S + \beta_5 \dot{S}^e \\
&\qquad + \beta_6 Y_w + \beta_7 P_m - \beta_2 \dot{r}_w]/\beta_1 && \text{(iii)}
\end{aligned}
\tag{3-70}
$$

and when it is floating they are

$$
\begin{aligned}
S = \{ &[\beta_3 j_4 (\gamma_2 j + \delta_1 \gamma_3) - j_4 \beta_1 j \gamma_4 + j_4 \beta_1 \gamma_3 \delta_2] P_{xw} \\
&+ j_4 (\gamma_2 j + \delta_1 \gamma_3)(\beta_5 \dot{S}^e - \beta_2 \dot{r}_w) - j_4 [f_s (\gamma_2 j + \delta_2 \gamma_3) \\
&- \gamma_1 \beta_1 j - k \beta_1 \gamma_3] \bar{Y} + j_4 [\beta_7 (\gamma_2 j + \delta_1 \gamma_3) - \beta_1 j \gamma_7 + \beta_1 \gamma_3 b_3] P_m \\
&+ j_4 [\beta_6 (\gamma_2 j + \delta_1 \gamma_3) - \beta_1 j \gamma_6 + \beta_1 \gamma_3 b_2 \alpha_2] Y_w - j_4 \beta_1 \gamma_3 C^* \}/H && \text{(i)}
\end{aligned}
$$

$$
Y = \frac{j_4}{H} [-\beta_4 (\gamma_2 j + \delta_1 \gamma_3) + \beta_1 (\gamma_5 j + \gamma_3 \delta_3)] \bar{Y} \tag{ii}
$$

$$
\begin{aligned}
P_d = \frac{j_4}{H} \{ &[(j\gamma_5 + \delta_3 \gamma_3)\beta_3 - \beta_4 j \gamma_4] P_{xw} - \beta_4 \gamma_3 C^* \\
&+ [(j\gamma_5 + \delta_3 \gamma_3)\beta_7 - \beta_4 j \gamma_7] P_m + (j\gamma_5 + \delta_3 \gamma_3)(\beta_5 \dot{S}^e - \beta_2 \dot{r}_w) \\
&+ [(j\gamma_5 + \delta_3 \gamma_3)\beta_6 - j\beta_4 \gamma_6] Y_w - [\beta_4 (k\gamma_3 - \gamma_1 j) \\
&+ n_2 f_s (\gamma_5 j + \delta_3 \gamma_3)] \bar{Y} \} && \text{(iii)}
\end{aligned}
\tag{3-71}
$$

where

$$
H = j_4 [\beta_1 (\gamma_5 j + \gamma_3 \delta_3) - \beta_4 (\gamma_2 j + \delta_1 \gamma_3)]
$$

We shall consider the fixed exchange rate case first, i.e. equations (3–70). The first equation tells us that in the long run the balance of payments depends only on the quantity of domestic credit that is created.[15]   A domestic credit expansion of 100 will eventually generate a balance of payments deficit of 100, the relationship is one-for-one. The following sequences in this relationship may be identified:

(i) When C rises by 100, initially the money supply will rise by 100.

(ii) This will generate an increase in domestic demand via equation (3–56) through two channels. First there will be a real balance effect along the lines of the discussion on pages 59–61. Secondly the increase in the money supply will have lowered interest rates via equation (3–8) and lower interest rates will stimulate domestic demand via equation (3–56).

(iii) The expansion of demand will generate inflation via equation (3–62) which will spread to export prices via equation (3–59).

(iv) As the price of exportables and non-exportables increases relative to overseas prices, the current account of the balance of payments will tend to go into deficit, and this tendency will be reinforced via the marginal propensity to import. In addition the capital account of the balance of payments will tend to go into deficit since domestic interest rates will have fallen.

(v) In the second 'period' the initial money supply increase of 100 will now be less – say 80 in view of a first 'period' balance of payments deficit of say 20. But even in the second 'period' there will be balance of payments deficits since domestic prices will tend to be out of line with world prices. Therefore, the money supply will continue to contract.

(vi) The contractions will continue until the cumulative balance of payments deficit is 100 since at this point domestic income, prices and interest rates will have reverted to their original position.

The second equation states that 'full employment' will eventually be restored. The reasons for this are essentially the same as those already discussed in connection with the *MGE* model in the closed-economy context. Equation (3–62) implies that prices will only stabilize when $Y = \bar{Y}$ in the absence of overseas inflation and the monetary assumptions imply that prices will be stabilized.

The third equation, i.e. equation (3–70 (iii)), essentially states that the price of non-exportables depends on overseas prices. If we assume that overseas export prices (P_{xw}) and import prices (P_m) move together and are related to a general overseas price index P_w, this would imply that the total derivative of P_d with respect to P_w was unity since $\beta_3 + \beta_7 = \beta_1$. Equations (3–57), (3–59) and (3–66) imply the following relationship for the aggregate price:

$$P = \delta_1 P_d + \delta_3 (P_w - S) + \alpha_2 Y_w \tag{3-72}$$

Substituting for P_d in terms of P_w from equation (3-70 (iii)) and noting that $\delta_1 + \delta_3 = 1$ implies that a one percentage change in P_w will induce the same percentage change in the aggregate domestic price level. In other words, when the exchange rate is fixed, the domestic price level (P) is dominated by overseas prices. This occurs through the following sequence:

(i) If P_w rises the balance of payments will improve so that the stock of money increases in the first 'period'.

(ii) The increase in the money supply will stimulate domestic demand and P_d and P_x will rise along the lines already considered. In addition the increase in P_w will generate cost inflation via equation (3-62) and will contribute directly to the domestic price level via equation (3-67).

(iii) This process will be repeated in the next 'period' and the balance of payments improvement will trigger another round of adjustment. The process will continue until domestic prices have risen in line with world prices for only then will the balance of payments position stabilize and the resultant process of monetary accumulation cease.

(iv) Thus, an increase in world prices generates balance of payments improvements during the adjustment process but not in the long run, while in the short run domestic prices might not relate closely to overseas prices although in the long run this will be the case.

Equation (3-70 (iii)) states that P_d depends on factors apart from P_w. Clearly if 'full-employment' output ($\bar{Y}$) increases, P_d will tend to fall in the long run. However, the remaining factors such as C and $\dot{r}_w$ play only a minor role through the implicit lag in the model. For example, a continuing domestic credit expansion of 100 will eventually lead to a continuing balance of payments deficit of 100. Therefore, eventually the money supply growth is zero. But in the interim the money stock will have grown and this will be reflected in a higher price level. A similar logic applies to the effects of $\dot{S}^e$ and $\dot{r}_w$ on P_d.

Since P depends upon P_w, Y tends to equal $\bar{Y}$, and the change in the money supply does not depend on domestic credit expansion, we may derive the solutions for the rate of interest via equation (3-8). If P_w rises by 10%, eventually P will rise by 10%. Equation (3-8) implies the demand for money should rise by 10% since $Y = \bar{Y}$, unless the rate of interest changes. But the rate of interest will also depend on overseas rates via the capital account of the balance of payments.

We now turn to the solutions for the main endogenous variables when the exchange rate is assumed to be flexible, i.e. equation (3-71). In the case of the exchange rate, the main result is that it varies proportionately with overseas prices. Assuming as before that P_{xw} and P_m are related to P_w and noting that $\beta_3 + \beta_7 = -\beta_4$ and that $\gamma_4 + \gamma_7 = -\gamma_5$ we may combine the coefficients on P_{xw} and P_m to equal HP_w, i.e.

$$\beta_3 j_4(\gamma_2 j + \delta_1\gamma_3) - j_4\beta_1 j\gamma_4 + j_4\beta_1\gamma_3\delta_2 + j_4[\beta_7(\gamma_2 j + \delta_1\gamma_3) - \beta_1 j\gamma_7 + \beta_1\gamma_3 b_3] = H$$

Thus, when the exchange rate is floating an increase in world prices of 10% would appreciate the exchange rate by 10% in the long run. The exchange rate will also depend on the domestic money supply (C^*); however, we shall reserve the issues here until we discuss equation (3-71 (iii)). $\bar{Y}$ will influence the exchange rate via its effects on the domestic price level (as shall be discussed) and variables such as $\dot{S}^e$ and $\dot{r}_w$ affect the exchange rate via the implicit lags of the stock–flow model as has already been discussed.

Equation (3-71 (ii)) implies that full employment is eventually achieved since the coefficient of $\bar{Y}$ in the numerator is equal to H, and the reasons for this outcome are the same as those already given in relation to equation (3-71 (ii)).

Equation (3-71 (ii)) implies that the overall domestic price level (P) depends on the money supply (C^*). This may be demonstrated as follows: Substituting for P_d and S in equation (3-72) from equations (3-71) for C^* we may write (ignoring other terms)

$$P = \frac{(-\delta_1 j_4 \beta_4 \gamma_3 + \delta_3 j_4 \beta_1 \gamma_3) C^*}{H} \tag{3-73}$$

Since $\delta_1 + \delta_3 = 1$ and $\beta_1 = -\beta_4$ the coefficient in the numerator may be written as $-\gamma_3 j_4 \beta_4$. However, H also equals $-\gamma_3 j_4 \beta_4$ since $\gamma_2 + \gamma_5 = 0$ (assuming $f_2 = 0$). Therefore, the domestic price level varies proportionately with the quantity of money, i.e. as in the closed economy model.

The analogue of equation (3-73) in terms of P_w is

$$P = -\frac{\beta_4 \delta_3 \gamma_3 j_4}{H} P_w = \delta_3 P_w \tag{3-74}$$

i.e. in view of the fact that P_w is a direct component of P in equation (3-57) and influences export prices which are also a component, via equation (3-59), world prices have an independent influence on the aggregate domestic price level.

The other determinants of P_d may be attributed to the implicit lags in the model as before and the volume of full employment output. The monetary influences on the exchange rate therefore occur via P_d and P_x. We defer further discussion of these relationships for the next chapter.

Finally, recalling the discussion on pages 66-8 and assuming that in the open economy case the demand for bonds varies inversely with the external rate of interest and positively with the expected rate of exchange rate appreciation, equation (3-20) continues to hold but in modified form:

$$P = \alpha M + (1 - \alpha)B + v(r_w - \dot{S}^e) \tag{3-75}$$

when the real exchange rate is assumed to be constant in equilibrium, i.e. when $P-S = P_w$. Thus portfolio balance effects generated by external interest rates may influence the price level even if the domestic money and bond stocks are unchanged.

CHAPTER 4

Extensions of the neoclassical model

Introduction

In this and the following chapter our principal purpose is to apply the macro-economic logic that has been constructed in the previous chapter to a series of policy interventions and exogenous influences. In particular we seek to identify the longer term equilibrium relationships between these factors and the following menu of endogenous variables:

(i) The balance of payments, when the exchange rate is assumed to be fixed, or

(ii) the exchange rate when it is assumed to be flexible

(iii) Employment or domestic economic activity

(iv) The price level or the rate of inflation

(v) Interest rates.

Hopefully, we shall cover most if not all of the policy initiatives that the authorities typically consider to be in their macroeconomic armory. These are:

(i) Tariffs

(ii) Import controls

(iii) Exchange controls

(iv) Incomes policy

as well as the more familiar policies:

(v) Fiscal

(vi) Monetary

(vii) Exchange rate intervention.

Our focus in this chapter is on the long term or equilibrium implications of the model that has been developed. All too often the respective authorities are pressurized into adopting macroeconomic policies for short term expediency; the longer term consequences are stored up for the future, which is hopefully beyond the next general election. A less cynical but equally disturbing possibility is that the authorities are unaware of the longer term consequences of their actions and that they believe that the partial equilibrium or short term effects are as much as need be considered for all practical purposes.

Or it may be argued that the long term is too remote and that the policy maker need only be concerned with a sequence of short term considerations.

In Chapters 6 and 7 we look into this view in greater detail and note that because of expectations the long run might not be so far off. To some extent
then, this chapter anticipates what is to follow in Chapter 7 insofar as we
emphasize the importance of long term macroeconomic responses to policy
initiatives.

However, before entering into this discussion we investigate the consequences of changes in some of the exogenous variables in the $MGEFB$ model,
e.g. overseas economic activity (Y_w) and prices (P_x). This will have the added
benefit of familiarizing the reader with its logic as well as shedding light on
what are after all the daily concerns of the macroeconomic analyst and policy
maker. Special attention is focused on the macroeconomic effects of energy
discoveries and/or energy price increases. To this end we extend the model to
incorporate a separate energy sector so that the macroeconomic interactions
can be separately identified.

Monetary policy

At the end of the preceding chapter we discussed the effects of domestic
credit policies and overseas prices on the macroeconomy. In fig. 4-1 we illustrate the nature of the time sequences that are implied by the $MGEFB$ model
when the exchange rate is assumed to be fixed. We assume that initially the
economy is in a long run steady state equilibrium. At time 1 the authorities
inject a fixed quantity of money into the economy, i.e. C_{t+1} is positive but
C is zero for all remaining periods. In practice this impulse may come from
a variety of sources such as an open market purchase of securities, a temporary
tax cut, etc. In period 1 the money stock rises as indicated. Output will be
stimulated via the real balance effect that ensues according to equation

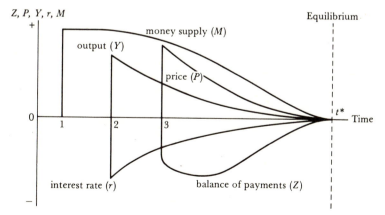

Figure 4-1 The sequence of macroeconomic adjustments to a monetary impulse

(3–57), while interest rates will decline according to equation (3–8) since the supply of money will exceed its demand. This decline in interest rates will further stimulate domestic demand. For our present illustrative purposes these reactions are assumed to begin in period 2.

In period 3 we assume that the inflationary and balance of payments effects are triggered. The price level responds to the pressure of demand in equation (3–63) while the balance of payments deficit (Z_{t+3}) is initially due to the weakening of the capital account which according to equation (3–54) will follow the decline in domestic interest rates. After period 4 the weakening balance of payments will be compounded by the deteriorating current account position that is implied by the expansion of demand and the deterioration in price competitiveness which will increase imports and reduce exports.

Once the balance of payments begins to deteriorate the money supply will begin to fall on the basis of equation (3–49) and the processes that have been triggered will be reversed. The monetary contraction will tend to raise interest rates as well as to lower domestic demand. Prices will begin to fall and the balance of payments deficit will begin to weaken as indicated in fig. 4–1. The balance of payments will continue to trigger domestic monetary and real adjustments as long as the deficit continues, which in turn feed back onto the balance of payments. Fig. 4–1 illustrates how as prices and output revert to their erstwhile levels via the balance of payments adjustments, these adjustments in turn become progressively smaller until eventually they disappear at t^* by which time the economy has reverted to its steady state.

In fig. 4–1 we have tended to assume that the adjustments will be monotonic. This need not be the case and it could happen that the solutions for the endogenous variables criss-cross the horizontal axis before settling down to their equilibrium values at t^*.

In fig. 4–2 we illustrate the juxtaposition between the current and capital accounts of the balance of payments during the transition. In other words

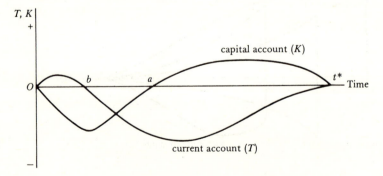

Figure 4–2 The relationship between the current and capital accounts

we break down the Z curve in fig. 4-1 into its two components. The capital account will tend to go into deficit as domestic interest rates fall following the monetary expansion, but as interest rates begin to return to their equilibrium level they will be rising and this will tend to generate arbitrage inflows on the capital account. Thus beyond some point (a) the capital account will begin to go into surplus during the adjustment process. By time t^*, $\dot{r} = 0$ since domestic interest rates will have come to rest in equilibrium and so capital inflows will cease.

We now turn to the current account of the balance of payments. The monetary expansion may initially strengthen the current account via the so-called J-curve effect. The domestic inflation will stimulate export prices so that there may be positive valuation effects that will benefit the current account temporarily. Because of marginal import propensities this effect may not occur, but in fig. 4-2 this possibility is illustrated. However, beyond point b the current account will go into deficit. But as prices begin to return to their original levels and as domestic economic activity begins to slacken the current account will tend to improve in the way indicated until eventually equilibrium is attained at t^*. Once again, non-monotonic adjustment profiles could produce more complex configurations than those illustrated in fig. 4-2.

The preceding analysis has been conducted under the assumption of a fixed exchange rate so that the balance of payments could play a critical role in the ensuing adjustment process. When the exchange rate is floating this adjustment route is sealed off and all the adjustments must occur within the economy itself. However during the transition the composition of the balance of payments between the current and capital accounts may alter while the overall balance of payments remains unchanged. In so far as the expansionary monetary impulse lowers interest rates the capital account may initially deteriorate as before and the illustration in fig. 4-2 may apply once more with the restriction that $K + T = 0$. Because $Z = 0$ the money generated during the impulse gets locked into the economy and so prices have to rise permanently to restore real balances to their equilibrium level while the exchange rate depreciates to equilibrate the balance of payments.

These theoretical results should have a familiar ring to them since they are not new and date back to 1752 when David Hume first established them. Thus the strength of these results does not lie in their novelty but in their antiquity and their robustness with respect to a wide range of specifications. The main contribution in Chapter 3 was to show how even under modern theoretical specifications these results continue to imply simple classical responses in the longer term. In so doing Chapter 3 spelt out the logic under which 'monetarism' will be valid and fills in a void which the 'monetarists' themselves had created. For the 'monetarists' had the unfortunate tendency of proposing their theory by way of highly simplified models of economic behavior which their critics rejected as being naive. Hopefully, it has now been shown that even more complex models produce the same results subject of course to the issues raised in connection with bond finance on pages 66-8 and 91.

The critical linkages in the *MGEFB* model that establish these results is the money demand function, equation (3-8), and equation (3-62), which relates the pressure of demand to inflation. Together these provide the crucial relationship between M and P. It is not even necessary to specify a relationship between wage inflation and the pressure of demand as in equation (3-48); real wage rates may be assumed exogenous. As long as prices depend on the money supply the constant real wage assumption implies that wage increases will follow price increases which in turn will produce cost inflation. However, monetary stability under such assumptions would generate price stability and thus wage stability. The absence of a Phillips Curve which permits real wage adjustments implies that there is no mechanism by which unemployment can equilibrate at a 'natural' rate. Instead, in the long run, unemployment is whatever it turns out to be - the goods markets may be in balance but not the market for labor. Nevertheless, the results for inflation, the exchange rate and the balance of payments continue to hold.

Even if inflation does not respond to the pressure of demand it is still conceivable that, when exchange rates are flexible, the same results obtain via speculative behavior in the foreign exchange market. An example of this may be found in the model presented by Ball, Burns and Warburton [1980] where increases in the money supply cause the exchange rate to fall which in turn triggers cost inflation. Import costs rise in domestic currency and competitors' export prices fall, putting upward pressure on wholesale and export prices respectively. These price increases then feed through the wage–price loop so that in equilibrium a 1% increase in the money supply generates a 1% fall in the exchange rate and a 1% rise in wages and prices. This result underscores the robustness of the results to quite radically different assumptions about economic behavior.

Overseas economic activity

Since we discussed the effects of overseas price changes on the domestic economy in the previous chapter, we concentrate here on the theoretical effects of a change in overseas economic activity (Y_w). At the partial equilibrium level this will raise the overseas demand for exports via equation (3–40) and stimulate domestic prices via equation (3–59). In the crude 'Keynesian' model this would trigger a domestic economic expansion via the multiplier which in turn would have a negative feedback onto the balance of payments. In the *MGEFB* model it is also necessary to take account of the monetary effects that are triggered by changes in overseas economic activity.

Let us assume that the exchange rate is fixed so that the following effects may be identified.

(i) An increase in Y_w will raise export demand and strengthen the balance of payments.

(ii) This will instigate two simultaneous inflationary effects. First, via equation (3-59) domestic prices will rise via the rise in export prices (P_x). Secondly, the pressure of demand will increase via the real balance effects and income-expenditure multiplier effects in terms of equation (3-56), generating inflation via equation (3-62).

(iii) These pressures will weaken the balance of payments and there will be a monetary contraction.

(iv) This will trigger (ii) in reverse.

(v) The final price increase will be such as exactly to offset the balance of payments benefits in (i) since this will establish a stable domestic monetary situation. Thus we find in equations (3-70) that in the long run the balance of payments does not depend on Y_w and that domestic economic activity (Y) is self equilibrating. However, prices will have to be higher to equilibrate the balance of payments and we would also find that the stock of money was slightly higher too in view of stock–flow technicalities.

A statistical illustration for the UK[1]

Inflation

The *MGEFB* model implies that prices will depend in the long run on the money supply as well as trend factors such as the rate of growth of output and possible secular changes in the velocity of circulation. On the other hand, cost increases may have a short term inflationary effect, but in the longer term they cannot exert an independent influence on the price level. To see this, let us assume that the money supply is fixed and that there has been an exogenous increase in costs, e.g. an oil price hike. Initially, via equation (3-56) this may raise prices but the price increases themselves will reduce real money balances and a negative real balance effect will occur via equation (3-56). Via equation (3-62) a deflationary syndrome would take place and the initial price increases would be reversed. Indeed, if the money supply is fixed, prices would have to revert to their initial values. If exogenous costs were constant and the money supply rose, one would expect prices to rise proportionately as previously discussed.

Thus whether the exchange rate is fixed or flexible one would expect the following relationships on the basis of our analysis:

(i) In the long run prices would vary in proportion with the money supply – i.e. the long run elasticity between money and prices would be unity.

(ii) In the long run prices would be invariant to exogenous costs – i.e. a long run elasticity between prices and these costs of zero.

If in the short term exogenous cost increases have an inflationary effect, (ii) implies that after a point the price–cost relationship will turn negative. Thus the hypothesis is that

$$\frac{\Delta P}{P} t = a + \sum_{i=0}^{J} b_i \frac{\Delta M}{M} t - i + \sum_{i=0}^{K} c_i \frac{\Delta X}{X} t - i + U_t \tag{4-1}$$

where

$$\sum b_i = 1$$
$$\sum c_i = 0$$

and

$\Delta P/P$: percentage change in prices

$\Delta M/M$: percentage change in money supply

$\Delta X/X$: percentage change in exogenous costs

U_t: randomly distributed error.

If the parameter a is zero this implies that the secular net growth in the demand for money is zero, for otherwise for a given money supply inflation would not have been zero. On the one hand the demand for money would tend to rise with secular economic growth, but on the other hand it may fall due to technological improvements in the uses of money, e.g. credit cards and other consumer banking services. If the secular net growth in the demand for money is positive this would induce a secular deflation and a would be negative. These theoretical prospects are illustrated using UK quarterly data where:

P is represented by the retail price index

M is represented by the narrow or M1 definition of the money supply

X is represented by unit import costs expressed in sterling.

Our objective here is to be illustrative rather than exhaustive in terms of alternative hypotheses of a subject as controversial as UK inflation, although the results themselves are suggestive enough. Our intention is to use real data to demonstrate the kind of macroeconomic relationships that we might expect.

The equation was estimated using constrained Almon lag estimation with both constraints in effects over the period 1952–75. The best results in terms of standard error of estimate were obtained by setting $J = 19$ or 4¾ years and $K = 23$ or 5¾ years. Both lag structures were approximated by a fourth order polynomial with front and end weights unconstrained. The restrictions were jointly and separately significant at the 95% level and the estimated lag structures are represented in figs. 4-3 and 4-4. Other statistical parameters are

$$R^2 = 0.79$$
$$\sigma = 0.0063$$
$$DW = 1.88$$

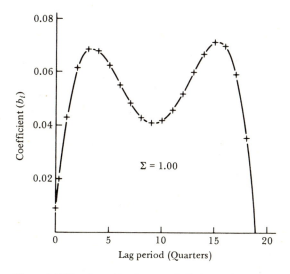

Figure 4-3 Distributed lag between inflation and monetary growth

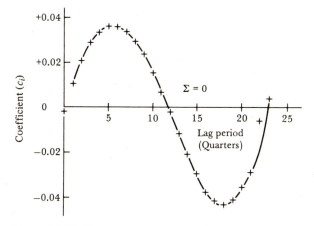

Figure 4-4 Distributed lag between inflation and import costs

while the constant term, which consists of three seasonal dummies was estimated as (t-values in parentheses):

$$\hat{a} = 0.00124 + 0.0024Q1 + 0.008Q2 - 0.0059Q3 = 0.00574$$
$$\quad\quad\quad (0.9)\quad\quad\;(2.9)\quad\quad\;(2.5)$$

In other words over the observation periods $\hat{a}$ was positive, implying negative secular growth in the demand for money, which generated an annual rate
of inflation of about 2¼% (i.e. $(4 \times 0.00574)100$)

For the present our main interest rests with figs. 4–3 and 4–4 and especially
the latter which indicates a strong-type relationship between price and exogenous cost inflation. This illustrates well our theoretical expectation that
cost inflation will have short term inflationary effects, but eventually beyond
the eleventh quarter the effects become deflationary and in the long term the
net inflationary effect is zero. On the other hand the long term elasticity
between P and M is unity. In chapter 7 we shall discuss some of the factors
that might influence the shape of the lag structures, especially in terms
of the dynamics induced by different forms of expectations generation. For
the moment we recall that the coefficients are of a reduced-form nature and
that they reflect a convolution of distributed lags.

Notice that we do not specify wage costs separately since these will be
endogenous to equation (3–22). However, just in the same way as exogenous
cost increases as represented by unit import costs do not exert long term
inflationary pressures but eventually induce deflation and associated unemployment, the same would be true for unrequited trade union wage increases. In
other words trade unions cannot cause inflation unless the authorities validate
these wage increases with expansionary monetary policies. Instead, trade
unions may cause unemployment.

The same result for the UK is illustrated by the following regression:

$$\Delta \log P_t = 0.65537 + \sum_{i=0}^{9} w_i \Delta \log P_w(t - i) - 0.08376 \log\left(\frac{P}{M}\right)_{t-1} \quad\quad (4\text{-}2)$$
$$\quad\quad\;\;(0.81)\quad\; i=0 \quad\quad\quad\quad\quad\quad\quad\quad (3.99)$$

$$\quad\quad - 0.15672 \log GDP_{t-1} + 0.0006911\,TIME$$
$$\quad\quad\quad (1.67)\quad\quad\quad\quad\quad\quad (1.34)$$
$$\bar{R}^2 = 0.7682, \sigma = 0.00779, DW = 1.7387, \text{observation period } 1966Q3\text{--}1978Q1$$

In this case P is represented by the deflator for final expenditure, P_w is represented by the world price of manufactures in sterling and M is the stock of
sterling M3. The estimation procedure follows Davidson et al. [1978] in which
case the long term or steady-state solution of the estimated equation is[2]

$$\log P = 7.8 + \log M - 1.87 \log GDP + 0.00082\,TIME \quad\quad (4\text{-}3)$$

i.e. the price level varies proportionately with the money supply and inversely with GDP. As GDP rises for a given quantity of money the price level falls (or rises less fast). Exogenous costs (i.e. ΔP_w) have a short term influence on inflation since they do not appear in the steady-state solution. $\Sigma w_i = 0.52146$ (estimated using a third degree Almon polynomial) so that over ten quarters a 1% increase in world prices raises UK prices by slightly more than ½%. However, these effects are reversed since, as P rises relative to M, equation (4-2) indicates that the resultant monetary disequilibrium will force prices downwards and that 8.3% of the disequilibria will be eliminated in each quarter.

More complex models may be fitted. For example, Beenstock and Longbottom (1980) show that equation (3-75) commands empirical support in the UK, suggesting that bond finance and world interest rates exert independent inflationary effects.

The exchange rate

When the exchange rate is floating it was shown that the exchange rate varies inversely with the supply of money in the long run. If, however, world money supply rises by 1%, world prices will rise by 1% and the exchange rate will rise by 1%. Therefore, we seek a proportionate long run relationship between the exchange rate and the supply of world money (M_w) relative to the UK money stock. This result is illustrated in terms of the following regression:

$$\Delta \log S_t = -0.3652 + 0.5259\,\Delta \log P_{wt} - 0.1358\log\left(\frac{SM}{M_w}\right)_{t-1} - 0.0014\,TIME$$
$$\quad\quad (2.3)\quad\quad (1.82)\quad\quad\quad\quad (2.23)\quad\quad\quad\quad\quad\quad (1.44)$$

$$(4\text{-}4)$$

$$\bar{R}^2 = 0.1044, \sigma = 0.0291, DW = 1.558, \text{observation period } 1971Q2\text{-}1978Q1$$

where S is represented by the effective exchange rate for sterling and M_w is the world money supply (for 18 countries) expressed in terms of foreign currency. Deriving as before the steady-state solution for the exchange rate gives:

$$\log S = -2.689 + \log\left(\frac{M_w}{M}\right) - 0.01\,TIME$$

$$(4\text{-}5)$$

i.e. in the long run the exchange rate varies directly with the relative supply of world money to UK money. The time trend reflects relative trends in velocity and GDP and implies that the trend rate of depreciation is 4% per year. Equation (4-4) was estimated over a period when the effective exchange rate was ostensibly floating and indicates that world prices have a short term impact on the exchange rate which is strikingly similar to the result in equation (4-2).

The balance of payments

When the exchange rate is fixed it was shown that the balance of payments on both current and capital accounts depends upon domestic credit expansion C. This theory implies that in the long run the UK money supply will adjust to the world money supply and that balance of payments deficits are a reflection of the adjustment of M to M_w. Therefore, imbalances between M and M_w will generate balance of payments disturbances. Whereas in equation (4-4) the relative price of money (i.e. the exchange rate) adjusts under floating exchange rates, when the exchange rate is fixed it is the quantity of money that adjusts. An illustrative result is reported in equation (4-6):

$$Z_t = 176.6 - 0.8187 C_t - 1799.6 \Delta \log r_{wt} - 1064.7 \log \left(\frac{M^*}{M_w}\right)_{t-1} \qquad (4\text{-}6)$$
$$\qquad (2.37)(4.21) \qquad (4.36) \qquad\qquad (1.15)$$

$\bar{R}^2 = 0.06372$, $\sigma = £250.93$ millions, $DW = 2.15$, observation period 1964Q3-1971Q1

where Z is the balance for official financing, C is domestic credit expansion and r_w is the 3 month euro-dollar rate. Equation (4-6) shows that 82% of DCE goes out over the balance of payments in the current quarter and that if external interest rates rise from 10% to 11% the balance of payments will deteriorate by £171 millions. M^*/M_w is the deviation of M/M_w from its trend, in which case equation (4-6) implies that, in the steady-state, $\log M = \log M_w$ plus a time trend as the monetary theory implies.

Since in practice sterling has not floated freely, a more general specification would endogenize exchange rates as well as the balance of payments and the resultant expression would be estimated over both exchange rate regimes. If M/M_w rises by 1% either the exchange rate must fall by 1% or M must fall by 1% via ensuing balance of payments deficits. An illustrative result of this joint approach is shown in equation (4-7):

$$\left(\frac{\Delta S_t}{S_{t-1}} + \frac{Z_t}{M_{t-1}}\right) = -7.415 + 108 \Delta \log P_{wt} - 61.856 \Delta \log M_t - 10.93 \log r_{t-1}$$
$$\qquad\qquad\qquad (0.65) \quad (2.67) \qquad\qquad (2.16) \qquad\qquad (4.03)$$
$$\qquad\qquad + 4.27 \log r_{w(t-1)} - 19.07 \log\left(\frac{MS}{M_w}\right)_{t-1} - 0.134\, TIME \qquad (4\text{-}7)$$
$$\qquad\qquad\quad (1.89) \qquad\qquad (2.72) \qquad\qquad\qquad (1.42)$$

$\bar{R}^2 = 0.337$, $\sigma = 3.57\%$, $DW = 1.46$, observation period 1964Q2-1978Q1

where r is represented by the 3 month local authority deposit rate. The steady-state solution of equation (4-7) is:

$$\log MS = 0.388 + \log M_w - 0.573 \log r + 0.224 \log r_w - 0.007\, TIME \qquad (4\text{-}8)$$

Equation (4-8) indicates that if world money supply increases by 1% then either the exchange rate rises by 1% or the money supply rises by 1% or some combination of the two, i.e. in accordance with the theory that has been developed. If UK interest rates rise this reduces the demand for money so that MS must fall in adjusting to equilibrium while the opposite occurs if overseas interest rates rise.

Output

An illustrative equation is reported for output. The real balance effect implies that output (represented here by GDP) will be constrained by the relationship between real balances ($m = M/P$) and real income. If real balances fall below their desired level in relation to income, aggregate demand will contract and vice versa. In the short term, however, aggregate demand may be influenced by accelerator effects, etc., and in an open economy it will be necessary to take account of the short term effects of changes in relative prices at home and abroad which will influence GDP via net trade and world economic activity (Y_w).

$$\Delta \log GDP_t = \underset{(7.22)}{0.3993} \, \Delta^2 \log GDP_t - \underset{(2.06)}{0.0714} \Delta \log \left(\frac{PS}{P_w}\right)_t + \underset{(3.38)}{0.1803} \Delta \log Y_{wt}$$
$$+ \underset{(3.34)}{0.00754} \log \left(\frac{GDP}{m}\right)_{t-1} \tag{4-9}$$

$\bar{R}^2 = 0.708, \sigma = 0.006, DW = 1.65$ observation period 1964Q3–1978Q1

The steady-state solution of equation (4.9) is simply $\log GDP = \log m$, i.e. the real money stock determines GDP. If, however, output is depressed (so that $Y < \bar{Y}$) prices will fall, real balances will increase and output will be stimulated via equation (4–9) so that in the steady-state for the model as a whole the full-employment or 'natural' rate of output will be achieved.

Equation (4–9) indicates that accelerator effects will be influential in the short run and that relative price movements and changes in overseas economic activity have significant effects on growth. If UK prices rise by 1% relative to world prices in common currency, GDP falls by 0.0714% in the short run. If world economic activity rises by 1%, GDP rises by 0.18% in the short run as UK exports rise and UK imports fall.

The feed-back from excess supply to wage rates is illustrated by equation (4–10):

$$\Delta \log w_t = \underset{(1.47)}{-0.0014} + \underset{(5.87)}{0.318} \Delta \log P_{t-1} + \underset{(2.08)}{0.2837} \Delta \log GDP_t$$
$$+ \underset{(1.74)}{0.167} \Delta \log \Pi_t + \underset{(5.87)}{0.3774} \log \left(\frac{\overline{GDP}}{GDP}\right)_{t-5} - \underset{(2.08)}{0.08835} \log \left(\frac{W}{P\Pi}\right)_{t-2}$$
$$+ \underset{(1.84)}{0.000231} TIME \tag{4-10}$$

$\bar{R}^2 = 0.685, \sigma = 0.0099, DW = 1.038$ observation period 1964Q2–1978Q2 where W refers to average earnings in manufacturing, Π represents productivity and $\overline{GDP}$ is the trend rate of growth of output. Thus if output is above its trend by 1%, wage growth will fall by 0.37%. The steady-state solution for the real wage rates is

$$\log\left(\frac{W}{P}\right) = 0.0158 + \log \Pi + 4.271 \log\left(\frac{GDP}{\overline{GDP}}\right) + 0.00261\,TIME \tag{4-11}$$

which suggests that real wages have risen faster than productivity by about 1% per year and that labor is inelastic in supply. In order to increase output by 1% above its trend, real wages have to be increased by 4.3% to attract the necessary labour.

Equations (4-1)–(4-11) show that the neoclassical model that has been proposed has prima facie empirical support in the UK context. Our purpose here has been the limited one of pointing out that in this essentially theoretical essay our concern is not with abstractions which, though interesting, are devoid of potential relevance. On the contrary, this brief empirical review is highly suggestive that the UK data support the neoclassical theory and that further empirical efforts will be most rewarding. At the same time the reported equations are intended to be illustrative rather than demonstrative of the neoclassical approach. Positively to demonstrate the validity of the neoclassical model for the UK is reserved for a later occasion and is beyond our present terms of reference.[3]

General policy principles

According to the *MGEFB* model, unemployment tends to be self-correcting while the balance of payments position reflects the authorities' domestic credit policies. This suggests that the authorities need not fear about unemployment and that the balance of payments will be healthy as long as the authorities do nothing to upset it. If the exchange rate is fixed, the *MGEFB* model indicates that inflation will be determined by external inflation while if the exchange rate is flexible the domestic monetary authorities will be responsible for inflation. In either case trade unions cannot determine inflation in the longer term.

This perspective dramatically alters the role of government in the macroeconomy as conventionally conceived, or at least as it has been conceived during the era of Keynesian macroeconomic activism. Instead of being benevolent interveners and the guardians of full employment, the new perspective may cast the authorities as being potential villains of the pax economica. When the exchange rate is fixed there is little that the authorities can do other than to upset the balance of payments and when the exchange rate is flexible there is little that they can do other than to upset price stability under the assumptions that have been made.

It should be recalled, however, that so far we have not discussed dynamic factors in any detail and that our preoccupation has been with long term macroeconomic responses. An alternative conception of macroeconomic policy is that the role of authorities should be to assist in disequilibrium situations, and as we have discussed in Chapter 2 this was one of the preoccupations of Keynes. However, these and related matters shall be taken up in Chapter 7 where macrodynamics are addressed directly.

We turn next to the relationship between the energy sector and the macroeconomy before going on to investigate the macroeconomic effects of the menu of policies that was previously mentioned. In Chapter 8 we shall return more fully to the issues in political economy that have been raised.

The energy sector and the macroeconomy

The nature of the model described in Chapter 3 may further be illustrated in relation to the advent of a national windfall. While this case is not of general applicability recent years have witnessed several such instances especially in relation to oil and oil prices. The OPEC price hikes of 1973–74 produced large benefits to the cartel members while of course the opposite was true in the oil-consuming countries. The macroeconomic effects of the price rise were rarely, if ever, explained in a satisfactory manner. On the one hand it was argued that they were inflationary, while on the other hand it was argued that they contributed significantly to the world-wide recession that began in 1974. An objective in this section is to explore some of the macroeconomic consequences of oil price hikes for both the producing and consuming countries according to the model previously described. We focus as much on the issues that confront the beneficiaries – an area that has been relatively ignored until now – as we do on the more familiar problems that confront the victims of the price hikes.

At the same time we focus on the related matter of oil discoveries which among the industrialized countries is a perhaps peculiar concern of the UK and Norway. However, with the peaking of US oil production in 1972 and the possibility that US oil output will decline significantly the converse macroeconomic influences could prevail in the US. Thus it seems that the macroeconomic analysis of an oil discovery may serve as a timely illustration of our basic model. Moreover, as with the case of the effects of the oil price hikes, there has been considerable confusion about the macroeconomic effects of oil discoveries.

Before entering into the analysis proper we note that what we have to say is not of course only applicable to oil but to any analogous situation where GNP increases or decreases for one reason or another. The macroeconomic effects of a general increase in GNP are summarized in equations (3-70) and (3-71) where $\bar{Y}$ does not have any long term balance of payments benefit (see equation (3-71 (i))), since, once the stock of real balances has adjusted upwards to its new equilibrium value, all further monetary adjustments will cease and so will any balance of payments improvements that might have occurred during this adjustment period. In a dynamic setting, however, faster secular growth will tend to engender a stronger balance of payments as the real balance effect sucks in nominal money balances over the balance of payments.

Equations (3-70 (ii)) and (3-71 (ii)) indicate that actual aggregate output moves in line with the full-employment level of output under either exchange rate regime (recalling the definition of H), while equations (3-70 (iii)) and (3-71 (iii)) indicate the familiar inverse relationship between prices and $\bar{Y}$, although it should be recalled that the processes will differ as between the fixed and floating exchange rate systems. Indeed, the process in equation (3-71 (iii)) is considerably more intricate, since the variability of the exchange rate triggers a more complicated set of interactions.

To discuss the macroeconomic implications of an energy (oil) discovery or an increase in the price of energy we augment the *MGEFB* model described in the previous chapter by formally adding a separate energy sector. However, since it is not germane to the analysis, the exposition is simplified by dropping the market for bonds and ignoring capital movements in the balance of payments. The balance of payments identity expressed in equation (3-50) is now modified to take account of net trade in energy (E):

$$Z \simeq X_w^d + P_x - (I + P_m - S) + (E + P_e - S) \qquad (4\text{-}12)$$

where P_e denotes the price of energy in terms of foreign currency. Like P_m, P_e is assumed to be exogenous. If the country is an energy exporter, E will be positive as indicated in equation (4-12). If the country was an energy importer it would be necessary to write $(S - P_e - E)$ as the energy component of the balance of payments.

We assume that energy exports are the residual between domestic production (E^s) and the domestic demand for energy:

$$E = E^s - E^d \qquad (4\text{-}13)$$

and that domestic energy demand varies directly with economic activity, including the energy sector itself, and inversely with the relative price of energy:

$$E^d = e_1 Y + e_2 E^s - e_3 (P_e - S - P_d) \qquad (4\text{-}14)$$

For our present purposes we assume that E^s is exogenous and is given by the natural endowment, although in practice the depletion profile is likely to depend on price expectations, policy, etc.[4]

It will also be necessary to modify the demand function for money as previously depicted in equation (3-2) to allow for the energy sector:

$$M^d = k_1 Y + k_2 E^s + P \qquad (4\text{-}15)$$

where the general price index expressed in equation (3-57) now includes the energy price:

$$P = b_1 P_d + b_2 P_x + b_3 (P_m - S) + b_4 (P_e - S) \qquad (4\text{-}16)$$

and where

$$\sum_{i=1}^{4} b_i = 1 \qquad (4\text{-}17)$$

Import volumes will now depend on activity in the energy sector in which case equation (3-64) may be rewritten as

$$I = -f_1 (P_m - P_d - S) - f_2 (P_m - S - P_x) + f_s Y + f_e E^s \qquad (4\text{-}18)$$

To simplify the exposition we postulate that in the non-energy sector actual output (Y) will converge on the full-employment level of output ($\bar{Y}$) according to the logic of the $MGEFB$. However, the dynamics of this process are likely to be influenced by the parameters of the energy sector since, for example, it would be necessary to incorporate net energy income itself in the effective demand schedule. Thus equation (3-56) would be reformulated as:

$$DD \simeq a_2 (M - P) + a_3 (Y + E^s) \qquad (4\text{-}19)$$

and energy prices would enter into the Phillips Curve relationship in equation (3-62) alongside import costs. Thus, as E^s rises, domestic demand would increase which, via the Phillips Curve, would generate short term inflationary impulses. In what follows, however, we focus on the monetary mechanisms that would lie behind such changes in effective demand.

We shall consider first the case when the exchange rate is fixed. Recalling the first row in equation (3-65), equation (4-12) may be rewritten as

$$Z \simeq \text{constant} - (e_3 + \beta_1) P_d + (1 - e_2 - f_6) E^s + (1 + e_3)(P_e - S) \qquad (4\text{-}20)$$

where the constant term reflects a range of exogenous variables that are not germane to our present discussion, such as overseas economic activity, (Y_w), import prices (P_m) etc. Thus domestic price increases have an additional adverse balance of payments impact via e_3 since this will encourage more domestic energy consumption via equation (4–14), reducing the surplus for export. It is also reasonable to assume that $1 - e_2 - f_6 > 0$ since energy discoveries are likely to raise energy exports. Finally, as the price of energy rises, the balance of payments will tend to improve due to the terms of trade benefit and the reduced domestic consumption of energy (e_3).

As E^s and P_e change, the balance of payments will alter and domestic monetary equilibrium will be disturbed. In equilibrium the rate of growth of the money supply would have to be equal to the rate of growth of the demand for money, i.e. equating equation (3–49) with the first time derivative of equation (4–15), recalling equations (4–16) and (3–59):

$$Z + C = k_2 \dot{E}^s + b_1(1 + b_2\alpha_1)\dot{P}_d + b_4\dot{P}_e - (b_2(1 - \alpha_1) + b_3 + b_4)\dot{S} \qquad (4\text{–}21)$$

For simplicity we shall assume that the energy endowment, the energy price and the exchange rate are fixed in which case $\dot{E}^s = 0$, etc. The model incorporated in equations (4–20) and (4–21) contains the principal balance of payments and monetary adjustments that are likely to occur. Exports, imports, domestic demand, etc., have all been substituted out and the remaining endogenous variables are the balance of payments itself and the domestic price level (P_d).[5] As in the previous chapter the links between the balance of payments and the monetary and real sectors imply a stock–flow adjustment mechanism and the general solution for the domestic price level derived from equations (4–20) and (4–21) is

$$P_d(t) = Ae^{-wt} + \frac{C + (1 - e_2 - f_6)E^s + (1 + e_3)(P_e - S)}{e_3 + \beta_1} \qquad (4\text{–}22)$$

where

$$w = \frac{e_3 + \beta_1}{b_1(1 + b_2\alpha_1)}$$

i.e. the model is stable for plausible parameter values,[6] and the solution for the balance of payments is

$$Z(t) \backsimeq -(e_3 + \beta_1)Ae^{-wt} - C \qquad (4\text{–}23)$$

The principal finding here is that since none of the energy parameters appear in equation (4–23) they do not influence the balance of payments in the long run, although the solution implies that in the short term this will not be true.

Monetary economists should find this solution intuitive enough since if indeed the balance of payments is a monetary phenomenon there would be no reason why a real phenomenon such as energy resources or the energy price should have any long term bearing on the balance of payments. In the UK, for example, where substantial oil deposits have recently been discovered the long term balance of payments effects of these discoveries is zero. This is so, because the monetary processes that are triggered by increases in E^s or P_e put upward pressure on domestic prices in general and thence onto export prices. Eventually oil exports replace other exports and import substitution to equilibrate the balance of payments. Otherwise equation (4-23) reminds us of the result already obtained in equation (3-70 (i)) that the balance of payments in the long run is equal and opposite to the rate of domestic credit expansion (C).

Equation (4-22) states that when the exchange rate is fixed the domestic price level varies directly in the long run with the supply of energy and its price. This reflects the implicit lag that has already been discussed in chapter 3 in relation to the long run effect of flow variables. Thus E^s and P_e influence P_d along the same lines as does domestic credit expansion (C). For example, when E^s rises the balance of payments will improve in the short term but not in the long term. During this adjustment the stock of money will build up so that given the demand for money function the equilibrium price level rises. This is a technical property of the model which in practice should not be important. The main result is that as in the basic model the domestic price level under fixed exchange rates is determined by world prices. This leaves the main effect of energy discoveries as the extra wealth with which society is endowed.

We now turn to the case where the exchange rate is flexible. Recalling equation (3-68) our two equation model now becomes

$$-(e_3 + \beta_1)P_d + (1 - e_2 - f_1)E^s + (1 + e_3)P_e - (1 + e_3 - \beta_4)S = 0 \qquad (4\text{-}24)$$

$$k_2E^s + b_1(1 + b_2\alpha_1)P_d + b_4P_e - (b_2(1 - \alpha_1) + b_3 + b_4)S = C^* \qquad (4\text{-}25)$$

The solution for S in the former equation will be the exchange rate that equilibrates the balance of payments, while the solution for P_d in the latter equation will be the price level that equates the demand and supply of money via the real balance effect. Notice that it is not necessary to complicate the model with dynamic factors since the absence of capital flows eliminates the stock-flow dimension from the problem and because the exchange rate is floating it is possible to assume that domestic monetary aggregates will be independent of the balance of payments which is zero by assumption.

The general equilibrium solution for the exchange rate may be solved as

$$S = \frac{e_3 + \beta_1}{b_1(1 + b_2\alpha_1)(1 + e_3 - \beta_4) + (b_3 + b_2(1 - \alpha_1) + b_4)(e_3 + \beta_1)} [k_2E^s + b_4P_e - C^*] \qquad (4\text{-}26)$$

while the solution for the domestic price level will be

$$P_d = \frac{1 + e_3 + \beta_4}{(1 + e_3 - \beta_4)b_1(1 + b_2\alpha_1) + (b_2(1 - \alpha_1) + b_3 + b_4)(e_3 + \beta_1)}$$

$$\times \left[C^* + \left[\frac{(b_3 + b_2(1 - \alpha_1) + b_4)(1 - e_2 - f_6)}{1 + e_3 - \beta_4} - k_2 \right] E^s \right.$$

$$\left. + \left[\frac{(b_3 + b_2(1 - \alpha_1) + b_4)(1 + e_3)}{1 + e_3 - \beta_4} - b_4 \right] P_e \right] \qquad (4\text{-}27)$$

As energy resources increase, equation (4-26) tells us that the exchange rate will tend to appreciate since the coefficient of E^s is positive.[7] However, equation (4-27) tells us that there will be two conflicting pressures on the domestic price level. On the one hand the higher exchange rate will create an excess supply of real balances and this will put upward pressure on the price level via the real balance effect. This factor is represented by the positive component in the coefficient on E^s in equation (4-27). On the other hand, the increase in E^s will raise the demand for real balances via k_2 and the ensuing excess demand for real balances will create a deflationary impulse. The net effect is indeterminate and will depend on the precise set of empirical circumstances. Analogous reasoning applies where the energy price itself changes, and as in the previous chapter S varies inversely with the money supply (C^*) while the price level varies in the opposite direction.

This discussion draws attention to the possible deflationary impact of an oil discovery. When the exchange rate is fixed this is unlikely to occur since money balances will tend to be sucked in via the balance of payments rather than through the process of a domestic deflation which increases the stock of real balances. When the exchange rate is flexible the balance of payments cannot act as a ready source of money balances although upward pressure on the exchange rate would tend to raise the stock of real balances. At the same time, and depending on the empirical circumstances, the economy might go into a deflationary syndrome to increase the stock of real balances. If this is considered to be undesirable the monetary authorities would have to intervene to increase the money supply according to the needs of the economy.

When the exchange rate is fixed it was argued that energy discoveries do not affect domestic prices since these are linked to world prices via monetary mechanisms. Therefore, exports do not automatically become uncompetitive and there is no threat of de-industrialization. To enjoy the wealth that is afforded by the energy discovery it is necessary to import more and it is these imports that enable the wealth to be enjoyed at all. But even if people insist on consuming exportables and exports become uncompetitive there will be no de-industrialization threat. All that happens is that manufacturers put their goods on trucks for the home market instead of ships for the world market. It is only when people insist on consuming non-traded output (services) that de-industrialization occurs, but as long as this is the revealed preference of the community such de-industrialization is in the social interest.

CHAPTER 5

Long term policy analysis

We now complete the task that was set in the opening paragraphs of the previous chapter by applying the neoclassical model that has been developed to the range of policy issues that was mentioned there. The effects of monetary policy have already been explored in Chapter 4. It therefore remains to consider tariffs, import controls, exchange controls, exchange rate policy, fiscal policy and incomes policy. We begin with the question of tariff policy.

The effects of a tariff

The conventional assumption is that a tariff will reduce imports, thereby aiding the balance of payments. However, this will trigger a series of monetary adjustments in view of the relationship that has been identified between the monetary sector and the balance of payments. These monetary adjustments will in principle affect domestic prices and expenditure which will repercuss in their turn onto the balance of payments. In this section we apply the model that has been developed to this problem in order to clarify the long term impact of a tariff on the macroeconomy.

We use the case of a tariff as an example of a current account intervention. Other comparable interventions might be export subsidization, subsidies to import substitution, etc.; however, the principles that apply in the case of a tariff would extend to these interventions too.

As in the previous section we assume that the economy will tend to full employment for reasons that have already been given. The demand for imports will have to reflect the presence of a tariff, so it is necessary to rewrite equation (3–64) as

$$I = -f_1(P_m - P_x - S) - f_2(P_m - P_x - S) + f_s Y - (f_1 + f_2)(1 + T) \qquad (5\text{-}1)$$

where $1 + T$ is an appropriate index of the tariff level (T). The higher the tariff, the less competitive will be imports in relation to exportables and other domestic output. The tariff will also raise the price of imports to residents and this will tend to raise the demand for real balances.

As in Chapter 4 it is not necessary to complicate the analysis by specifying a market for bonds, and so we may rewrite the expression for the balance of payments from equation (3-65) as

$$Z \doteq -\beta_1 P_d + (f_1 + f_2)(1 + T) + \text{constant} \tag{5-2}$$

while the analogue of equation (5-2) as the equilibrium condition in the domestic money market will be

$$Z + C = b_1(1 + b_2\alpha_1)\dot{P}_d + b_3\dot{P}_m + b_3(1 + T) - (b_2(1 - \alpha_1) + b_3)\dot{S} \tag{5-3}$$

For simplicity we assume that the exogenous variables are fixed so that the general solution for the domestic price level (P_d) is

$$P_d(t) = Ae^{-vt} + \frac{C + (f_1 + f_2)(1 + T)}{\beta_1} \tag{5-4}$$

where

$$v = \beta_1/b_1(1 + b_2\alpha_1)$$

i.e. once more the model is stable,[1] and the solution for the balance of payments is

$$Z(t) \doteq -\beta_1 Ae^{-vt} - C \tag{5-5}$$

This last expression states that in the long run the balance of payments is independent of the tariff level although tariffs may have a temporary balance of payments effect. How does this occur? In the first instance the tariff will reduce imports and raise domestic prices. The resultant improvement in the balance of payments will then increase the money supply and this will tend to generate a series of inflationary real balance effects. On the other hand the demand for money will rise by $b_3\Delta(1 + T)$ due to the increase in post-tariff import prices and this will tend to generate deflationary impulses. Eventually the former impulse will prevail over the latter since it represents an accumulating flow while the latter represents a once and for all stock effect. Full employment and monetary equilibrium can only prevail when the price level has risen high enough to offset the contributions of the tariff to the balance of payments. As equation (5-4) demonstrates, when $1 + T$ is increased a positive price response is induced with an elasticity of $(f_1 + f_2)/\beta_1$.

Instead the balance of payments in the long run is equal and opposite to domestic credit expansion since according to the model we have postulated the balance of payments acts as an escape valve for nominal money balances that are not in demand. We should note that the tariff will generate revenues for the authorities and this may induce them to reduce domestic credit creation since the government borrowing requirement is lower. If C falls, a tariff would have a favorable balance of payments effects in the long run but not for the usual partial equilibrium reasons, but because the authorities agreed to alter their monetary policies in response to increased revenues. In this case monetary policy rather than commercial policy is responsible for the balance of payments improvement.

We now turn to the case where the exchange rate is floating. Under these circumstances the exchange rate will be determined on the basis of the equilibration of the balance of payments which, as the analogue of equation (5-2), may be adapted from equation (3-68) as

$$-\beta_1(P_d + S) + (f_1 + f_2)(1 + T) = 0 \tag{5-6}$$

which is an adaptation of equation (4-24), and domestic monetary equilibrium will prevail when the demand for money equals its supply.

In the floating exchange rate case, where the money supply is not influenced by balance of payments flows equation (5-3) becomes

$$b_1(1 + b_2\alpha_1)P_d + b_3(1 + T) - (b_3 + b_2(1 - \alpha_1))S = C^* \tag{5-7}$$

The solutions of this model for P_d and S are

$$P_d = \frac{\beta_1 C^* + (b_2(1 - \alpha_1) + b_3)(f_1 + f_2\beta_1)(1 + T)}{\beta_1(b_2(1 - \alpha_1) + b_3 - b_1(1 + b_2\alpha_1))} \tag{5-8}$$

$$S = \frac{\beta_1 C^* + (b_1(1 + b_2\alpha_1)(f_1 + f_2) + \beta_1 b_3)(1 + T)}{\beta_1(b_2(1 - \alpha_1) + b_3 + b_1\beta_4(1 + b_2\alpha_1))} \tag{5-9}$$

The latter expression indicates that a tariff will tend to boost the exchange rate while P_d may either rise or fall depending on the sign of $f_1 + f_2 - \beta_1$.[2] This ambiguity is analogous to that previously discussed in relation to equation (4-27). On the one hand the tariff will generate deflationary impulses since the post-tariff price level will initially be higher and real balances will be eroded. On the other hand the appreciated exchange rate will tend to increase real balances via the reduction in import prices and the price of exportables. The net effect may go either way, but it is apparent that a tariff applied under floating exchange rates could exert a deflationary effect on the economy. When the exchange rate is fixed this possibility does not arise since the extra demand for money is met via the balance of payments. This suggests that when the exchange rate is flexible the deflationary effects of a tariff might be balanced by an expansion of the money supply as an act of policy.

In summary, an increase in tariffs will

(i) improve the balance of payments in the short run but not in the long run when the exchange rate is fixed,

(ii) stimulate economic activity in the short run but not in the long run under either regime,

(iii) generate inflationary pressures when the exchange rate is fixed,

(iv) however, if the exchange rate is floating, the effects could be deflationary.

Such results could not be obtained from a Keynesian model of an open economy. Perhaps of particular importance is the first result, but this merely confirms a neoclassical theorem which dates back to David Hume over two hundred years ago.

Import controls

Whereas a tariff leaves the actual volume of imports as an endogenous variable to be determined in the light of the tariff, import controls or quantitative restrictions would imply that the volume of imports (I) was exogenous and a policy instrument of the authorities. Like a tariff, import controls might be regarded by the authorities as a means for strengthening the balance of payments directly or as a device for stimulating domestic demand and employment. In this latter context we should point out straight away that the model that we have developed would imply that as employment stimulants, tariffs and import controls are unnecessary. This is because the Phillips Curve mechanism implies that full employment would eventually be restored, as was demonstrated in the previous chapter. The question remains, however, whether this natural process can be accelerated by stimulating domestic demand through tariffs and import controls. We defer this discussion until Chapter 7 since it relates more generally to dynamic issues in demand management. In the meanwhile, we merely note that import controls and similar policy interventions will inevitably change the dynamic structure of the model since certain structural parameters are either over-written or modified by these policies. Our present preoccupation, however, is with the statics or long run tendencies of the model that are implied by these various policy interventions.

We also omit any detailed analysis of the implications of these policy interventions for allocative efficiency. This raises a range of microeconomic issues that lie beyond the purview of the present study. Nevertheless, a number of comments are in order. As a general policy principle interventions within the market framework are desirable when they are correcting for some market distortion that is impeding the overall allocative efficiency of the economy. For example interventions that stimulate factor mobility, the dissemination of information, the recognition of external economies and diseconomies, etc., will contribute to improved economic performance. It therefore has to be asked whether the implications for microeconomic efficiency of the various macro-motivated policy interventions are likely to generate benefits that are larger than their social costs.

Occasionally policy makers consider this issue. For example prices and incomes policies are sometimes criticized for introducing rigidities into the economy which will inhibit allocative efficiency. However, this does not always eliminate such policies in practice. As a general rule, the issue of allocative efficiency is not seriously considered, if at all. To a large extent this may be atributed to the convention of dichotomizing between micro- and macroeconomics and the theory of macroeconomic policy has on the whole failed to integrate micro and macro policy concerns. Although no systematic attempt at this integration is attempted in this study, we shall return to this issue in Chapter 7 where the integrating principle is considered to be the speed of macroeconomic adjustment as a correlate of intertemporal resource misallocation, and the impact of macroeconomic intervention on this parameter.

If import volumes are controlled at I^* it will be necessary to replace equation (3–64) by

$$I = I^* \tag{5-10}$$

in which case the determinants of the balance of payments may be written as

$$Z \doteq -e_1(P_x + S) + P_x - I^* + S - P_m \tag{5-11}$$

Notice that while the volume of imports is fixed, the value of imports need not be since the price of imports may vary through changes in P_m or S. The conditions for domestic monetary equilibrium are

$$Z + C = b_1(1 + b_2\alpha_1)\dot{P}_d + b_3\dot{P}_m - (b_2(1 - \alpha_1) + b_3)\dot{S} \tag{5-12}$$

If the exchange rate is fixed $\dot{S} = 0$. Substituting for P_x in equation (5–11) from equation (3–59) and solving this simultaneous system for P_d yields

$$P_d(t) = Ae^{vt} + \frac{C - I^*}{\alpha_1(e_1 - 1)} \tag{5-13}$$

where

$$v \doteq \frac{(1 - e_1)\alpha_1}{b_1(1 + b_2\alpha_1)}$$

Thus the stability condition[3] would be that $e_1 > 1$. This implies that the balance of payments in the long run will equal

$$Z(t) \simeq \alpha_1(1 - e_1)Ae^{vt} - C \qquad\qquad (5\text{-}14)$$

If the stability condition is fulfilled this implies once more that the balance of payments is equal and opposite to the rate of domestic credit expansion. In other words controlling imports has no long run balance of payments benefit.

This apparent paradox would not disturb the monetary economist since Z is a monetary phenomenon and I is a real phenomenon. Typically I^* would be reduced as the authorities attempt to improve the balance of payments or to stimulate domestic demand. This would initially improve the balance of payments and the money supply would increase over time. As equation (5-13) indicates, this will tend to raise domestic prices and thence export prices since there will be an excess supply of money. This process will continue until prices have risen high enough to offset the initial balance of payments improvements since this will restore domestic monetary equilibrium. In this new equilibrium the value of exports will fall by an amount equal to the controlled fall in the volume of imports. We therefore conclude that import controls will not serve as a long term balance of payments palliative and that they will be inflationary. They will also distort the allocation of resources within the economy at large.

If the exchange rate is floating it is difficult to imagine why the authorities would seriously consider import controls. However, it is possible that imports might be controlled for employment purposes. In this case the model may be simplified down to

$$(1 - e_1)\alpha_1(P_d + S) - I^* = 0 \qquad\qquad (5\text{-}15)$$

$$b_1(1 + b_2\alpha_1)P_d - (b_3 + b_2(1 - \alpha_1))S = C^* \qquad\qquad (5\text{-}16)$$

which implies that

$$P_d = \frac{(b_3 + b_2(1 - \alpha_1))I^* - (1 - e_1)\alpha_1 b_1(1 + b_2\alpha_1)C^*}{\alpha_1(1 - e_1)(b_3 + b_2(1 - \alpha_1)) - b_1(1 + b_2\alpha_1)} \qquad\qquad (5\text{-}17)$$

$$S = \frac{\alpha_1(1 - e_1)C^* - b_1(1 + b_2\alpha_1)I^*}{\alpha_1(1 - e_1)(b_3 + b_2(1 - \alpha_1)) - b_1(1 + b_2\alpha_1)} \qquad\qquad (5\text{-}18)$$

For normal responses, e.g. P_d varies directly with C^*, the denominator as a whole must be negative. Under these circumstances equation (5-17) states that as imports are increasingly controlled – i.e. as I^* is reduced, P_d increases while equation (5-18) states that the exchange rate will appreciate.

In summary, therefore, neoclassical analysis suggests that import controls (below the market-determined level) will

(i) improve the balance of payments in the short run but not in the long run when the exchange rate is fixed,

(ii) stimulate economic activity and employment in the short term but not in the long term, and

(iii) generate short run as well as long term inflationary pressures.

Exchange controls

Whereas import controls, tariffs, etc., are current account restrictions, exchange controls are capital account restrictions. It is most probably the case that exchange controls have been less widely discussed than current account controls and at the political level they have received considerably less attention than their current account counterparts. For example the General Agreement on Tariffs and Trade has no parallel as far as capital transactions are concerned other than fairly vague political commitments to capital market liberalization. Although exchange controls have been significantly reduced over the years, extensive controls and regulations remain as testified by the IMF's annual review of exchange controls.

The purpose of exchange controls is to benefit the balance of payments and as in the previous sections we apply the model that has been developed in Chapter 3 to explore the macroeconomic implications of exchange controls. We notice first of all that the controls usually apply to outward capital movements that might be initiated by domestic economic agents. The international portfolio behavior of foreign economic agents is usually beyond the jurisdiction of domestic regulations. Under these circumstances the authorities may only attempt to control half the capital account.

Furthermore it is necessary to distinguish between stocks and flows. The authorities may either permit a given annual outflow on the capital account or they may set a limit to the foreign currency positions of domestic economic agents. Recalling equation (3-52) we therefore have two main policy situations:

(i) $\dot{B}_w$ = constant
(ii) B_w = constant

while B_f, overseas holdings of domestic bonds, will be unconstrained. In theory, however, the domestic authorities could control these too but this is not usually practiced.

To explore the macroeconomic effects of either of these policies we may modify the *MGEFB* model described in Chapter 3 by altering equation (3-52). If B_w is a constant that is determined by policy, $\dot{B}_w$ will be zero, therefore in either case the parameters q_3 and q_4 would be set to zero. If the exchange controls are stock-related, i.e. B_w is a constant, we may deduce straight away that in the longer term the balance of payments will not be affected since in equations (3–65) and (3–68) only $\dot{B}_w$ matters, via Z. In other words, since only the flow of foreign owned bonds enters the model and not the stock, a stock-related exchange control cannot make any longer term difference to macroeconomic status. Likewise the removal of such exchange controls would not have any adverse longer term consequences either. There would naturally be short term consequences and if B_w were reduced the balance of payments on the capital account would strengthen temporarily.

Let us assume that the exchange rate is fixed and that the authorities are assumed to impose a stock-related exchange control that requires the reduction of B_w outstanding by 100. According to the *MGEFB* model the following sequence of events is likely to take place.

(i) Initially the balance of payments will improve by 100.

(ii) But this will add to the money supply via equation (3–49).

(iii) Domestic interest rates (r) will fall via equation (3–28) since the supply of money has grown relative to demand, triggering inflationary pressures via equations (3–56) and (3–62) in terms of real balance and interest rate effects.

(iv) At the same time the non-controlled part of the capital account of the balance of payments will weaken as interest rates fall via equation (3–51).

(v) The pressures in (iii) will weaken the current account so that the domestic money supply will tend to fall due to balance of payments outflows.

(vi) This stock–flow syndrome will persist until the cumulative balance of payments outflow equals the initial inflow. At the new equilibrium the balance of payments will have reverted to its original state while the domestic price level will have fallen all the way back from its initial increase. The nature of the implied time profile is illustrated on fig. 5–1 where the solid lines refer to the balance of payments (Z) and the broken lines the domestic price level (P). By the time the balance of payments effect is zero the money stock will have reverted to its original level. Fig. 5–1 draws attention to the fact that the initial balance of payments improvement will be followed by a temporary period of balance of payments deficit and price inflation.

(vii) Because the demand for domestic bonds has been artificially increased domestic interest rates will be lower in the new equilibrium.

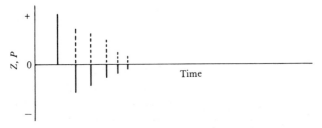

Figure 5–1 Time profile of balance of payments and prices

We now turn to the case of a flow-related exchange control, i.e. where $\dot{B}_w$ is constrained by policy. In many respects this is analogous to an import control except, whereas an import control would stimulate domestic demand directly, a flow-related exchange control would only do so indirectly via its effects on the monetary sector. In terms of equation (3-65), $\dot{B}_w$ would now become an exogenous variable along with Y_w, $\dot{r}_w$, etc., and the qualitative relationship between $\dot{B}_w$ and the endogenous variables such as the balance of payments and the price level would be broadly the same as for the other exogenous variables. In other words, in equation (3-70) the only exogenous determinant of the balance of payments would remain the rate of domestic credit expansion while the price of domestic output would only be influenced by $\dot{B}_w$ insofar as the technicality of the stock–flow effect discussed on page 90 applied. Thus, if previously the free-determined value for $\dot{B}_w$ had been 200 and $\dot{B}_w$ is constrained to be 100 via a flow-related exchange control the balance of payments would initially improve by 100. Eventually the other components of the balance of payments would weaken by 100 so that the final state of the balance of payments remains unaltered. Exports will be less and imports more since the price level will tend to be higher while the freely-determined component of the capital account should remain unaltered in the long run since the change in the interest rate differential $(\dot{r} - \dot{r}_w)$ will be unchanged. During the adjustment period, however, the freely-determined component of the capital account will tend to deteriorate temporarily since the expansionary monetary impact of the exchange control would tend to lower domestic interest rates relative to overseas interest rates.

We may conclude, therefore, that the removal of a flow-related exchange control would not have any adverse longer term balance of payments effects. During the adjustment period, however, there may be deflationary effects which would tend to strengthen the rest of the balance of payments in a compensatory fashion. Finally, we note that the dynamics of the model implied by equation (3-67) will be altered since q_3 and q_4 will be zero under either version of exchange control policy.

Devaluation

Especially since the 'floating' of the US dollar in 1971, the polarized typology between fixed and floating exchange rates has become unrealistic, but such a polarity could re-emerge in the future. Especially among the industrialized countries the majority of exchange rate regimes are characterized by 'managed' exchange rates where the authorities buy and sell foreign exchange with the objective of influencing the exchange rate but where the exchange rate itself is not fixed. Less charitable commentators refer to this as 'dirty' floating in contrast to 'clean' floating where there would be no official intervention at all.

We shall not consider here why the authorities might wish to influence the exchange rate or what the pros and cons of 'managed' floating might be, since this discussion is deferred to the remaining chapters. Instead we investigate the positive economics of 'managed' floating in terms of the $MGEFB$ model.

When the exchange rate is fixed it is, as it were, perfectly 'managed' since a fixed rate is an extreme case of exchange rate management. Under these circumstances the balance of payments and thus the change in reserves is endogenous to this particular exchange rate objective. More generally the change in reserves may be considered as an instrument of policy whose objective is to influence the exchange rate in the first instance. As the authorities run down their reserves of foreign exchange in support of domestic currency, the exchange rate will tend to appreciate and vice versa. Thus we may recast Z as the exogenous policy instrument while S would become endogenous to the system.

We first consider the effects of exchange policy under a regime of pegged exchange rates which was the case described by equation (3-65), where the exchange rate (S) appears as an exogenous variable. The short run effects of a devaluation are obvious enough from the structural equations that have been specified in Chapter 3. Assuming the Marshall–Lerner conditions are fulfilled (i.e. $\beta_4 < 0$) a devaluation would tend to improve the current account of the balance of payments. Equation (3-53) further implies that the capital account will improve for one time period since $\dot{S} < 0$ on account of the devaluation.

The stronger current account will directly stimulate aggregate demand and employment along conventional Keynesian lines. In addition the current and capital account improvements will increase the money supply which in turn will depress the rate of interest and aggregate demand will be further stimulated.

The long run effects of devaluation on the economy are recorded in equation (3-70). The first of these equations indicates that in the long term the balance of payments is completely independent of the exchange rate. The second implies that the equilibrium level of output does not depend on the exchange rate either. The third equation states the devaluations have a proportionate inflationary effect (since $\beta_4 = -\beta_1$ according to equations (3-66 (i)) and (3-66 (iv)).

How does this arise? The short term effects expand the money supply in the way already described and effective demand is increased. This in turn will trigger price rises which will affect in part the competitive edge that was provided by the devaluation. In addition, apart from demand–pull inflation there will be cost push inflation since import costs will have increased. As long as the balance of payments benefits from the devaluation, inflationary pressures will persist and in each period the domestic price level will rise. The rise continues until domestic prices have risen in proportion with the devaluation as implied by equation (3-70 (iii)). At this point the competitive edge is lost entirely and the balance of payments effect is zero. During the adjustment period the cumulative balance of payments benefits will have bid up the domestic money stock by an amount proportionate to the devaluation. This must be so because the price level has risen by a proportionate amount and the demand for money function implies a proportionate relationship between the money supply and the price level. The exchange rate is therefore neutral in the long run and the price level is determined by the world price level when expressed in common currency.

It should be emphasized that although equation (3-74) implies that the domestic price level eventually moves proportionately with the world price level this does not necessarily confirm the so-called 'law of one price'. This law states that the price of a homogeneous commodity in one country should equal its price in another country, otherwise arbitrageurs would be able to profit by buying at the cheaper price in one country and selling at a profit in another. The law is therefore concerned with the relationship between prices of traded goods that is generated by trade theory rather than the relationship between general price levels that is implied by monetary theory. For the 'law of one price' to obtain it is necessary that α_1 as defined by equation (3-60 (i)) be equal to zero in which case export prices in equation (3-59) depend entirely upon competing prices abroad. This typically happens when $e_1 = \infty$, i.e. when the elasticity of substitution in demand between internationally traded goods is infinite.

Equation (3-74) states that regardless of the value of α_1 and e_1, i.e. regardless of whether the 'law of one price' is fulfilled or not, monetary theory implies that the domestic price level will vary proportionately with the world price. The smaller is e_1, the weaker will be the trade and therefore the monetary linkages between currency areas and the longer will it take for long run price proportionality to hold, as may be seen by exploring the roots to equation (3-64) and (3-69).

It should also be pointed out that just because the balance of payments is insensitive to the exchange rate in the long run it cannot be assumed that a separate exchange rate is of no practical use and that currency independence should be abandoned in favor of monetary unification. On the contrary, although in the long run exchange rates are neutral, in the short term they provide an important additional degree of freedom for the economy to adjust to random shocks. For example a random surge of world prices would lead to a temporary exchange rate appreciation sheltering the economy from inflationary pressures. This protection would not have been forthcoming under monetary union. Exchange rate separation should only be given up if there are compensatory economic and political benefits. Long run neutrality should not be taken as an argument for ignoring the role of short run exchange rate adjustments.

Exchange rate intervention

Abstracting from Y, r and the unrelated exogenous variables of the *MGEFB* model we may, as before, express the model in terms of two equations that determine the exchange rate and prices (P_d) simultaneously. Equilibrium in the foreign exchange market will require that

$$-\beta_1 (p_d + S) - \beta_s \dot{S} = Z \qquad (5\text{-}19)$$

i.e. the net supply of foreign exchange from the market, the current account plus the capital account, must equal the net demand of foreign exchange by the monetary authorities (Z). Equilibrium in the domestic money markets will require that the growth in the supply of money will equal the growth in the demand for money:

$$C + Z = b_1(1 + b_2\alpha_1)\dot{P}_d - (b_3 + b_2(1 - \alpha_1))\dot{S} \qquad (5\text{-}20)$$

Thus the more the authorities support the exchange rate net, i.e. the smaller is Z, the greater will be the net monetary contraction to which the domestic economy has to adjust. The respective solutions for the exchange rate and price are:

$$S(t) = Ae^{-jt} - \frac{[b_1(1 + b_2\alpha_1) + \beta_1]Z + \beta_1 C}{\beta_1 b_1(1 + b_2\alpha_1)} \qquad (5\text{-}21)$$

$$P_d(t) = Be^{-jt} + \frac{(C + Z)}{b_1(1 + b_2\alpha_1)} \qquad (5\text{-}22)$$

where

$$j = \frac{-\beta_1 b_1(1 + b_2\alpha_1)}{\beta_1(b_2(1 - \alpha_1) - b_3) - \beta_s b_1(1 + b_2\alpha_1)}$$

The stability condition will require that $j > 0$. In what follows, however, we focus on the particular integrals or the long term solutions of the model.

Equation (5-21) states that the equilibrium relationship between the exchange rate and intervention will be positive while domestic credit expansion will tend to depress the exchange rate. Thus as Z falls the authorities lend more net support to the exchange rate and the exchange rate will tend to appreciate. Equation (5-22) indicates that such a policy would also be deflationary since the price level will tend to fall. When the authorities intervene in the foreign exchange market to support the currency, the following conceptual stages may be identified:

(i) The exchange rate will appreciate and the money supply will tend to contract via equation (3-49) since Z falls.

(ii) The appreciated exchange rate will reduce exports and increase imports triggering a deflationary effect while a second deflationary impulse will be generated by the negative real balance effect.

(iii) On the other hand the appreciated exchange rate will tend to lower the domestic price level directly and this would generate inflationary real balance effects.

(iv) But since equation (5-19) must hold, if S rises, P_d must fall and the deflationary impulses must predominate.

Thus exchange rate support may be temporarily deflationary. We should also point out that in the nature of things exchange rate support cannot be continued indefinitely since foreign exchange reserves are finite. Technically speaking the authorities may prevent the exchange rate from appreciating by accumulating reserves indefinitely but they obviously cannot afford to reverse this procedure.[4] In Chapter 7 we shall return to this discussion, where dynamic considerations are explicitly examined.

Fiscal policy

In this and the next section the analysis no longer requires the specification of an open economy model since it is not germane to our subject matter, and so we conduct our investigations in terms of the simpler idiom of a closed economy. In the case of fiscal policy the main analytical issue is the stock–flow phenomena that are generated by government expenditure, taxation and the financing of the public sector. Thus government expenditure is essentially a flow while the way in which it is financed will tend to alter the stocks of financial assets in the economy.

To introduce this notion we posit the simplest of models. Thereafter, we shall progress to more sophisticated models where the same general principles hold. We represent the volume of government expenditure by G and the price level by P. Thus in current prices the logarithm of government expenditure is represented as $G + P$ which for the moment we assume is financed by the printing of money. Thus the change in the money supply will be

$$\dot{M} \simeq G + P \tag{5-23}$$

For further simplicity we assume that the economy is at full employment $(Y = \bar{Y})$. Thus from equation (3-2) the growth in the demand for money will depend on the growth in the price level. The equilibrium condition in this model will therefore be

$$\dot{P} = G + P \tag{5-24}$$

i.e. where the growth in the demand for money equals the growth in its supply. The general solution for the price level will be

$$P(t) = Ae^t - G \tag{5-25}$$

where A is an arbitrary constant reflecting the initial conditions (P_0). We may therefore rewrite equation (5-25) as

$$P(t) = (P_0 + G)e^t - G \tag{5-26}$$

Thus, the rate of inflation is

$$\dot{P}(t) = (P_0 + G)e^t \tag{5-27}$$

and the greater is the volume of government expenditure, the greater will be the rate of inflation. The logic incorporated in this model is straightforward. First, in any given time period government expenditures will increase the quantity of money because of the financing assumption. This will raise the price level via the real balance effect and in the next period government expenditure in current prices will be higher due to the interim inflation. This will require a further injection of money into the system; and so the inflationary process will continue.

Alternatively the authorities might resort to taxation instead of the printing press to finance their expenditure. The public sector's borrowing requirement (R) will be the difference between its expenditure in current prices and its tax receipts $(Y + P + T)$, where T represents the income tax rate.

$$R \triangleq s(G + P) - (Y + P + T)(1 - s) \tag{5-28}$$

where s is the share of expenditure in R. If the budget is balanced, i.e. if $R = 0$, equation (5-28) will imply that

$$G = T + Y \tag{5-29}$$

If this last condition is fulfilled, $\dot{M} = 0$ and government expenditures will not be inflationary. In other words, in the present context, what matters is not the volume of public expenditure or the tax rate, but the monetary implications of fiscal policy. As long as the budget is balanced there will be no inflation since monetary growth will be zero. If it is less than balanced the rate of inflation will be

$$\dot{P}(t) = [P_0 + sG - (T + \bar{Y})(1 - s)]e^t \tag{5-30}$$

From this it emerges that, apart from the political issues associated with the size of the public sector's involvement,[5] the rate of inflation depends on how this involvement is to be financed. In practice, it is most probably the case that resort to inflationary finance will be greater, the larger the public sector's involvement. However, the model makes it quite explicit that nothing may be directly inferred from the volume of public expenditure regarding inflation; the critical factor in this regard being financial policies and subsequent monetary growth.

If we extend the model to include bonds the authorities may meet the borrowing requirement either by open market sales (B) or through the processes of domestic credit creation (C). Thus we have an additional identity to consider:

$$R \simeq \dot{B} + C \qquad\qquad (5\text{-}31)$$

According to this formulation, monetary expansion will not only depend on the borrowing requirement but on open market policies too. Open market sales will reduce the money supply while open market purchases will increase it. Having laid bare the principles we wish to consider in the context of the rudimentary MG model, in the remainder of this section we describe a more general model in which the elements of fiscal policy are activated. First, equation (3-55) has to be rewritten as

$$Y = wDD + G(1 - w) \qquad\qquad (5\text{-}32)$$

where $1 - w$ is the share of G in Y. Private sector demand (DD) is assumed to be determined as before in equation (3-56) except that it is now necessary to specify disposable income in view of direct taxation, while indirect taxation will raise final prices. If we denote T as the direct tax rate and V as the indirect tax rate we may rewrite equation (3-56) as

$$DD \simeq -a_1 r + a_2(M - P - (1 + V)) + a_3(Y + (1 - T)) \qquad\qquad (5\text{-}33)$$

Thus an increase in the indirect tax rate raises final prices and induces a negative real balance effect, while an increase in the direct tax rate will have deflationary effects since it will lower disposable income.

The borrowing requirement of the government (R) is the difference between money expenditures and receipts

$$R \simeq s(G + P) - (Y + P + (T + V))(1 - s) \qquad\qquad (5\text{-}34)$$

where government direct and indirect tax revenue is represented by $Y + P + (T + V)$.[6] Raising either of the tax rates will raise government tax receipts and reduce the borrowing requirement, but there will also be macroeconomic feedback effects to consider which we shall discuss presently.

Notice that because bonds have been incorporated into the model it has been necessary to specify a rate of interest (r) and below we relax the assumption held in the rudimentary model that $Y = \bar{Y}$.

To close this model we note as in equation (3–62) that the rate of inflation is hypothesized to depend on the pressure of demand:

$$\dot{P} = j_4(Y - \bar{Y}) \tag{5-35}$$

and that equations (3–8) and (3–10) imply that domestic monetary equilibrium will prevail when

$$k\dot{Y} + \dot{P} - j\dot{r} = C \tag{5-36}$$

The model that has been proposed may be rewritten as

$$\begin{bmatrix} \alpha & 0 & \beta \\ -j_4 & D & 0 \\ kD + (1-s) & D + (1-2s) & -jD \end{bmatrix} \begin{bmatrix} Y \\ P \\ r \end{bmatrix} = \begin{bmatrix} -a_2 w(1+V) + wa_3(1-T) + (1-w)G \\ -j_4\bar{Y} \\ sG + (s-1)(T+V) - \dot{B} \end{bmatrix} \tag{5-37}$$

where

$$\begin{aligned} \alpha &= 1 - w(a_2 k + a_3) & \text{(i)} \\ \beta &= w(a_1 + a_2 j) & \text{(ii)} \end{aligned} \right\} \tag{5-38}$$

and D is once more the differential operator. The determinant of the system is

$$det = -(k\beta + \alpha j)D^2 - \beta(j_4 + 1 - s)D + j_4\beta(1 - 2s) \tag{5-39}$$

i.e. the model entails two roots x_1 and x_2 and it is likely that at least one of these roots will be positive since inflationary deficit financing implies an unstable price level as in equation (5–27). The general solution for the price level implied by this model is

$$P(t) = A_1 e^{x_1 t} + A_2 e^{x_2 t} + A_3 \tag{5-40}$$

where

$$A_1 = \frac{P_0 e^{x_2} - P_1 - A_3(1 - e^{x_2})}{(e^{x_2} - e^{x_1})(1 - 2s)} \qquad \text{(i)}$$

$$A_2 = \frac{P_1 - P_0 e^{x_1} - A_3(1 - e^{x_1})}{(e^{x_2} - e^{x_1})(1 - 2s)} \qquad \text{(ii)} \right\} \tag{5-41}$$

$$A_3 = (1 - s)\bar{Y} - sG + (1 - s)(T + V) + \dot{B} \qquad \text{(iii)}$$

Differentiating equation (5–40) with respect to t implies that the relationship between the rate of inflation and the exogenous variables is:

$$\dot{P}(t) = \frac{-A_3[(1 - e^{x_2})x_1 e^{x_1 t} + (1 - e^{x_1})x_2 e^{x_2 t}]}{(e^{x_2} - e^{x_1})(1 - 2s)} \qquad (5\text{-}42)$$

This last expression is the analogue of equation (5-30) in the model except that we omit the initial conditions (P_0 and P_1). If, say, higher government expenditures, ceteris paribus, add to the rate of inflation as before, the coefficient of $-A_3$ in equation (5-42) will have to be positive. Under these circumstances higher tax rates and open market sales would tend to have a depressing effect on the rate of inflation.

We may now attempt to verbalize the principal analytical themes in this model of fiscal policy in a fully specified macroeconomic setting, and we consider both the short term and long term factors:

Direct taxation

(i) An increase in the direct tax rate (T) will initially reduce disposable income which will depress aggregate demand in the private sector via equation (5-33). This is the traditional Keynesian effective-demand relationship and in the short term the familiar multiplier mechanism would tend to operate.

(ii) Since we assume government expenditure, etc., to be constant, the first stage will tend to induce price deflation via equation (5-35) since the economy will have fallen below its erstwhile state of full employment.

(iii) However, there will be an additional deflationary effect since the increased tax revenues will tend to reduce the money supply if financial policy is not altered. For the borrowing requirement will be smaller via equation (5-34), in which case domestic credit (C) will tend to be expanded at a lower rate.

(iv) This will induce deflationary or negative real balance effects and interest rates will tend to rise further reducing aggregate demand in the private sector.

(v) Had the increase in T been for one period only, the economy would have become relatively depressed, but as the price level fell this would have increased the stock of real balances along the lines discussed in the previous chapter until full employment was eventually restored. Under these circumstances a policy of temporary fiscal tightness would trigger a protracted monetary adjustment process which extended beyond the time span of the fiscal policy itself, and a reversal of a fiscal initiative could not be expected to unwind the previous deflation in effective demand over a comparable time period until the monetary equilibrium of the economy had been restored through the dynamics of the real balance effect. Thus fiscal initiatives which in their nature affect the flow of financial assets also have the important macroeconomic effect of upsetting the stock equilibrium in the monetary sector as a consequence of which even temporary fiscal policies will tend to generate monetary reverberations for perhaps a considerable time.

(vi) If, however, the increase in T is permanent, the economy will experience a permanent leakage of money balances and a permanent deflationary real balance syndrome will be generated. If the implied rate of monetary contraction was greater than the rate of price deflation, the volume of real balances would decline exponentially and eventually the economy would grind to a halt and there would be mass unemployment.

(vii) Assuming away this stability problem the rate of price deflation would have to be such that the volume of real balances was left unchanged by the fiscal leakage under consideration. For, according to the monetary mechanisms in the model that has been proposed, full employment would be associated with a given volume of real balances.

Indirect taxation

(i) Like direct taxation, indirect taxation will have a depressing effect on the money supply over time since in each period the authorities will receive a flow of revenue from indirect taxation. As indirect taxation (V) increases, the government's borrowing requirement decreases via equation (5-34) which for given open market operations will reduce monetary growth via equation (5-31).

(ii) Thus the processes identified in relation to direct taxation and the adjustment of the price level to compensate for the loss of real balances would tend to apply in the case of indirect taxation too.

(iii) However, indirect taxation introduces an additional factor as may be seen in relation to equations (5-33) and (5-36). As V rises, the post-tax price level will rise. This will have two effects. First, the volume of real balances will fall and this will reduce aggregate demand via equation (5-33). Secondly, interest rates will tend to rise since the demand for money will have risen reflecting the high post-tax price level. As interest rates rise aggregate demand will fall yet further as indicated by equation (5-33).

(iv) As the economy reverts to full-employment equilibrium it will have to experience an additional deflationary syndrome that is implied by (iii). At full employment the pre-tax price level will have to be lower to compensate for the tax-inflated price level so that the full-employment volume of real balances will be restored.

Expenditure policy

(i) Government expenditure (G) will directly affect economic activity via equation (5-32). To evaluate the macroeconomic effects of government expenditure it is necessary to make an assumption about how it is to be financed. Broadly speaking, the authorities have three choices. First they might finance themselves out of taxation (T or V). Secondly, they might sell government debt ($\dot{B}$) and finally they might expand domestic credit (C) – or 'print money'. In practice the authorities are likely to combine these options, in which case the macroeconomic consequences could be quite complex.

(ii) If the authorities choose to balance the budget, R will be zero via equation (5-34) so that via equation (5-31) monetary aggregates will be unchanged; tax leakages from the money supply are exactly balanced by the government expenditures themselves. Under these circumstances the real balance effect would be zero and public expenditure would appropriately replace private expenditure at full employment. In practice the matter might be complicated by the balanced budget multiplier if revenues are raised via direct taxation since, even if the initial volume of real balances is unchanged, demand-pull inflation would tend to follow since Y is greater than $\bar{Y}$. Under these circumstances prices would rise via equation (5-35) and the volume of real balances would be reduced. This inflationary process would continue until full employment was restored.

(iii) Alternatively the authorities might balance the budget by raising indirect taxation. However, we have already observed that as V increases a negative real balance effect will be triggered. At full employment DD must fall by the increase in G and in practice this will be achieved via an adjustment in the price level and interest rates from equation (5-33).

(iv) If the authorities do not balance the budget, and print money instead, the macroeconomics are essentially the same as those already discussed in relation to the rudimentary model expressed by equations (5-23)–(5-27); i.e. an inflationary spiral will be triggered. We therefore concern ourselves instead with the case where the borrowing requirement is financed through sales of government debt. At full employment DD must fall by the increase in G and the principal adjustment variable will be the rate of interest. The sales of government debt will tend to raise the rate of interest and this will reduce DD via equation (5-33). In practice the price level might have to adjust too, despite the assumption that initially the volume of real balances is unchanged since $\dot{B} = R$. This will occur if the initial increase in the rate of interest is insufficient to reduce DD by an amount equal to the change in G. If this happens a real balance effect will be set in motion and adjustments will continue until prices stabilize once again at full employment. This argument assumes that bond finance can successfully 'crowd-out' expenditure by the private sector without any long term inflationary effects. At this juncture in particular it is worth recalling the caveat raised in connection with equation (3-20) that 'crowding out' through bond finance may be inflationary, depending upon the assumptions made about portfolio behavior.

Prices and incomes policies

To explore the main macroeconomic principles involved with prices and incomes policies we revert to the model of money, goods and employment (*MGE*) that has been described in Chapter 3. Critics have often argued that such policies do not work; however, there are at least two possible interpretations to this claim. The first is that even while the policy is being applied inflation is not affected. The second is that once the controls or restraints are removed prices catch up to what they otherwise would have been in the absence of the policy and that during this transition inflation even accelerates.

In what follows we concern ourselves more with the second claim than the first. If prices and incomes policies are merely voluntary they may be ignored. If they are mandatory and conditions of law and order prevail they will be effective. But even under these circumstances there may be loop-holes around the law. For example, wages may be supplemented by various perks while prices may be 'increased' by quality reductions. As in the previous sections of this chapter we do not explore the effects of such policies on allocative efficiency although the effects of relative price and wage rigidities that are implied by such policies are likely to be detrimental to the efficient functioning of the economy as a whole.

Nevertheless, it is important to point out that neoclassical analysis suggests that an incomes policy would tend to generate persistent unemployment insofar as it adversely affects the wage differential enjoyed by skilled workers. This possibility is illustrated on figs. 5-2 and 5-3, where the supply and demand schedules for labor that were described in fig. 3-4 are drawn for unskilled and skilled employment. The free market schedules are D_u, S_u, D_s, S_s, and the associated free market wage rates are w_u and w_s, at which L_{u1} of unskilled labor is supplied and demanded and L_{s1} of skilled labor is supplied and demanded. There is a wage differential in favor of skilled workers of $w_{s1} - w_u$.

The government is assumed to impose an incomes policy which has the

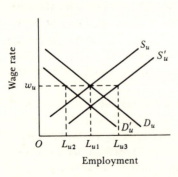

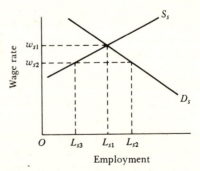

Figure 5–2 Unskilled employment sector   Figure 5–3 Skilled employment sector

effect of narrowing the differential enjoyed by skilled workers. On figs. 5-2 and 5-3 this is represented by a fall in the skilled wage rate from w_{s1} to w_{s2} while unskilled wage rates are left unchanged at w_u. Clearly other configurations could be envisaged, e.g. w_u may be revised relative to w_s, etc., but the same principles would apply. At w_{s2} firms demand L_{s2} of skilled labor but only L_{s3} will be supplied, so that the supply of skilled employment falls by $L_{s1} - L_{s2}$. A proportion of these will decide to join the ranks of the unskilled work force since the premium they get as skilled workers is insufficiently high, in which case the supply schedule of unskilled workers shifts from S_u to S'_u as indicated on fig. 5-2. At the same time, however, the demand for unskilled workers will fall from D_u to D'_u, since the supply of skilled employment has fallen and since there is a complementarity in production between the skilled and unskilled work force.

The demand for unskilled workers contracts to L_{u2} while the supply rises to L_{u3}, in which case incomes policy generates $L_{u2} - L_{u3}$ of unemployment among the unskilled work force. So much for the distorting effects of incomes policy as a structural component of the economy. We now turn to the relationship between incomes policy and inflation.

We may illustrate our main arguments with respect to the levels of wages (W) and prices (P) rather than rates of inflation, and we assume that the quantity of money (M) is fixed in a closed economy. From the *MGE* model the full employment real wage rate (or the wage rate at the natural rate of unemployment) is $w^* = W^*/P^*$ where P^* is the price level consistent with full employment $(Y = \bar{Y})$ for the given quantity of money. If M increases, P^* and W^* will increase along the lines already discussed in Chapter 3 and the determinants of w^* are illustrated on fig. 3-4.

If an incomes policy reduces the nominal wage rate below W^* an excess demand for employment will develop. It might be argued that if wage rates are lowered prices might follow suit since costs will be lower. In an inflationary context the argument would be that, as the rate of wage inflation is controlled via the incomes policy, price inflation will eventually decelerate and that this in turn will further decelerate wage inflation via a wage–price spiral. In a monetary economy, however, prices will not fall because the quantity of money is fixed by assumption, in which case there will be no real balance effects that might be expected to trigger a deflationary price syndrome. On the contrary, prices may even rise. This may happen since the lower real wage rates may reduce the volume of employment supplied, so that aggregate output falls below $\bar{Y}$. If under these circumstances the quantity of money is unchanged, P will rise above P^*. We therefore arrive at the ironical conclusion that incomes policies will tend to induce into the economy both latent and actual inflationary stimuli. The pressure of demand will tend to increase and the economy will be more buoyant than it was previously.

Once the controls are taken off W (or $\dot{W}$), the latent inflationary pressures will be activated and W will rise back towards W^*. In other words, as long as the money supply is unchanged general macroeconomic equilibrium will require that $P = P^*$, in which event $W = W^*$. If, however, during the period of wage restraint the money supply is lowered by the same percentage reduction as wages themselves, P^* will fall so that when the restraint is lifted wages will not revert to their original level since in the meanwhile W^* will have fallen in line with the restrained level of wages.

We may conclude from this that if the money supply is unchanged the benefits of an incomes policy will not be lasting. If, however, monetary policy is altered to reflect the objectives of the incomes policy, the effects will be lasting. They will be lasting not because of the incomes policy but because of the monetary policy. If the money supply is reduced, wage rates would in any event have fallen to their new value with or without the incomes policy.

Analogous reasoning applies to price controls or combinations of wage and price controls. The essential analytical point is that, as long as the money supply is unaltered, when the restraints are eventually lifted the real balance effect will push both P and W back to their original values of P^* and W^*. Thus prices and incomes policies in the longer term cannot exert an independent effect on the level of wages and prices; only monetary policy can determine these aggregates.

Thus if in practice monetary growth has been at an annual rate of 10% and wages and prices have been restrained to grow at an annual rate of 5% when the freely determined growth rate would have been say 8% (allowing for secular output growth), the termination of the restraints will be followed by inflation in excess of 8% per annum during the adjustment process. If the restraints had been in operation for two years, at the end of this period the level of wages and prices will be 6% (i.e. $2 \times (8-5)$) below their equilibrium value as determined by the level of the money supply and output. If it takes a further two years for W and P to catch up to their equilibrium values the average rate of inflation over this period will be 11% (i.e. $8 + 6/2$) per annum. Thereafter the rate of inflation will revert to its trend rate of 8%.

If instead monetary growth is gradually reduced to 7% per annum over the period of restraint, the equilibrium rate of inflation will fall to 5%. However, average monetary growth over this two-year period may have been in excess of 7% so that when the restraints are lifted inflation will be greater than 5% over the adjustment period. Thereafter, the steady state rate of inflation will be 5% per annum.

It should be noted that as the real balance effect unwinds itself during the post-restraint adjustment period the economy will be relatively buoyant.

Summary and concluding remarks

In this and the previous chapter we have applied the intellectual apparatus that was developed in Chapter 3 to a broad range of macroeconomic policies in order to determine their theoretical impact on the macroeconomy in the short and long runs. The range of policy options is hopefully sufficiently broad as to be representative of the principal policy options that the authorities tend to review. Our menu covered monetary, fiscal and exchange rate policy as well as a variety of controls and interventions such as import controls, exchange controls, prices and incomes policies and tariffs. We also explored how an energy sector might be integrated into our basic model and discussed the balance of payments and monetary linkages that are involved in this integration.

For convenience, the qualitative impact of these policies on the balance of payments, inflation, unemployment and the exchange rate are summarized in the table below. The detailed arguments that lie behind the various signs was of course the principal concern in this chapter and cannot be repeated here. Instead we note that a crucial analytical factor is the specification of a rudimentary monetary sector in the basic model which implies a stock–flow interaction between the balance of payments, the monetary sector and the real sector of the economy. We also note that in the model there is a built-in tendency for labor markets to clear and it is for this reason that the long run unemployment effects of the various policy interventions are zero. In the short term, however, these policies are likely to have an impact on unemployment in the way indicated.

These results are naturally a reflection of the theoretical model that has been deployed and it is emphasized that the model itself is essentially built on neoclassical assumptions. In the main, however, the qualitative results do not depend on the parametric detail of the model. A different income propensity, or export demand elasticity, would not have made any substantive difference especially in the longer term equilibrium context. The model would have tended to full employment and the balance of payments would have in any event depended on domestic credit creation. In the short term or disequilibrium context, parametric detail would be more important and would obviously influence the precise behavior of the macroeconomy over time.

In practice the parametric detail of macroeconometric models will differ. However, models that are built on neoclassical foundations will tend to behave along the lines that have been indicated – and this will tend to cover a wide class of actual models. If, on the other hand, models depart from neoclassical assumptions, by dichotomizing the real and monetary sectors and/or by assuming that wages and prices do not respond to demand and supply pressures, the deductions that have been drawn would clearly not hold. But such departures do not seem to represent the main stream of contemporary macroeconomic design.

Table 1 *Summary of policy effects*

Effect		1	2	3	4	5	6	7	8	9	10	11	12
Balance of payments	short run	−	−	+	+	+	+	na	(−)	(+)	(?)	(−)	(−)
	long run	0	−	0	0	0	0	na	(−)	(+)	(0)	(0)	(0)
Inflation or price level	short run	+	+	?	?	+	+	−	+	−	?	?	−
	long run fixed exchange rate	0	0	+	+	+	0	na	(+)	(−)	(0)	(0)	0
	floating exchange rate	+	+	+	+	+	+	−	−	−	0	0	0
Unemployment	short run	−	−	?	?	+	+	−	+	−	?	+	+
	long run	0	0	0	0	0	0	0	0	0	0	0	0
Exchange rate	short run	−	−	+	+	+	+	+	(−)	(+)	(?)	(−)	(−)
	long run	−	−	+	+	+	+	+	(−)	(+)	(0)	(0)	(0)

Key: Increases in:
1. Money supply
2. Monetary growth
3. Oil discovery
4. Tariff
5. Import controls
6. Exchange controls
7. Exchange intervention
8. Government expenditure – financed by monetary growth
9. Taxation
10. Government expenditure – financed by open market sales
11. Wages restraint
12. Price restraint

( ) not directly discussed in text.

The adjustment processes that have been incorporated into the analysis reflect the Phillips Curve hypothesis and the stock–flow interactions that are implied by the integration of monetary and income–expenditure approaches to macroeconomic behavior. As it happens, these are unavoidable dynamic features. Apart from this, no detailed attempt was made to discuss macro-dynamics and their implications for policy. These considerations are taken up in the following chapters.

CHAPTER 6

The rational expectations hypothesis

So far we have refrained from discussing the role and influence of expectations in the neoclassical model that was developed in Chapter 3. However, in Chapter 2 it was argued that Keynes regarded expectations as something of a will-of-the-wisp and that he regarded them as a primary cause of disruption in the economy. As such he rightly drew attention to the case for stabilization policies by the authorities to offset market failure: it was in the social interest to protect society from itself; where the market feared to tread it was the duty of government to fill the breach.

There are at least two possible interpretations of the Keynesian view. The first is that people are irrational in the sense that they disregard information that will help them make reliable forecasts of the future. The second is that expectations are dominated by herd instincts – if everybody expects everyone else to believe that the future depends on some will-of-the-wisp then it will be positively rational for the individual to act on such impulses even if this happens to be socially irrational. This is the analogy of Keynes' beauty competition where nobody is really interested in beauty itself but only in some arbitrary hunch about what has pretensions to beauty, as described in Chapter 2.

A constant theme in this and the next chapter where the role of expectations is explored is that neither of these interpretations is reasonable and that the second interpretation has been a considerable source of confusion in the exposition of the rational expectations hypothesis. The first interpretation implies that people do not mind if they make persistent and systematic errors in their forecasts which fly in the face of homo economicus or rational man, and that instead they have a sado-masochistic desire to be wrong. How people in fact behave is of course an empirical matter but this interpretation has very little a priori appeal. As for the second interpretation, it must be asked where the will-of-the-wisps originate. Either a hunch is the rational deduction of a relevant model in which case it is not a will-of-the-wisp or it will be deemed irrelevant by both society and the individual and will not influence expectations. In the case of the beauty competition the individual can only select the woman he finds most beautiful and the winner will reflect average opinion. In the case of economic markets each individual can do no more than to take a cool and logical view of the future. If we all behave that way there will be no will-of-the-wisp; in this instance society is no more than the sum of its parts and there is no external force of madness that dictates how events will unfold.

Historical perspective

In view of the significance that is attached to the rational expectations hypothesis (REH) in Chapter 7, the present chapter is largely devoted to an exposition of the basic principles that lie behind REH. In view of our interest in macroeconomic policy this exposition distinguishes the positive as well as the normative principles of REH since some of the normative principles may not have been always clearly understood. In particular there has been growing concern with the positive question (e.g. Sargent and Wallace [1976], Fischer [1977]) of whether or not discretionary monetary policies which are fully anticipated by economic agents along the lines of REH can influence macroeconomic activity or market behavior in general. Questions of this nature are clearly crucial, but as far as policy is concerned what matters is not so much whether rational expectations will offset some or all of the intended effects of government interventions, but whether the authorities are socially justified in intervening whatever the degree of offset may appear to be.

, Our approach in considering this normative issue will be to regard government intervention in the markets it intends to influence as speculation on the tax-payers' behalf. In other words, if the expected costs of the speculation are less than the benefits, intervention will be justified, where the welfare calculus is conceived from the point of view of the tax-payer who would have to foot the bill of any speculative losses on the part of the authorities. Hopefully, this treatment of discretionary policies will serve to clarify some of the basic issues that are raised when a government or some other authority intervenes in a market in the ostensible interests of the public at large.

Before we enter into these and related issues it is as well to consider how theoretical and empirical approaches to expectations have developed over the last two decades or so. Our intention here is not to present a full historical survey of the treatment of expectations in economics, no matter how interesting an issue this may be. By and large macroeconomics has been both taught and practiced in the absence of any reference to the role of expectations and their determinants despite the importance that Keynes attached to them.

Curiously enough, concern with the determination of expectations arose as a by-product of the econometric revolution of the 1950s in particular. Econometric model-builders saw the need for the specification of expected values in their models, which because they could not be directly observed had to be proxied by an appropriate measure or indicator. It was largely in this way that

Nerlove [1958] invented the theory of adaptive expectations where individuals'
expectations were assumed to react to the gap between actual values and previous expected values. The simplest first-order model of adaptive expectations
is specified as

$$_tP^e_{t+1} - _{t-1}P^e_t = a(P_t - _{t-1}P^e_t) \tag{6-1}$$

where $_{t-j}P^e_{t+k}$ is the price expected to prevail in period $t + k$ as of time
$t - j$. P_{t-j} denotes the actual price at time $t - j$. Equation (6-1) hypothesizes
that the expectations change or adapt to past errors. If, e.g., it were hypothesized that demand for an inventory (D) depended on the expected capital
gain:

$$D_t = b(_tP^e_{t+1} - P_t) \tag{6-2}$$

then, when equation (6-1) is repeatedly substituted into equation (6-2), the
result may be expressed in terms of observable variables only as:

$$D_t = b(a-1)P_t + b(1-a)P_{t-1} + (1-a)D_{t-1} \tag{6-3}$$

In other words it is not even necessary to specify the expectations themselves,
but merely how they adapt to events over time. In this way the expected price
becomes an infinite regress in terms of the 'irritants' that cause the expectations
themselves to change.

The ingenuity of Nerlove's hypothesis has been fully recognized and the
hypothesis itself has no doubt been applied on innumerable occasions. Nevertheless, the a priori justification for the adaptive expectations hypothesis was
never closely considered. Why, for example, should speculators be expected
to behave according to equation (6-1) in the first place? Is it reasonable to
react blindly to one's errors, as this hypothesis implies, regardless of any
extraneous information about the future upon which speculators and investors
might change? These are of course rhetorical questions which undermine the
a priori plausibility of the hypothesis since the hypothesis departs from the
usual economic principles of rationality and efficiency that lie behind so much
of economic theory. Conceived of in this way, the adaptive expectations hypothesis is little more than a behavioral rule of thumb that owes no allegiance
to economic theory, but whose popularity was most probably related to the
econometric technology of the day. This technology incorporated the specification of lagged endogenous variables as in equation (6-3)[1] which was well
suited to the transformations implicit in the adaptive expectations hypothesis.

The symbiosis between econometric technique and the theory of expectations is further exemplified by the apparent relationship between the development of the Almon [1965] technique for estimating distributed lags and

the extrapolative theory of expectations as developed by Modigliani and Sutch [1966]. In its most general form this theory of expectations may be expressed as

$$_tP^e_{t+1} = v \sum_{j=0}^{J} A_j P_{t-j} + (1-v)B(P_t - \bar{P}_t) \qquad (0 \leqslant v \leqslant 1) \qquad (6\text{-}4)$$

where $\bar{P}$ is the 'normal' price level to which prices might be expected to return. Equation (6-4) states that the expected price is a weighted average of an extrapolation of previous price trends and an assumption that prices will regress towards their 'normal' level. This 'normal' level is further hypothesized as

$$\bar{P}_t = \sum_{h=0}^{H} C_h P_{t-h} \qquad (6\text{-}5)$$

Substituting equation (6-5) into equation (6-4) implies that the expected price is a distributed lag in terms of past prices. When this result is in turn substituted into the model, e.g. into equation (6-2), the ensuing result is ideally suited to the Almon lag method of estimation, which facilitates the specification of moving averages of the appropriate variables. A further gloss on this approach to the modeling of expectations has been to apply the techniques developed by Box and Jenkins [1970], where expected values may be proxied by an autoregressive moving average process rather than moving averages alone.

The extrapolative–regressive theory of expectations, like the adaptive expectations hypothesis, does not have any obvious allegiances to economic theory. What, for example, is the economic basis for assuming the existence of a 'normal' price level to which the world might return; or why is it reasonable to extrapolate current price trends? Once more, these are behavioral questions, although, like the adaptive expectations hypothesis, the extrapolative–regressive approach has been popular enough.

It is most probably fair to say that until very recent times (about 1973) the specification of expectations was more the concern of the econometric model builder rather than the economic theoretician. The expectations hypotheses that have been summarized here, or variations on them, seemed to be plausible enough behavior and thus a reasonable way to express unobservables in terms of observables. Yet it would seem that a double standard was being applied. For example, the econometric model builder commissioned to provide forecasts of the price of apples would most probably construct a model of the supply and demand curves of the apple market which he would then use to solve for the price of apples in terms of the assumptions about the exogenous variables and the predetermined variables. There may also be a speculative demand for apples which depended on the expected price of apples in the future, or farmers' behavior might in part depend on expected rather than actual prices. These expected prices could be proxied along the lines of the adaptive or extrapolative–regressive hypothesis, but this would imply that speculators and farmers followed a different price forecasting methodology than our econometric modeler. Whereas our modeler might be criticized for forecasting apple prices by way of a 'black box', it has not seemed to matter that he ascribes 'black box' methodologies to the various participants in his model. So there is one rule for the official price forecaster and another for forecasters or speculators that form part of his model, a state of affairs which is clearly unsatisfactory if not hypocritical. Moreover, actual speculators who will stand to lose if they get things wrong are likely to take advantage of every means available in order to take the best possible view of the future. This would seem to preclude an extrapolative or adaptive approach. Rather speculators would stand to benefit from a rational examination of what is likely to determine prices in the future (i.e. in the same spirit as our econometric modeler) instead of doggedly reacting to past mistakes or crystal gazing into past price movements. It is precisely this assumption that forms the basis of the rational expectations hypothesis.

It is self-evident that the dynamic properties of econometric models could be heavily influenced by how we proxy the unobservable variables. Both the adaptive and extrapolative–regressive hypothesis will inject given forms of dynamic behavior and will affect the eigenvalues of the system. Consequently, it is impossible to foretell, even in principle, how expectations are likely to influence economic behavior. It is quite possible that these behavioral models of expectations could render unstable the model as a whole, or the dampening characteristics might be very weak. Indeed, anything could happen to the dynamics of the model.

Policy makers or their advisors, under these circumstances, might understandably seek to play with these models in order to see whether they can improve the way in which the economy (as represented by the model) operates. If the lags are long or, worse still, if the roots are unstable, the authorities might regard themselves as the guardians of stability and will seek to invent policy tactics that will be stabilizing. Or as new information becomes available the authorities will avail themselves of it on the assumption that economic agents themselves are unable to do so since this is implied by the various behavioral hypotheses. If indeed speculators and economic agents at large behaved as these hypotheses imply, the authorities could clearly intervene in the economy in what seemed to be a beneficial manner. But this merely amounts to saying that if the market is wrong or that it is not making efficient use of the information that is available, the authorities should act in the public interest by counteracting these defects.

The political economy of these behavioral theories of expectations is therefore formidable. What might have appeared as an innocuous enough assumption
about the specification of expectations is also a rationale for an entire political
economy based on discretionary macroeconomic policies. In this way, from
being a backwater in the profession, expectations are propelled into the front
line of economic issues in relation to macroeconomic policy and stabilization
policy in general.

The rational expectations 'revolution'

It is precisely this realization that has been the basis of a minor revolution in
relation to REH. Interest in REH took off in 1973 or thereabouts in the
academic literature[2] and at the present time it is evident that this interest is
intensifying as researchers engage in a variety of issues that relate to REH.
The main issues would appear to be:

(i) Positive economics - if expectations are formed rationally what are the
effects of policy interventions likely to be? The issue here is that as economic
agents learn about the authorities' strategies they will tend to anticipate their
intended effects, in which case the final effects of these strategies could differ
from the intended effects.

(ii) Normative economics - if expectations are formed rationally ought the
authorities to intervene? The issue here is when is a speculative act by the
authorities on the taxpayers' behalf justified when taxpayers themselves
choose not to engage in these acts?

(iii) Hypothesis testing - does the evidence support REH and is REH
empirically superior to competing hypotheses about the formation of expectations?

(iv) Techniques - how might models that incorporate REH be solved? The
issue here is that numerical methods for solving dynamic linear or non-linear
simultaneous equations systems (e.g. the Gauss–Seidel technique) have been
backward looking, i.e. the solution for each period was obtained so that the
current solution depended only on past solution values. In this way one arrived
at the chain rule methodology of forecasting. In contrast, REH requires a
forward looking numerical methodology since, via REH, current solution
values depend on future solution values as well as past solution values.

Most efforts have been concentrated at (i)[3] and (iii)[4] although the situation
is changing very rapidly. The present study is primarily concerned with (ii)
although to achieve this it will be necessary to evaluate the positive economics
first. Much of the theoretical research into the positive economics has been
concerned with rational expectations about inflation and the efficacy of discretionary monetary policies under these conditions (e.g. Sargent and Wallace
[1976]). Relatively little attention has been paid to rational expectations in

open economies although Minford [1978, Chapter 6], Dornbusch [1976], Barro [1978] and Calvo and Rodriguez [1977] have explored various aspects of REH in relation to the market for foreign exchange. A full macroeconomic application of REH in the context of an open economy would require, inter alia, the specification of expectations in relation to both inflation and the exchange rate. This is indeed the subject matter in the next chapter.

Oddly enough REH was conceived by Muth [1961] in the microeconomic context of supply and demand, yet it would seem that its most enthusiastic application has been in relation to macroeconomic issues of employment and inflation and it has become something of a burning issue with regard to the principles of macroeconomic policy. In recent years, and especially in connection with the debate about the so-called 'New International Economic Order',[5] there has been renewed interest in the age-old matter of the desirability of commodity price stabilization policies. While this problem relates closely to the one considered by Muth in his seminal work, it is ironical that REH has not been seriously applied in relation to this debate. In the later sections, therefore, where we recall the principal elements of REH in the context of a heuristically simple model, we choose the commodity price stabilization problem as our illustrative example.

It is puzzling that, despite its publication in 1961, REH lay dormant for more than ten years. The reasons for the explosion of interest in REH since 1973 are also unclear; although one may hazard a guess. It is possible that the REH 'revolution' was related to the growing dissatisfaction with demand management policies as they had been practiced after the Second World War. By the beginning of the 1970s it was becoming increasingly obvious that policies never seemed to have their intended effect. Since this was an implication of REH, it was brought off the shelf, dusted down and applied in a new context. But, whatever the causes, the 'revolution' may well be as significant as far as macroeconomic policy is concerned as was the Keynesian revolution, and the 1970s could well go down in the annals of the history of economic thought as the dawn of a new era.

The essence of REH is the assumption that the expectation of a variable X is equal to its expected value as determined by the relevant economic model in which X is determined and based on all the information Ω which is available at the time the expectation is formed. Thus

$$_{t-j}X_{t+k}^{e} = E_{t-j}(X_{t+k}/\Omega_{t-j}) \tag{6-6}$$

where $E_{t-j}(X_{t+k}/\Omega_{t-j})$ is the conditional expected value of X_{t+k} given the information available at the time $t-j$. Since rational expectations use up all the available information they are optimal and efficient; they constitute the best possible view of the future in the sense that no better forecast could be made. Rational expectations could just as easily be considered as neoclassical expectations since they are founded on the familiar neoclassical principles of optimization and efficiency. If equation (6-6) is not fulfilled, information will be used inefficiently and the market will have correspondingly failed.

A simple commodity model

Our purpose in this section is to recall the basic principles, both positive and normative, of REH in relation to a very simple model of a commodity market. In view of our later use of REH in the macroeconomic context, this exercise should serve as a basis for understanding what is to follow. Simple as this essentially expositional model might be, it is directly relevant to various aspects of commodity price stabilization, which has once more become a political issue in the context of the so-called North–South dialogue. The model distinguishes supply, demand and speculation.

The basic principle of REH is that expected prices etc. are the solutions of the appropriate model in the sense of equation (6-6). In other words, speculators are assumed to base their prognostications on some meaningful economic forecasting methodology – a familiar enough concept to economists. In so doing, speculators would also have to take into account the effects of their own rational expectations on future prices since REH would be a distinctive and intrinsic feature of the model. For the present we assume that an appropriate consensus model exists. Later on we shall discuss this assumption more thoroughly.

The speculative flow demand for a commodity in period t will be equal to the change in desired inventories ΔQ_t. At the end of period t speculative inventories (Q) are assumed to depend upon the expected capital gain $_tP^e_{t+1} - P_{t-1}$:

$$Q_t = e(_tP^e_{t+1} - P_t) \tag{6-7}$$

where, as before, $_tP^e_{t+1}$ is the price expected at time t to prevail in the next period (P is normalized about unity).[6] Therefore, the flow of speculative demand may be written as:

$$\Delta Q_t = e(_tP^e_{t+1} - P_t - _{t-1}P^e_t + P_{t-1}) \tag{6-8}$$

Consumer demand is assumed to vary inversely with the current price

$$D_t = -aP_t \tag{6-9}$$

and production is assumed to depend on the expected current price, i.e. there is a single period gestation lag

$$S_t = b_t - {}_1P_t^e \tag{6-10}$$

In equilibrium, supply and demand are equal

$$S_t = D_t + \Delta Q_t \tag{6-11}$$

According to the rational expectations hypothesis, i.e. applying equation (6-6), the expected price is equal to its expected value in terms of the appropriate model:

$$t - {}_iP_{t+1}^e - i = E_t - {}_i(P_{t+1} - i/\Omega_t - i) \quad i = 0, 1 \tag{6-12}$$

The dynamic structure of this model is intentionally simple. In practice the supply function is likely to be quite complex and storage, transactions costs, etc., would influence speculative behavior.

If the model is indeed appropriate, the expected price should be an unbiased estimate of its future value in which case we may use $E(P_{t+1})$ and P_{t+1} interchangeably for all t. This does not imply that speculators always make the right forecasts; only that they do so on average.

Using these assumptions, the market clearing conditions in equation (6-11) imply the following second order difference equation in the price under perfect foresight:

$$eP_{t+1} - (2e + a + b)P_t + eP_{t-1} = 0 \tag{6-13}$$

the roots of which will come in reciprocal pairs.[7] Consequently, one root must be greater than unity and the other less than unity. If we rule out speculative bubbles, i.e. in the long run speculators cannot dominate the market, the greater root may be ignored (or it is eliminated because it does not satisfy the boundary condition that price cannot become zero or go to infinity). This implies that the price will tend (in this model) to be a first-order Markov process since the future price will depend only on the present price via the single stable root, in which case speculators will realize that on this basis

$$t - {}_1P_t^e = \lambda P_{t-1} \tag{6-14}$$

where λ is the stable root. This then is the model that speculators will use according to REH. Substituting this relationship into the overall model for expected prices implies the following first order difference equation in the price level

$$P_t = \left(\frac{e(1 - \lambda) - \lambda b)}{e(1 - \lambda) + a}\right)P_{t-1} = \lambda P_{t-1} \tag{6-15}$$

which is the dynamic behavior of prices when expectations are assumed to be formed rationally.

In other words, for any initial disequilibrium situation (i.e. where $P_t \neq P_{t-1}$), the price level will monotonically return to equilibrium since the coefficient on P_{t-1} must always be less than unity. As the coefficient on P_{t-1} approaches unity the interval of disequilibrium prices will approach zero. Notice that, as e approaches infinity, λ will approach unity and the coefficient on P_{t-1} will approach unity too. That is, as the slope of the speculation schedule becomes infinite, prices are always perfectly stabilized by market forces when expectations are formed rationally.

These possibilities are illustrated in fig. 6-1 where it is assumed that until time t_0 the market has been in long run equilibrium, i.e. $P_{t-1} = P_{t-2}$, etc. = 0. At time t_0 the price is shocked out of equilibrium so that $P = P_1$. The shock is assumed to be temporary and to last for one period only. If $\lambda = 1$, rational speculation causes the price to fall back to equilibrium immediately; speculators do not tolerate any price that deviates from its long run value $\bar{P}$. If $\lambda < 1$ it will take time for the effects of the shock to die out. Curve (i) assumes that the shock effects die out more quickly than they do in the case of curve (ii). In reality, the market will be repeatedly shocked to different degrees from one period to the next and in each case REH implies that a stable impulse response pattern such as in fig. 6-1 will result. At any point in time the price level will reflect the entire history of current and past shocks according to equation (6-16):

$$P(t) = \sum_{i=0}^{\infty} \lambda^i \epsilon_{t-i} \qquad\qquad (6\text{-}16)$$

where the ϵs represent the disturbances. According to equation (6-16) the more recent disturbances will have a greater influence on the current price than the more remote ones.

Since the value of e – the shape of the speculation schedule – has such a

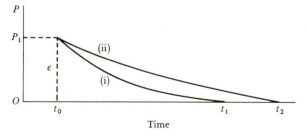

Figure 6-1 Random shocks and price movements

critical bearing upon λ, in the next section we focus more closely on the determinants of e. In particular we seek the conditions under which e tends to infinity.

The speculation schedule

Since speculation is an important aspect of REH, in this section we consider the fundamental parameters that determine speculative responses. In particular we focus on the relationship between the elasticity of speculation and the risks that are inherent in speculative activity. By the elasticity of speculation we refer to the change in the volume of speculative inventories that are induced by changes in expected capital gains.

Expected speculative capital gains may be written as

$$G = Q(P^e - P) \tag{6-17}$$

i.e. the difference between the expected price and the current price multiplied by the inventory.[8] The representative speculator is assumed to be averse to risk and his expected utility function $E(u)$ is of the conventional form:

$$E(u) = H(G, \sigma_g^2) \tag{6-18}$$

where σ_g^2 is a measure of the expected risk on the speculative portfolio,

$$\sigma_g^2 = Q^2 \sigma_p^2 e \tag{6-19}$$

and where $\sigma_p^2 e$ is the variance of the expected price. The usual principles of risk aversion imply that $\partial H / \partial G > 0$, $\partial H / \partial \sigma_g^2 < 0$. Even assuming that the speculator was not constrained by a budget, aversion to risk would prevent him from assuming an infinitely large speculative inventory. Maximizing expected utility with respect to Q gives

$$\frac{dE(u)}{dQ} = \frac{\partial H}{\partial G}(P^e - P) + \frac{2\partial H}{\partial \sigma_g^2} Q^* \sigma_p^2 e = 0 \tag{6-20}$$

in which case the optimal portfolio is given by

$$Q^* = e(P^e - P) \tag{6-21}$$

where

$$e = -\frac{\partial H}{\partial G} \bigg/ \frac{2\partial H}{\partial \sigma_g^2} \sigma_p^2 e > 0 \tag{6-22}$$

e is the slope of the speculation schedule since it relates the desired portfolio with the expected capital gain. Equation (6-22) shows the underlying determinants of this very important parameter; it varies directly with the preference for expected profits and inversely with the degree of risk aversion and expected risk. Absolute risk aversion or a subjective evaluation or risk that was infinite would set e to zero. The obverse would hold when either of these parameters were zero.

While it may be reasonable to assume that $\partial H/\partial G$ and $\partial H/\partial \sigma_g^2$ are parameters, the same cannot be said for $P^e - P$ and $\sigma_p^2 e$ which are likely to vary over time. If the expected price is the solution of a model whose parameter estimates are reasonably stable over time, it may be plausible to assume that $\sigma_p^2 e$ is a parameter too. In contrast, the expected price is likely to vary over time as new events unfold, in which case in this presentation we focus on P^e, assuming $\sigma_p^2 e$ to be constant. However, where necessary we shall recall that e may vary, especially in the context of changes in the model that are induced by policy changes.

From equation (6-22) we may deduce that e will tend to infinity and thus λ will tend to unity as

(i) $\partial H/\partial G = \infty$

(ii) $\partial H/\partial \sigma_g^2 = 0$ $\qquad\qquad\qquad\qquad\qquad\qquad$ (6-23)

(iii) $\sigma_p^2 e = 0$

The first condition states that investors get limitless satisfaction from capital gains. The second states that they do not care at all about risk, i.e. they are completely unaverse to risk. The third states that they do not think that there is any risk to be averse to. In general none of these extreme conditions is likely to prevail, in which case λ will be less than unity and the price level would not be perfectly stabilized by the market. Instead, in the context of our simple model any exogenous shocks, e.g. harvest failures, changes in tastes, etc., that disequilibrated prices would reverberate through the market for some time before equilibrium prices prevailed once more. This hesitation by the market is explained in terms of risk aversion in an uncertain world; while on the whole speculators think that equilibrium prices will eventually prevail they do not know what random shocks await them round the corner and so they do not back their expectations to the hilt. If indeed there are no further random shocks and in each period speculators go half-way in backing their expectations there would be a geometric convergence of the price to its equilibrium value over time as illustrated in fig. 6-1.

The determinants of risk

Having drawn such attention to the relationship between e, λ and $\sigma_p^2 e$ it remains to consider the factors that might influence $\sigma_p^2 e$. REH does not claim that speculators will make accurate or correct forecasts of future developments since this would only be possible in a deterministic world when in fact the world is stochastic. Therefore, the best that can be hoped is that speculators do not make any avoidable mistakes, which will be achieved if expectations are formed according to equation (6-12); the error in expectations will be

$$\epsilon_t = P_t - E_{t-1}(P_t/\Omega_{t-1}) \tag{6-24}$$

which is the difference between the rationally expected price and the realized price P_t. It therefore follows that $\sigma_\epsilon^2 = \sigma_p^2 e$, ϵ_t and therefore its variance will depend upon the random disturbances that affect the market. In terms of the model set out in equations (6-7)–(6-12), ϵ_t will depend on ϵ_{1t}, ϵ_{2t} and ϵ_{3t} which are respectively the random disturbance terms to equations (6-8), (6-9) and (6-10). The greater their variance the greater will be $\sigma_p^2 e$ unless of course there happen to be negative covariance terms. If a buffer stock authority were to intervene in the hope of stabilizing prices on the basis of some feedback rule such as

$$B_t = hP_{t-1} + \epsilon_{4t} \tag{6-25}$$

where B_t represents the intervention and ϵ_{4t} is a random disturbance term, it follows that unless there are negative covariances between ϵ_3, ϵ_2 and ϵ_1 that σ_ϵ^2 will be increased. This in turn will increase $\sigma_p^2 e$, which will reduce e, which will reduce $|\lambda|$. The reduction in $|\lambda|$ will slow down the natural stabilizing effects of the market. We may conclude then that a stochastic stabilization rule such as equation (6-25) will have the counter-productive effect of destabilizing the market when expectations are formed rationally. We shall return to this issue later. In the meanwhile we note that the intuitive reason for this reaction is that the intervention itself injects additional uncertainties into the market place and that this confuses the market which responds by proceeding with more caution and hesitation.

Unstable roots and the boundary condition

An unfortunate amount of confusion prevails over the apparent instability and indeterminacy of models that incorporate rational expectations. The issue is basically quite simple yet much has been made of the matter in the literature. In the illustrative example provided in this chapter it was shown that equation

(6-13) has two roots, one of which is unstable, while the other is not, so that the general solution for P is

$$P(t) = A_1 \lambda_1^t + A_2 \lambda_2^t \tag{6-26}$$

which implies that as $t \to \infty$, $P \to \pm \infty$. Muth [1961, p. 326] disposed of the matter rather abruptly: 'For a bounded solution the coefficient of the larger root vanishes; the initial condition is then fitted to the coefficient of the smaller root.' This if $|\lambda_2| > 1$, $A_2 = 0$ and A_1 is determined by the initial condition as usual. Sargent and Wallace [1975, p. 248] in a slightly different context ruled out the unstable root on the grounds of 'a terminal condition that has the effect of ruling out "speculative bubbles"'. Perhaps the clearest statement of the issue has been made by Minford [1978, pp. 156-9] where he argues that experience teaches us that prices do not generally explode, in which event such information becomes an intrinsic part of the model itself.

Nevertheless, in his review of rational expectations Shiller [1978] makes two assertions. The first concerns the stability issue or the value of A_2 – 'these models may explode rather than converge on a rational expectations mechanism because the expectations mechanism held at time t influences the behavior of y_t and hence the revised expectations mechanism in time $t + 1$. Because of the arbitrary nature of the adjustment mechanism, we cannot say in general which models will explode and which models will not' [p. 38]. The second concerns the possibility that REH solutions are indeterminate or, as Shiller puts it [p. 33], 'We are left with a fundamental indeterminacy for the solution of rational expectations models, and an infinity of potential solutions for all but those degenerate models which yield zero order difference equations.' This indeterminacy reflects the possibility that investors will have different hunches at different times. On the one hand if such collective hunches exist it will be rational to build them into expectations, but on the other hand since these hunches are generally not known in advance it is impossible to form rational expectations today.

Both of these issues are related. Models of rational expectations tend to generate apparent instability for the simple reason that the way they are specified allows for the possibility of an unstable syndrome of self-fulfilling expectations. If the current price depends on the expected price and if say the price is initially expected to rise by 10%, P_t will rise by 10%. Assuming that in fact this expectation is fulfilled, i.e. that $P_{t+1} = {}_tP_{t+1}^e$, the initial expectation gets locked into the system and prices always remain 10% higher. This can be seen by considering the case of a model of rational expectations where the only participants are speculators, i.e. in the illustrative model $a = b = 0$. In this case equation (6-13) becomes

$$P_{t+1} - 2P_t + P_{t-1} = 0 \tag{6-27}$$

which has a single root $\lambda = 1$. Thus if P_{t+1} is expected to rise it will rise and it will stay there in the absence of further changes in expectations so that $P_{t+2} = P_{t+3} = \ldots = P_{t+1}$. At the heart of the matter is a bootstraps theory of expectations where speculators choose the latest will-of-the-wisp and it is this that creates the impression of instability and indeterminacy.

But this is not what REH is all about, for an essential component of the hypothesis is that speculators do not go off on wild goose chases of their own making. They know that in fact a and b are not zero and that there is an underlying genuine demand and supply for the commodity in question. In the case of apples for example their ultimate purpose is consumption and not just for speculative transactions. The only conceivable reason why speculators attach any value at all to apples is because they know that apples fulfill a real need in society, and it is precisely this knowledge that ties the price of apples to the long run equilibrium $\bar{P}$ at which supply and demand are in balance. In the absence of such a logic P would indeed be indeterminate and unstable as Shiller claims. But the fact is that such a market logic exists and this explains why speculators are there in the first place. According to REH, will-of-the-wisps cannot dominate the market and speculators do not get carried away by their own enthusiasm. Self-fulfilling bubbles are precluded from REH even if they might be conceptually meaningful. But such behavior would be the deduction of some other theory, not REH.

This matter is reminiscent of Keynes' beauty competition. It is the appreciation of genuine beauty that prevents the selection of some ogress, and it is this which serves as a centre of gravity for the judge's choices. So it is with speculators and investors whose centre of gravity is the underlying logic of supply and demand which provides commodities and financial assets with an intrinsic value rather than one that hangs off the bootstrap of some arbitrary speculative whim. Just as a migratory flock of birds traces out enigmatic but purposeful patterns across the sky as each bird pursues its own destiny, so do individual speculators and thence the market as a whole follow some common logic that creates the effect of mass movement. It is the instinct of the individual rather than the instinct of the herd that matters in the end.

It is this outlook on market behavior that requires the elimination of the unstable root. The outlook suggests that in the limit $P(t) \to 0$ (recalling that P is expressed in this chapter as a deviation from its equilibrium), therefore it follows that $A_2 = 0$ in equation (6-26). Below, we shall return to the same issue but from a slightly different angle.

REH does not imply that the unstable root will be operational for a while until the market realizes that it has taken the wrong path. Instead, it suggests that right from the outset speculators will reject the unstable path since they understand that it has nothing to do with underlying market forces. This is illustrated in fig. 6-2 where, as in the case of fig. 6-1, it is assumed that at t_0

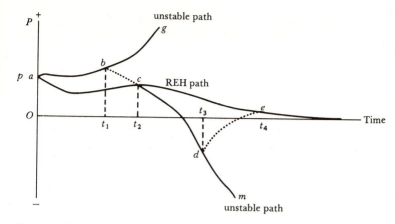

Figure 6-2 Stable and unstable paths under rational expectations

there has been a single random shock which raises P from zero to a. The stable REH path is given by ace. When the unstable path is fitted to the initial condition it produces (say) abg which implies that P eventually goes off to infinity. It could be argued that the market travels along abg until say at time t_1 it realizes that it has gone wrong. It then travels along bc in order to get back onto the REH path which it reaches at t_2. It may then follow the unstable path once more which, when fitted to the new set of initial conditions at t_2, produces cdm. In fig. 6-2 it is assumed that the market travels down this path until at t_3 it makes another correction to the REH path which is represented by de; and so on until equilibrium is reached when $P = 0$.

According to this argument the actual path oscillates around the REH path under the assumption that it takes time before the market realizes that it must have gone wrong. In this case the path becomes $abcde$ rather than ace. This is naturally an interesting theoretical possibility but is incompatible with REH, which maintains that at t_0 the optimal path ace can be established.

Moreover, REH implies that speculation will stabilize models that are unstable when speculation is ignored. For example if the model is

$$\left.\begin{array}{l} S_t = b_1 P_t + b_2 P_{t-1} \\ D_t = -a P_t \\ D_t = S_t \end{array}\right\} \tag{6-28}$$

i.e. supply responds to current and lagged price, there will be a single root equal to $-b_2/(b_1 + a)$. If $b_2 > b_1 + a$ the model will be unstable. If, however, we add to this equations (6-8) and (6-12) and eliminate the unstable roots as before the model will become stable. This implies that speculators do not believe that it was in fact globally unstable. If, however, they believed that it was in fact globally unstable it would be rational to expect such behavior and REH would indeed produce a genuinely unstable path.

Further considerations

The simple model so far discussed does not imply any oscillatory price behavior because the final form of the model, i.e. equation (6-15), was only a first order process. In general, higher order processes will prevail and oscillatory price behavior could be implied. For example, if because of gestation lags, supply unavoidably depended on past prices, it may be the case that the supply equation should be written as:

$$S_t = \sum_{j=0}^{J} b_j P_{t-j} \tag{6-29}$$

in which case equation (6-13) would be rewritten as

$$eP_{t+1} - (2e + a + b_0)P_t + (e + b_1)P_{t-1} + \sum_{j=2}^{J} b_j P_{t-j} = 0 \tag{6-30}$$

This would inevitably imply a more complex dynamic structure that would form the basis of rational expectations and equation (6-15) would become a difference equation of the Jth order (at the most since some of the roots may not satisfy the boundary conditions).

If, however, e is infinite once more and the limits of equation (6-30) are taken with respect to e we obtain

$$P_{t+1} - 2P_t + P_{t-1} = 0 \tag{6-31}$$

as the difference equation that rational speculators look to in forming their expectations. The root of this is $\lambda = 1$, in which case equation (6-14) would be applicable once more. Substituting this for P^e in our more complicated model would still imply that $P_t = P_{t-1}$. In other words, even if the structural equations of the model are dynamic in terms of price, perfectly held rational expectations will smooth out price oscillations; the equilibrium price will always prevail. Of course, e is generally finite, in which event the final form of the model would be some difference equation with a maximum order of J.

The integration of the rational expectations hypothesis into dynamic economic models has fairly specific implications for disequilibrium price behavior. Let us assume that the price of a particular commodity has been in equilibrium at $P = 0$ in fig. 6-3. At t_0 there is a shock, e.g. a harvest failure, that raises the price level to P_1. In our conceptual experiment speculators do not know that

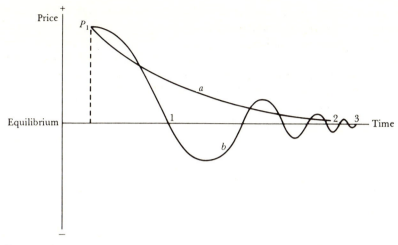

Figure 6-3 Dynamic price adjustment under rational expectations

in the future there will be no further shocks. If they were sure of this, it would be rational for them to sell immediately, because the price would be expected to fall back to P^* in the next period. But in reality, they are not sure and so the price will grope its way back to equilibrium. Curve a is the adjustment path implied by the simple model and is taken from fig. 6-1 while curve b is the path implied by the more complicated model. In the former case the adjustment path is monotonic, in the second case it may be oscillatory. It can be shown that the smaller is e the more oscillatory the adjustment path is likely to be.[9]

If the equilibrium price is Pareto optimal what is the status of disequilibrium values of P; aren't they in some sense suboptimal? It would naturally be for the best if there were never any unanticipated exogenous shocks, but this never arises. We therefore have to try to conceive of optimal price behavior in a dynamic stochastic world. If expectations are formed rationally then the price profiles implied by the rational expectations hypothesis are optimal in the sense that ex ante in terms of expected utility the market could not have produced a better set of prices.

Rational expectations and efficient markets

There is a fairly obvious affinity between REH and the efficient markets hypothesis which states that the current price of speculative assets will reflect all the available information about the future.[10] It is in this sense that a market is considered to be efficient, for otherwise it would be wasting information. But REH would seem to be the more general hypothesis, since it allows for the possibility of those autocorrelated price movements which reflect the principles of risk aversion and uncertainty that have already been discussed. In other words the observation of autocorrelations in the respective time series does not necessarily testify to market inefficiency since it could equally reflect dynamic adjustment processes under REH. The cautious use of information which is an appropriate and efficient form of behavior would seem to be a more meaningful criterion for judging the efficiency of speculative markets than a pre-occupation with identifying random walks. Instead, the requirement of REH is that errors in expectations should not be autocorrelated, i.e. $E(\epsilon_t \epsilon_{t-i}) = 0$ for all $i > 0$ in equation (6-24) since persistent error implies that the market is not learning from its mistakes and is therefore not behaving rationally.

Stabilization policies

So far the model that we have been discussing assumed no intervention on the part of a stabilization authority. In this section we consider the positive and normative economic issues that are raised where say a buffer stock authority attempts to influence the price and when expectations are formed rationally.

For example, in our simple model where the free market final form is given by equation (6-15) what would happen if the authorities sought to intervene on the basis of some optimal feedback rule? For argument's sake, let us assume that the authorities have a stockpile and that storage costs are zero. During time t their intervention rule should only depend on P_{t-1} since P_t is independent of P_{t-2}, P_{t-3} etc. in this simple model. The intervention rule may therefore take the form[11]

$$B_t = hP_{t-1} \tag{6-32}$$

and equation (6-11) would become

$$B_t + S_t = D_t + \Delta Q_t \tag{6-33}$$

If this rule is deterministic, it would be noted by our rational speculators who would incorporate the authorities' behavior into their expectations. Equation (6-13) would become

$$eP_{t+1} - (2e + a + b)P_t + (e - h)P_{t-1} = 0 \tag{6-34}$$

and the stable root is

$$\lambda = \frac{(2e + a + b) - [(2e + a + b)^2 - 4e(e - h)]^{\frac{1}{2}}}{2e} \tag{6-35}$$

The partial derivative between λ and h is

$$\frac{\partial \lambda}{\partial h} = -[(2e + a + b)^2 - 4e(e - h)]^{-\frac{1}{2}} < 0 \qquad (6\text{-}36)$$

The sign of this derivative must be negative since in the model that has been proposed there are no complex roots. We may therefore conclude that a stabilization rule such as equation (6-32) has the effect of slowing down speculative reactions under REH. As it were, the market compensates for the initiative taken by the authorities on its behalf. Therefore, rational expectations will offset some of the intended effects of the intervention rule, which was conditional on the free market value for λ, or $\lambda(1)$. On the basis of $h(1)$, $\lambda(1)$ becomes $\lambda(2)$ and an $h(2)$ is required; and so on. In other words, in determining their intervention rule the authorities must take account of the fact that their own behavior will change the model and consequently the appropriate intervention rule. In a related context Lucas [1976] has discussed the inadequacy of fixed parameter models when policy is assumed to alter.

How, in principle, can the authorities allow for this? Since we have invented the hypothetical assumption that the buffer stock is costless (as a heuristic device) it follows that the authorities should set h in such a way that the final form of the model becomes $P_t = P_{t-1}$. For then disequilibrium behavior would always be eradicated instantaneously by the combined efforts of the market and the stabilization policy. Equation (6-15) may be rewritten on the basis of equations (6-32)-(6-34) as

$$P_t = \frac{e(1 - \lambda(h)) - \lambda(h)b + h}{e(1 - \lambda(h)) + a} P_{t-1} \qquad (6\text{-}37)$$

But it is clear from equations (6-37) and (6-36) that the coefficient on P_{t-1} declines as h increases, in which case stabilization dampens the stabilizing characteristics of the market under REH.

Therefore the optimal feedback rule in the presence of rational expectations is to set $h = 0$, i.e. to have no feedback rule at all. But if in addition the feedback rule is stochastic, stabilization rules could even be destabilizing since as we have already noted in equation (6-22), the higher is $\sigma_p^2 e$, the lower is e and the greater will be the destabilizing tendencies in the model since the coefficient on P_{t-1} in equation (6-15) varies directly with e. In general, stabilization rules will be stochastic and in practice they could be highly irregular. If expectations are formed rationally, stabilization policies could easily have a net destabilizing effect on prices.

Normative applications of REH

So much for a very brief look at some of the positive economics of intervention in a market where expectations are formed rationally. It would seem though that even these considerations raise doubts as to whether intervention is likely to be worthwhile in practice. But these are not the main normative considerations. Instead the main normative principle would appear to be as follows: If the market itself is not prepared to speculate at the margin, on what basis might the authorities intervene or speculate on the market's behalf? For when the authorities buy and sell commodities it is on the assumption that the prevailing prices are wrong, and so they are in effect speculating when they intervene.

At the margin, speculators in the aggregate will have balanced the advantages of spending the additional cent on their speculative positions against the risks that this incurs. Ex ante, their expected utility is maximized. The question is, would they be happy to underwrite any losses of an agency that undertook to speculate on their behalf? In the absence of externalities the answer must surely be 'no' for otherwise they would have been engaging in these speculations themselves i.e. without the need for the agency. Or if the agency was considered likely to make a profit, it must be asked how if expectations are formed rationally this can be so. These and related issues are illustrated in fig. 6-4.

The curves $U_1, U_2, \ldots,$ represent the community indifference curves based on equation (6-18). OL_1 is the market's perception of the relationship be-

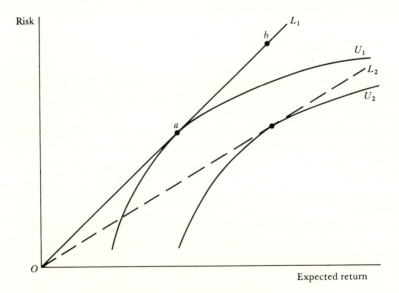

Figure 6–4 Intervention policies under rational expectations

tween expected return and risk; the greater the speculative portfolio, the greater the expected return but also the greater is the exposure to risk. Ordinarily, when expectations are formed rationally the market would select their speculative portfolio at the tangency of U_1 and OL_1, at a. If, however, the authorities intervene on behalf of the market, e.g. at b, the community would be driven onto a lower indifference curve since everybody has exposed themselves to more risk than they wish and since ultimately the market itself has to underwrite the mistakes of the authorities.

If the market's perception of OL_1 is correct, a is socially optimal and b suboptimal. But if the market's perception of OL_1 is wrong this situation could be reversed. Two main conditions may be identified.

(i) Externalities in risk: It may be the case that there is a divergence between private and social risk, e.g. as in risk pooling. However, our assumption is that the market has already provided for efficient risk pooling facilities and that these institutions are already reflected in OL_1. But if for some reason there are risks that cannot be pooled in this way, and the true social trade-off is given by OL_2, it would be appropriate for the authorities to speculate on society's behalf. The optimum under these circumstances is given by c, i.e. at the tangent of U_2 and OL_2. In other words the authorities should consider how the market would have behaved had it perceived the true trade-off of OL_2 instead of OL_1.

(ii) Externalities in information: It may be the case that the authorities have information which it is legitimate for them not to divulge, e.g. related to matters of national security, etc. This too could drive a wedge between the social and private trade-off between risk and expected returns, except this time it is due to the higher social expected return than to the lower social risk. If the effect of this wedge is to generate OL_2 as the social trade-off function the optimum intervention would be determined once more at c on fig. 6–4.

In general it is difficult to conceive why there should be a divergence between the private and social perceptions of the trade-off function. At least, it would seem that the burden of proof rests on the shoulders of those who claim that such divergences exist.

Thus the foregoing discussion suggests that, even if it were the case that the authorities could intervene to stabilize the system as a matter of positive economics, ex ante this would not necessarily be justified on normative grounds since it is necessary to form an assessment of the risks that such policies implicitly incur in a stochastic world in relation to the public's attitude towards these risks. All this of course is in the context of REH. Outside this context, i.e. where expectations are not formed rationally, the principles of policy intervention would be less clear-cut. But if the market is taking arbitrary views about the future and the intervention agency can form more rational views, it seems likely that intervention could in principle improve matters since it is correcting for a deficiency in the market.

Appropriate model

The previous discussion has been couched in terms of the admittedly rarified assumption that the appropriate model is known. Unfortunately, the truth of the matter is that the appropriate model is seldom known although there may be a range of models that seem plausible enough.

As far as the principles of policy intervention are concerned, this is not as problematic as it might appear unless the authorities feel that their appropriate model is more appropriate than everyone else's. If people's views about the future differ on account of differences between their models, trading will take place in speculative markets and the best horse will win. In this way speculation under REH will weed out the losers and encourage the winners.

In this context, the authorities must decide whether they wish to 'race' their own model. If they are confident that their's is the best model this is fair enough, but it is most probably true to say that this is not what motivates interventionist strategies. Nevertheless, this constitutes a reasonable criterion for intervening: if the authorities can accumulate sufficient profits on their speculations to justify the risks involved and which do not reflect any monopolistic advantages they have, intervention would seem reasonable as long as it was consistent with the community's aversion to risk. On the whole, however, it would appear that intervention agencies have been singularly unsuccessful in these respects.

Rational expectations and market failure

In neoclassical economics the orthodox criterion for official intervention in market situations is when the market has failed. In static economic analysis it is necessary to review the intersection of supply and demand to determine whether the market equilibrium is efficient or socially desirable. If it is not there will be a prima facie case for government involvement to produce a more efficient or socially desirable equilibrium based upon the classical principle of Pareto optimality. Market failure in the static sense tends to occur when either there are divergences between private and social costs or when there are divergences between private and social benefits. Individuals will collectively seek to equate marginal costs and benefits at the private level when in fact it would have been in the collective interest to equate marginal costs and benefits at the social level. Market failure would also occur if, at the private level, agents are behaving irrationally or inefficiently, e.g. they choose inefficient technologies. However, in this case inefficiencies may be more apparent than real since the agents concerned may have good reasons for choosing what seem to be inefficient technologies.

These principles have been repeatedly spelt out in numerous textbooks on public finance and require no further elaboration here. Nor is it necessary to elaborate upon the orthodox solution to market failure where shadow pricing techniques, such as those described in Little and Mirrlees [1977], may be used to inject the appropriate market signals into the market place. Policy in public finance may then be used to set the structure of taxes and subsidies and if necessary direct controls and licences to narrow the divergence between the private and social interest that is created by static market failure. Such policies must inevitably be evaluated at the micro-level; indeed, shadow pricing has traditionally been regarded as part of the discipline of microeconomic analysis. Market failure has no obvious analogue at the macro-level yet employment, the exchange rate and other macroeconomic objectives, and the use of fiscal, monetary and other policies to achieve these objectives begs the question of the micro-foundations of macroeconomic policy. We shall indeed be returning to this theme in Chapters 7 and 8.

So much for market failure and its remedies at the static or equilibrium level. What if anything would constitute market failure at the dynamic or dis-equilibrium level and what if anything would serve as an appropriate remedy? This is an important question since in many cases markets are in disequilibrium and it is appropriate for the government to consider how it might act, if at all, in the social interest in such disequilibrium states. We may use the simple commodity model that was described earlier in this chapter as a basis for discussion of this issue.

The principle of market failure in the disequilibrium case hangs on whether or not expectations are formed rationally. If expectations are formed rationally, disequilibrium states will be efficient and optimal. If expectations are not formed rationally there will be market failure in the classic sense and disequilibrium states will be inefficient and suboptimal. That is to say that REH may be used to explain the behavior of speculative markets in disequilibria along the lines previously indicated and, as long as agents are using all the information at their disposal as REH requires, then it must be the case that the disequilibria and imbalances that result are efficient. They are efficient in the sense that, in a stochastic environment where risk cannot be ignored, the disequilibrium values relate as closely as possible to their equilibrium Pareto-optimal values. Indeed the only reason why there are any divergences from these Paretian values is the uncertainty that exists and agents' aversion to risk which causes legitimate market hesitation, as previously described. Thus, when e is finite on account of risk aversion according to equation (6-22), it follows that λ is less than unity, so that the effects of random shocks upon market behavior tend to persist for some time. But at each point in time during the adjustment period speculative positions are efficient since, according to the analysis of fig. 6-4, agents are incurring as much risk and expectation of gain as they desire. It is in this sense that we may speak of disequilibrium Pareto-optimality and the price paths illustrated in fig. 6-3 are optimal.

We therefore arrive at the important conclusion that, under REH, adjustment paths are optimal. If, however, adjustment paths diverge from their REH paths we may correspondingly speak of market failure at the disequilibrium level. Indeed, as was argued in Chapter 2, Keynes rejected REH and put the case for intervention in terms of market failure along such lines. If $x^*(t)$ is the optimal path for variable x that is implied by REH (e.g. the solution for $P(t)$ in equation (6-15)) market failure will occur if

$$x(t) \neq x^*(t) \tag{6-38}$$

i.e. if there is a discrepancy between the actual behavior of the variable and its warranted behavior as implied by REH. If this inequality condition is fulfilled it means that market forces do not fully reflect all the information that could bear upon the market situation. This would arise if expectations are extrapolated or adaptive, i.e. where agents are assumed to make systematic errors in their predictions. In other words market failure occurs when agents do not take the best posssible view of the future, which is analogous to the case of static distortions when perceived prices diverge from their shadow values.

It may arise, however, that even though each agent is assumed to have rational expectations there is a divergence between private and social risk in which case REH paths may not be socially optimal. That is to say the risk facing society as a whole is less than the sum of risks facing each individual. Neoclassical economic analysis suggests that whenever such situations arise, and wherever risk can be diversified away, the market will supply risk bearing services, e.g. insurance, unit funds, etc. Therefore for REH paths to be suboptimal it is necessary that there is a divergence between private and social risks which are non-diversifiable. In practice it is difficult to conceive of such situations. For example, in the case of the illustrative model of supply and demand the risk element reflects random shocks such as harvest failures, wars, technical change, etc., which affect everybody concerned. Presumably, up to a point, insurance against some but not all risk would be forthcoming; thereafter risk cannot be diversified and divergences between private and social risk are zero.

If the inequality condition in equation (6-38) is fulfilled there would be a prima facie case for official intervention, e.g. by a buffer stock authority to correct for market failure along conventional and orthodox lines. The objective would then be to intervene in such a way that $x(t) = x^*(t)$. This may be done directly by open market purchases and sales or it may be done indirectly by the uses of taxes and subsidies to stimulate the appropriate market responses.

An alternative formulation: the method of undetermined coefficients

We now return to the simple commodity model set out in equations (6-7)–(6-12) in order to discuss the influence of random shocks under REH from a slightly different perspective. In the previous discussion disturbances to equilibrium states generated shock waves such as those illustrated in fig. 6-3. In the present section we show how a history of disturbances will influence market behavior. Although the two approaches are logically equivalent, both presentations seem worthwhile since REH analysis is often posed in terms of the latter idiom. For example, this is how Muth [1961] presented his analysis and it may be of assistance if for the sake of completeness the alternative formulation is presented.

To save time the minimum of exposition is provided since the ground has already been covered, and primed equation numbers refer to their original counterparts. Thus equation (6-7′) is the re-specification of equation (6-7) when the random disturbance terms are made explicit. The model thus becomes

$$Q_t = e(_tP^e_{t+1} - P_t) + u_{1t} \tag{6-7′}$$

$$D_t = -aP_t + u_{2t} \tag{6-9′}$$

$$S_t = b_t - {}_1P^e_t + u_{3t} \tag{6-10′}$$

where the us are the random disturbance terms such that $E(u_i) = 0$. Substituting these equations into equation (6-11) produces

$$(b + e)E_{t-1}P_t - eE_tP_{t+1} + (a + e)P_t - eP_{t-1} = u_t \tag{6-13′}$$

where

$$u_t = u_{2t} - u_{3t} + u_{1t} - u_{1t-1} = \sum_{i=0}^{\infty} w_i \epsilon_{t-i} \tag{6-39}$$

and where $E(\epsilon_t) = 0$, $E(\epsilon_t \epsilon_{t-j}) = 0$. Since the ϵs are exogenous the reduced form for P_t may be written as

$$P_t = \sum_{i=0}^{\infty} \Pi_i \epsilon_{t-i} \tag{6-40}$$

where the coefficients Π are functions of e, a, b and the ws. Equation (6-40) is the relationship that is sought since it tells us how the current price responds to the entire history of random disturbances and thus may be compared with equation (6-16). It only remains to determine the Πs. From equation (6-40) it follows that

$$E_t P_{t+1} = \Pi_0 E_t \epsilon_{t+1} + \sum_{i=1}^{\infty} \Pi_i \epsilon_{t+1-i} = \sum_{i=1}^{\infty} \Pi_i \epsilon_{t+i-1} \tag{6-41}$$

$$E_{t-1} P_t = \sum_{i=1}^{\infty} \Pi_i \epsilon_{t-i} \tag{6-42}$$

Equation (6-13$'$) may therefore be rewritten as

$$(b+e) \sum_{i=1}^{\infty} \Pi_i \epsilon_{t-i} - e \sum_{i=1}^{\infty} \Pi_i \epsilon_{t+1-i} + (a+e) \sum_{i=0}^{\infty} \Pi_i \epsilon_{t-i}$$

$$\tag{6-43}$$

$$-e \sum_{i=0}^{\infty} \Pi_i \epsilon_t \epsilon_{t-i-1} = \sum_{i=0}^{\infty} w_i \epsilon_{t-i}$$

Collecting terms in ϵ_{t-i} from equation (6-43) produces the following set of identities

$$
\left.
\begin{array}{ll}
\epsilon_t & : (a+e)\Pi_0 - e\Pi_1 = w_0 \\
\epsilon_{t-1} & : -e\Pi_0 + (2e+b+a)\Pi_1 - e\Pi_2 = w_1 \\
\epsilon_{t-2} & : -e\Pi_1 + (2e+b+a)\Pi_2 - e\Pi_3 = w_2 \\
\quad \cdot & \quad\quad\quad \cdot \\
\quad \cdot & \quad\quad\quad \cdot \\
\quad \cdot & \quad\quad\quad \cdot \\
\epsilon_{t-j} & : -e\Pi_{j-1} + (2e+b+a)\Pi_j - e\Pi_{j+1} = w_j \\
& \quad j = 3, 4, \ldots
\end{array}
\right\} \tag{6-44}
$$

Equations (6-44) show that in our example a time pattern is induced in the relationship between the Πs which in this case happens to be a second order difference equation. Working examples of higher order systems may be found in Bell and Beenstock [1980]. In principle there are an infinite number of equations in (6-44) to solve for the infinite number of unknown values of Π. But this is not very helpful. In practice it is likely that beyond a point, say w_k, the $w s$ are zero, in which case there will be a homogeneous difference equation of the form

$$-e\Pi_k + (2e+a+b)\Pi_{k+1} - e\Pi_{k+2} = 0 \tag{6-13'}$$

which is exactly analogous to equation (6-13). The general solution to equation (6-13$'$) is

$$\Pi(k+j) = A_1 \lambda_1^j + A_2 \lambda_2^j \quad j = 0, 1, 2, \ldots \tag{6-45}$$

where, as before, the roots come in reciprocal pairs so that one is stable while the other is not. Equation (6-45) is used to solve for the Πs for Π_k, Π_{k+1}, . . . , etc., for given values of the arbitrary constants. It therefore remains to determine A_1 and A_2 and Π_0, Π_1, . . . , Π_{k-1}, which makes $k + 2$ unknowns. However, we have so far not used the $k + 1$ initial equations from (6-44) since the homogeneous difference equation only commenced with the $(k + 2)$th term. It appears that we are an equation short but the boundary condition that $\Pi_j \to 0$ as $j \to \infty$ bridges the gap so that everything squares in the end.

This boundary condition is analogous to the one discussed in relation to the original presentation. Whereas previously it was applied to prevent prices from exploding following a random shock, for reasons already discussed at length, in the present context it is applied to prevent shocks from a long time ago from exerting an infinitely large influence on current prices. If the Πs were to tend to infinity it would imply that the current price was infinitely large. Since prices in general are not at infinity it follows that the boundary condition is a self-evident restriction to apply.

equations		unknowns	
(i) unused identities:	$k + 1$	(i) Arbitrary constants:	2
$w_0, w_1, \ldots w_k$		A_1, A_2	
(ii) boundary condition:	1	(ii) Unexplained reduced form coefficients:	k
$\Pi_j \to 0$ as $j \to \infty$		$\Pi_0, \Pi_1, \ldots \Pi_{k-1}$	
Total	$k + 2$	Total	$k + 2$

For convenience the solution system is summarized in the table. No matter how complicated the model, the same solution system will apply for linear systems. k may vary and the number of arbitrary constants may vary but the solution principle is always the same. If $k = 0$ the homogeneous difference equation starts straight away so that all the Πs may be solved from equation (6-45). The boundary condition implies, as before, that $A_2 = 0$, in which case the solution for the Πs is

$$\Pi_i = A_1 \lambda_1^i \qquad i = 1, 2, \ldots \tag{6-46}$$

which implies that in the simple commodity model the Πs decline geometrically. The effect of a simple random shock is to produce a price profile such as in fig. 6-1; the alternative presentation produces precisely the same result as before.

CHAPTER 7

Macroeconomic policy and rational expectations

I The theory of macroeconomic policy

In Chapters 3, 4 and 5 we proceeded by abstracting from the complicating role of expectations in macroeconomic policy discussion. Thus we have been explicitly assuming that expected prices, wage rates, exchange rates, etc., are constant and predetermined. This important simplification has enabled us to focus on the long term properties of the theoretical models that have been proposed as well as the policy implications that these properties generate. In so doing, we violate the fairly obvious fact of economic life that expectations in general, and expectations about macroeconomic aggregates in particular, are variable, if not volatile. A comprehensive analysis of policy must explicitly recognize the positive and normative roles that expectations play in the macroeconomy; it must integrate long term or equilibrium notions with short term or disequilibrium behavior which reflects, inter alia, the influence of expectations on macroeconomic adjustment.

In this chapter the assumption of fixed or exogenous expectations is relaxed within the long term equilibrium models that have been posited. Instead, expectations are endogenized under various assumptions and the effects of and rationales for alternative macroeconomic policies are explored. In this way, we arrive at comprehensive rather than partial analyses of macroeconomic interventions. In particular, we focus on the endogeneity of price and exchange rate expectations, and, as before, we proceed from the simpler models of closed economies to the more complex models of small open economies.

We have already introduced and reviewed in Chapter 6 the positive and normative issues that are raised when expectations are endogenized within dynamic economic models. Therefore, in what follows that chapter is taken as read. In the present chapter we also explore the implications of the 'behavioral' and 'rational' hypotheses about the formation of expectations, although greater attention is focused on the rational expectations hypothesis (REH).

Principal policy issues

Before we embark on the analytical discussion which follows, it is as well to pause and consider what the objectives of policy makers might reasonably be in the new context that we are about to define. The macroeconomic models that we have been postulating have been essentially neoclassical. Wages and prices have been assumed to respond to the pressures of excess demand, the demand for money has been linear homogeneous in prices, macroeconomic markets have been assumed to clear and be self-equilibrating, and in one form or another real and financial assets have been assumed to be substitutes for each other in varying degrees. Because of their self-equilibrating nature, it was shown that in a fundamental sense activist or discretionary macroeconomic policies were redundant in neoclassical models. Full employment – or the 'natural' rate of unemployment – would *eventually* be restored. When the exchange rate was fixed, the balance of payments *eventually* responded to changes in domestic credit policies while prices *eventually* moved in line with changes in world prices. When the exchange rate was flexible, prices *eventually* reflected domestic monetary policy. It was also argued that the authorities could not exert any longer term influence over real variables. Instead, they could exert extensive influence over nominal variables such as the balance of payments, the exchange rate and prices, in which context they were in a position to do perhaps more harm than good.[1]

The operative word here is 'eventually'. The principal policy issue is whether or not the authorities can speed up the adjustment process through macroeconomic policy in a fashion that does not jeopardize social welfare, e.g. to speed up the eventuality of full employment without creating any untoward side-effects in the process. However, it shall be argued that such policies cannot be assessed in the absence of a clear understanding of the causes for the macroeconomic disequilibrium in the first place. Timing is therefore the essence of macroeconomic policy in dynamic neoclassical models – can the authorities legitimately help a decentralized economy to adjust more easily to macroeconomic disequilibria? For example, let us assume that the economy is under-employed, i.e. $Y < \bar{Y}$ (continuing with the previous notation).[2] Thus in each period (t) society will forgo output equal to $\bar{Y} - Y(t)$. Within the neoclassical framework that we have been using, quantity disequilibria will reflect absolute and relative price disequilibria. If say in the MG model[3] the full-employment price level, given a fixed quantity of money, is $\bar{P}$ (i.e. where $Y = \bar{Y}$), but the actual price level is greater than $\bar{P}$, there will be negative real balance effects, as previously discussed, and the economy will enter a period of recession. During this period Y will be less than $\bar{Y}$ as the economy grinds through the trauma of restoring the price level to $\bar{P}$ along the lines discussed in Chapter 3. In the absence of further shocks that might cause the price level to deviate from its equilibrium level or path the real resource loss to the economy will be the value of the output forgone during the adjustment process, or

$$Q = \int_0^{t^*} (\bar{Y} - Y(t))e^{-\delta t}\, dt \tag{7-1}$$

where t^* denotes the time when Y eventually returns to its equilibrium level of $\bar{Y}$ and δ represents some appropriate social rate of discount.

If the authorities can accelerate the recovery of output to $\bar{Y}$, Q will tend to be smaller and social welfare will have been improved. In practice, society does not only attach importance to the minimization of resource losses. It also reveals a strong preference for price stability, and a more general criterion functional for policy analysis would include the imputed resource loss resulting from inflation:

$$Q = \int_0^{t^*} (\bar{Y} - Y(t)) + J(\dot{P}(t))e^{-\delta t}\, dt \tag{7-2}$$

where $J(\dot{P}(t))$ expresses this imputation in terms of real resources. Since inflation in our model would tend to accelerate if $Y > \bar{Y}$, equation (7-2) would not necessarily imply that $Y > \bar{Y}$ constituted a net social benefit.

One could construct yet more complex policy criterion functionals which included balance of payments and other objectives appropriately weighted and which could be minimized with respect to various policy instruments using optimal control methods.[4] However, this raises broader issues to which we shall return later. In the meanwhile, it is argued that the principal legitimate arguments in the criterion functional should be inflation and output forgone; the balance of payments, interest rates, etc., are of no intrinsic social value, although practically they might serve as intermediate rather than final policy objectives for the authorities. Also, if the valuation of investment did not properly reflect its future stream of consumption, it would be necessary to replace Y in equation (7-2) by consumption itself. But, in the present aggregative context this is only a detail.

Causes of disequilibrium

Following the discussion in Chapter 3, several sources of macroeconomic disequilibrium behavior may be identified, and it has been repeatedly noted that, although the structural equations in the models that have been presented are instantaneous, i.e. containing no distributed lags, the general equilibrium solutions have been nonetheless dynamic.[5] These sources are:

(i) The Phillips Curve. The Phillips Curve is narrowly concerned with the relationship between wage inflation and unemployment. In the present context we use this term to cover the general response of both wages and prices to situations of excess demand.[6] If, as in equation (3-25), price inflation depends on the level of output, while the model as a whole implies that in equilibrium the price level and the level of output will be related, a first order adjustment process will be implied. The model will be dynamic and disequilibrium situations will exist since the Phillips Curve implies that there is no instantaneous elimination of excess demand, and for sound microeconomic reasons related, e.g., to job search principles.

(ii) Stocks and flows. Changes in stocks of financial assets, and especially money, were shown to alter expenditure either via real balance effects or via substitution effects between real and financial assets. In open economies, stocks of financial assets will depend on the financial flows that are related to the balance of payments when the exchange rate is fixed.[7] Therefore the balance of payments will trigger portfolio adjustments and a first order dynamic process will be induced. For example, the price level will cause the money supply to change via its effects on the current account of the balance of payments. The changed money supply would in turn affect prices along the lines discussed. When the exchange rate is flexible, the observation that the current account depends on the level of the exchange rate while the capital account depends on the change in the exchange rate implies a first order adjustment process.

Thus Phillips Curves and the stock–flow logic of open monetary models combine to form second order dynamic processes. Indeed, in the models that have been so far developed, these were the principal dynamic adjustment elements. Next, we consider two additional dynamic elements that have so far not been incorporated into the analyses of Chapters 3, 4 and 5 but which were identified in Chapter 6.

(iii) Distributed lags. Lags in the structural equations[8] would initially alter the dynamic structure of the model as a whole. A first order lag in any of the equations cited in the *MGEFB* model would have transformed a second order system into a third order system. The order of the system as a whole (O) is equal to the sum of the orders of the individual equations in a simultaneous system;

$$O = \sum_{k=1}^{K} O_k \tag{7-3}$$

In large scale models O may be large and the dynamics of the model extremely complex.

(iv) Expectations. It was shown in Chapter 6 that both rational and extrapolative expectations altered the dynamic structure of the system, but in different ways. Insofar as expectations are themselves expressed as distributed lags the dynamic effects will be qualitatively the same as in (iii). However, because rational expectations are forward-looking and future developments are anticipated (up to a point), disequilibrium behavior may be reduced and the dynamic structure of the model simplified.[9]

For all these reasons, economic models will tend to be dynamic and adjust over time. Once a disequilibrium situation has been established, it is likely that the economy will remain in disequilibrium for some time, even if in the neoclassical specification there is a self-correcting tendency.

Macroeconomic policy and the principle of market failure

It shall be argued that the principles of macroeconomic intervention should be the same as the principles of microeconomic intervention. In microeconomic markets intervention is socially desirable when there is market failure in one form or another[10] which prevents the economy from attaining Pareto-optimality. For example, external diseconomies may be taxed in the social interest while subsidies may be used to counteract factor immobilities. These are, of course, time-hallowed principles of public policy which in microeconomic contexts are used day-in day-out all over the world.

However, macroeconomic policy has not been traditionally perceived in this way. Rather, the tendency has been to regard monetary policy, fiscal policy, etc., as levers that may be pulled to affect different macroeconomic aggregates regardless of (and sometimes despite) their effects, both long run and short, on the functioning of the main macroeconomic markets such as the markets for goods, employment, foreign exchange, money, etc. This 'assignment' philosophy of macroeconomic policy was discussed in Chapter 1. However, it implicitly dichotomizes the rationales for government involvement in micro- and macroeconomic markets. Governments do not see as their role the maintenance of full employment in micro markets such as textiles, shipbuilding, etc., yet for employment as a whole this is not so.

If, indeed, macroeconomic policy is to be devised along the same principles as microeconomic policy – what does the concept of market failure in the macroeconomic context mean? Let us return to equation (7–1), where it was argued that if the economy had been shocked out of a situation of full employment, i.e. $Y < \bar{Y}$, the neoclassical assumptions with which we have been working would imply an eventual restoration of equilibrium at full employment. The critical issue, in this example, is whether the existence of less than full employment or disequilibrium is a reflection of failure in macroeconomic markets. If it is, there would be a prima facie case for government intervention to counteract the underlying market imperfections and to raise social welfare in the process according to the orthodox theory of public intervention.

First impressions might indicate that such conditions are indeed implied in equation (7–1), for otherwise an efficient set of markets would restore prices and quantities to their equilibrium values straight away. It might be argued that, in an efficient market structure, prices and quantities cannot be 'wrong', an efficient market is always 'right'. Therefore, unemployment is either a reflection of market failure or there is a measurement problem, e.g. the 'natural' rate of unemployment has shifted.

In Chapter 6, however, it was argued that in a stochastic world where speculators (and economic agents more generally) are risk averse, the restoration of equilibrium prices and quantities could take some time even when expectations were formed rationally. In other words, the persistence of disequilibrium situations is compatible with rational market structures in the sense that economic agents are not systematically acting on the basis of mistaken views about the future. REH under perfect certainty would discount underlying lag structures that were attributed to structural elasticities and equilibrium would be restored straight away. However, under the less restrictive assumptions of imperfect certainty where risk aversion with respect to rational but risky expectations introduces an element of inelasticity into speculative responses, equilibrium would not be restored straight away. Thus disequilibrium behavior is compatible with REH when foresight is not perfect.

But does imperfect foresight or uncertainty amount to a market imperfection that justifies government intervention of a countervailing nature? This issue has already been discussed at length in Chapter 6[11] where it was argued that risk and risk aversion are real economic phenomena that should be respected by policy makers. The hesitation that is inherent in market adjustments under REH is natural enough and it would be inappropriate for policy makers to undertake risks on behalf of economic agents which they themselves are unwilling to undertake independently. If I act on the unbiased probability that a given economic event is going to happen tomorrow, it would be inappropriate for the government to supplement my actions on my implicit behalf. It may, however, claim that my probability estimates were biased and that this indicated market failure, but that would be a different matter.

In other words, even if all markets work perfectly smoothly and expectations reflect all the currently available information (and in that sense are rational, optimal and efficient), disequilibria in economic markets will tend to persist. But this would not constitute market failure and could not be regarded as a sufficient condition for government intervention, for what real sense has the market failed? Risk aversion is a plausible state of mind which the authorities should respect.

If, however, expectations are not formed rationally, e.g. they are formed adaptively or extrapolatively, there will be a case for government intervention along the conventional lines of market failure. Irrational expectations will generate 'wrong' prices and quantities, and the authorities may intervene in a socially productive manner. In this chapter we therefore take it as obvious that either in micro- or macroeconomic markets the authorities will have a positive stabilization role to play when expectations are not formed rationally. The precise optimal policy would then depend on the details of the market imperfections themselves.

The micro-foundations of macroeconomic policy

Therefore the crude approach to the theory of macroeconomic policy that is implied by equation (7-2) is rejected. While the setting of targets for employment, inflation, etc., characterizes the conventional approach to macroeconomic policy formation in academic and finance ministries alike it is unorthodox in the sense that it has no self-evident relationship with the principles of market failure upon which neoclassical orthodoxy requires all official intervention to be based. Instead, as argued in Chapter 6, the case for official intervention or stabilization must emanate from a detailed microeconomic analysis which identifies areas of market failure and Paretian suboptimality at both the static and dynamic levels. The apparent dichotomy between the theory of macroeconomic policy and the theory of microeconomic policy is false although, especially in the post-war era, this dichotomy has degenerated into a habitual mode of thought. Indeed, in a fundamental sense there is no such thing as a separate and independent theory of macroeconomic policy. Instead it is necessary to put the theory of macroeconomic policy on a microeconomic footing; macroeconomic policy cannot be considered in a vacuum.

Market failure thus emerges once more as the basic organizing principle for assessing policy at both the micro and macro levels. Indeed, as argued in Chapter 2, this was Keynes' modus operandi in attacking classical economics in the *General Theory*; he sought to show how market failure affected the macroeconomy. Whether one agrees with him or not his approach was orthodox since he tried to establish a new basis for political economy on the assumption that market failure was the rule rather than the exception. Nevertheless, in the post-war period this methodological orthodoxy fell into disuse and Keynes' economics was effectively replaced by the political economy of control and assignment developed by Meade, Tinbergen, Mundell and others. Such Keynesian political economy implicitly or inadvertently took it for granted that macroeconomic markets required permanent government assistance to make them function efficiently and a de facto dichotomy between micro and macro analysis became established.

How and why this dichotomy arose is unclear and would serve as a fascinating issue in the history of economic thought. For the present, however, the issue itself is merely raised; its resolution lies clearly beyond the mandate of the present essay. The approach in the remainder of this chapter is therefore to revert to grass roots and to base the case for macroeconomic intervention on the principle of market failure, which was the theme developed at length in Chapter 6. In the case of disequilibrium situations this amounts to basing policy on the inequality condition established in equation (6-38). If the macroeconomy is off its REH path the market will have failed and there will be a prima facie case for government intervention along familiar orthodox lines.

II The closed economy

In this section the main focus is on the augmentation of the models considered in section I of Chapter 3 when expectations are endogenized. The objective is not to augment all the models seriatim but to illustrate the basic principles that are involved when such an augmentation is carried out. In particular we seek to clarify the dynamic implications of endogenizing expectations in terms of REH which, as argued in Chapter 6 and section I of this chapter, provides a benchmark for evaluating whether the economy is functioning efficiently and whether government intervention is required to offset any manifestations of market failure.

In section III we investigate what happens when expectations are endogenized in the context of some of the open-economy models described in section II of Chapter 3. Here again the purpose is to illustrate basic principles rather than to be exhaustive or taxonomic.

In certain cases it will be necessary to reconsider some details of theoretical specification which arise when expectations are endogenized in terms of REH but which may be ignored otherwise. In principle, REH may be applied to any model where expectational variables appear. However, if agents are assumed to form their expectations rationally in the sense of equation (6-6) it may be sensible to modify certain behavioral equations so that agents are also assumed to respond rationally to the signals that they perceive. In particular it may be necessary to drop the assumption that aggregate supply is fixed at $\bar{Y}$ and to reconsider the Phillips Curve hypothesis and the associated hypothesis of price formation.

In Chapter 6 it was shown that REH models may either be presented in the format of equations (6-7)–(6-15) or equivalently they may be presented in terms of the stochastic format of equations (6-34)–(6-46). In this chapter we shall slip between both of these formats in the interest of familiarizing the reader with the various approaches.

The policy frustration hypothesis

It may be as well to begin with the issue first raised by Sargent and Wallace [1975] as to whether discretionary monetary policy can have any real impact upon the economy when expected prices are formed according to REH. Sargent and Wallace did not consider the normative issue as to whether under REH employment stabilization policies were justified, but the issue in positive economics of whether the authorities could use monetary policy to stabilize employment at all. Their conclusion was that under REH any stabilization of real variables was not feasible since rational expectations frustrate the objectives of monetary policy; the monetary authorities are impotent with regard to the control of real output and employment.

This startling conclusion is intuitive enough. In a quantity theory framework, agents expect changes in the money supply to be neutral in the long run. If experience shows that the authorities expand monetary policy during recessions and contract it during booms agents will build this information into their expectations. Say, for example, Y has fallen below $\bar{Y}$ by 5% and that the authorities are expected to increase the money supply by 5% in order to stabilize output. Agents will respond by raising prices by 5% so that real balances are left unchanged and output is unchanged. They do this because they understand from the quantity theory that prices will in any case rise by 5% and, since each individual wishes to be on the right side of the market, prices will tend to rise straight away. Thus the intentions of monetary policy are beaten even before they get off the ground.

The basic issue may be demonstrated as follows. Aggregate demand (Y^d) is assumed to depend upon the expected real rate of interest:

$$Y_t^d = -a(r_t - {}_{t-1}P_{t+1}^e + {}_{t-1}P_t^e) + u_{1t} \tag{7-4}$$

i.e. the expected rate of inflation (when expectations are measured at time $t - 1$, although the details of timing are unimportant) is represented by ${}_{t-1}P_{t+1}^e - {}_{t-1}P_t^e$. Aggregate demand is also assumed to depend upon a random disturbance u_{1t} which may be serially correlated although this is not material to the analysis either. Y^d may also be specified to depend upon real money balances but since this is not germane to the matter in hand we ignore this too.

Sargent and Wallace assume that aggregate supply is equal to the 'natural' level of output ($\bar{Y}$) if expected prices and actual prices in the current period are equal:

$$Y_t^s = \bar{Y} + b(P_t - {}_{t-1}P_t^e) + u_{2t} \tag{7-5}$$

Thus entrepreneurs have to plan their production on the basis of expectations about future prices. If actual prices are greater than expected prices each producer thinks that profitability is greater than expected and so increases output as a consequence. u_{2t} is a random disturbance term. The equilibrium condition is for aggregate demand to equal aggregate supply:

$$Y_t^d = Y_t^s \qquad (7\text{-}6)$$

which produces an *IS* curve. The *LM* curve in this simple model is represented by the familiar money demand function:

$$M_t = P_t + kY_t - jr_t + u_{3t} \qquad (7\text{-}7)$$

Clearly this model is the REH equivalent of the *MGB* model described by equations (3-8)–(3-11). The quantity of money is assumed to be exogenous and to depend on government policy.

The reduced-form for the price level is

$$P_t = \frac{-\bar{Y} + u_{2t} - u_{1t}}{d} + h_{t-1}P_t^e + \frac{a}{d}_{t-1}P_{t+1}^e - \frac{a}{jd}u_{3t} + \frac{a}{jd}M_t \qquad (7\text{-}8)$$

where

$$d = a(1 + b(k + 1))/j \qquad \text{(i)}$$
$$h = \left(\frac{b + \frac{kab}{j} - a}{}\right)/d \qquad \text{(ii)} \qquad \Biggr\} \qquad (7\text{-}9)$$

So far nothing has been said about the formation of the expected price level which in equation (7-8) is assumed to be predetermined. If we apply REH in accordance with equation (6-6) the expected price level may be hypothesized as:

$$_{t-i}P_t^e + k = E_{t-i}(P_t + k/\Omega_{t-i}) \qquad (7\text{-}10)$$

Applying equation (7-10) to (7-8) for $_{t-1}P_t^e$ produces

$$E_{t-1}P_t = \frac{-\bar{Y}}{d} + hE_{t-1}P_t + \frac{a}{d}E_{t-1}P_{t+1} + \frac{a}{jd}E_{t-1}M_t \qquad (7\text{-}11)$$

which states that the conditional expectation of the price level depends upon future price expectations and the expected money stock. The random disturbances disappear since $E_{t-1}(u_{it}) = 0$. Subtracting the expected price level from the actual price level produces

$$P_t - E_{t-1}P_t = \frac{u_{2t} - u_{1t}}{d} - \frac{a}{jd}u_{3t} + \frac{a}{jd}(M_t - E_{t-1}M_t) \qquad (7\text{-}12)$$

We may now use equation (7-12) to determine the effect of monetary policy upon output by substituting $P_t - E_{t-1}P_t$ into equation (7-5)

$$Y_t = u_t + \frac{ba}{jd}(M_t - E_{t-1}M_t) + \bar{Y} \qquad (7\text{-}13)$$

where

$$u_t = u_{2t} + \frac{b(u_{2t} - u_{1t})}{d} - \frac{bau_{3t}}{jd} \qquad (7\text{-}14)$$

Equation (7-13) contains the important result that the influence of the money supply on output depends upon the discrepancy between the actual money supply and the expected money supply. Next we assume that the authorities attempt to stabilize output about its 'natural' rate on the basis of a policy feedback rule such as

$$M_t - M_{t-1} = \beta(\bar{Y} - Y_{t-1}) + u_{4t} \qquad (7\text{-}15)$$

where u_{4t} is a random disturbance term with zero mean, i.e. the authorities increase the money supply during recessions and vice versa. The rational expectation of the money supply may be derived from equation (7-15) as

$$E_{t-1}(M_t/\Omega_{t-1}) = M_{t-1} + \beta(\bar{Y} - Y_{t-1}) \qquad (7\text{-}16)$$

in which case $M_t - E_{t-1}M_t = u_{4t}$ and equation (7-13) may be rewritten as

$$Y_t = u_t + \frac{bau_{4t}}{jd} + \bar{Y} \qquad (7\text{-}17)$$

Thus the systematic part of monetary policy does not affect output since β does not appear in equation (7-17). Y depends upon u_4 but this is a random factor over which the authorities do not have any systematic control. We may therefore conclude as Sargent and Wallace that under REH monetary policy is ineffective.

Slight modifications to the model will, however, alter this important conclusion. For example, if, as in Lucas [1972], equation (7-5) is replaced by

$$Y_t^s = \bar{Y} + b(P_t - E_{t-1}P_{t+1}) + u_{2t} \qquad (7\text{-}18)$$

equation (7-17) becomes

$$Y_t = u_t + \frac{ba}{jd}(\beta E_{t-1}Y_t - \beta Y_{t-1} + u_{4t}) + \bar{Y} \qquad (7\text{-}19)$$

in which case Y_t depends upon β and output is influenced by the systematic component of monetary policy. The Lucas supply hypothesis assumes that entrepreneurs hold back production in anticipation of more favorable prices at a later date. However, McCallum [1978a] has shown that, if $E_{t-1}P_{t+1}$ is discounted as seems appropriate by the rate of interest, the Sargent and Wallace superneutrality proposition emerges once more.

The essential point to note is that the Sargent and Wallace result is not robust; it is easy to make plausible assumptions which cause it to break down. The superneutrality proposition stands and falls by a relationship such as equation (7-5) which states that output depends on the current error in price expectations. Since according to REH this must be a random variable, the authorities are powerless to exploit the relationship. Once such a relationship is replaced the superneutrality proposition vanishes. For example Fischer [1977, p. 198] assumes that wage contracts are fixed for two periods at a time so that the aggregate supply function becomes

$$Y_t^s = \frac{1}{2} \sum_{i=1}^{2} (P_t - E_{t-i}P_t) + u_{2t} \tag{7-20}$$

in which case aggregate supply no longer depends upon a current error in expectations of the price level. The lagged values of expected prices reflects the assumption that wage rates are fixed on the basis of a moving average of price expectations. Consequently, policy action taken at time $t-1$ cannot be fully reflected in wage rates as would be the case in equation (7-5), and so monetary policy may systematically influence real wage rates and then aggregate supply under REH.

The same applies to the model proposed by Phelps and Taylor [1977] where firms set prices in advance of the period in which they sell their output. Once firms have set their prices the authorities can alter monetary policy without it having any effect on prices in the current period. As it were, advanced price setting provides monetary policy a temporary harbor from the frustrating effects of REH. These assumptions lead Phelps and Taylor [p. 171] to suggest an aggregate output equation of the form:

$$Y_t = \alpha_0 + \alpha_1 E_{t-1}P_t + \alpha_2 P_{t-1} + \alpha_2 M_t + u_{2t} \tag{7-21}$$

It comes as no surprise, therefore, that these studies violate the superneutrality result since they break with the form of aggregate supply equation that is given by equation (7-5). The Fischer and Phelps–Taylor studies introduce elements of price stickiness into the basic model. However, McCallum [1978b] shows that even if prices adjust slowly superneutrality may still prevail. The important thing to note is that McCallum [p. 423] operates with an aggregate supply function such as in equation (7–5). Therefore, no matter how he complicates the model it is bound to produce the superneutrality result. In contrast Minford and Peel [1978], who do not assume wage-price stickiness, generate an output equation that violates equation (7–5) from which it follows that monetary policy cannot be superneutral in their model.

It follows from this discussion that whether or not the superneutrality proposition holds depends critically on the underpinnings of the output equation in the model. It should go without saying that the theoretical underpinnings of macroeconomic models is a crucial area for study. However, our main concern is not with the issue of whether or not the authorities can influence real variables in the economy, but even if they can it remains to be seen whether they should deploy this ability. In the meanwhile we may make some rather obvious observations on the superneutrality issue. If, on the basis of the model, agents expect monetary policy to be neutral in the short run (it is assumed that in the long run there is no doubt about its neutrality) then it will indeed be neutral in the short run. If, instead, they expect monetary policy to be non-neutral in the short run then it will indeed be non-neutral in the short run. Therefore under REH everything turns on the properties of the model itself. But even if macroeconomic policies are non-neutral it is clear that the response of the economy under REH to policy changes will differ from its response when expectations are not formed rationally. This issue has obviously been brought out by equation (6–37) where it was shown that the effects of policy intervention are modified by REH. If the authorities seek a certain real effect they must allow for the fact that agents will take into consideration the systematic components of the authorities' behavior. We shall return to this theme later.

The money and goods model

We now return to the basic quantity theory model described in Chapter 3 and explore its behavior when the demand for money is assumed to vary inversely with the expected rate of inflation and where such expectations are formed rationally in the light of the model. The nature of the problem requires us to switch from the differential equation mode that was adopted in Chapter 3 to the difference equation model.[12] However, the underlying specifications are essentially the same, in which case the minimum of exposition is necessary. Thus equation (3–2) may be rewritten as

$$M_t^d = P_t + kY_t - h(_tP_{t+1}^e - P_t) \qquad (7-22)$$

where $_tP_{t+1}^e$ is the price level expected in time t to prevail in the next period. Given the logarithmic presentation, $_tP_{t+1}^e - P_t$ represents the expected rate of inflation.

We continue with equation (3-4) in assuming that the actual rate of inflation depends on the pressure of demand:

$$P_t - P_{t-1} = c(Y - \bar{Y})_t \tag{7-23}$$

and that demand itself depends on real balance effects augmented by expectations as in equation (7-22). Therefore, equation (3-3) is modified to:

$$Y = \bar{Y} + b(M - M^d) \tag{7-24}$$

where M is the exogenously determined supply of money. If the supply of money is greater than the demand for money, expenditure will tend to be higher. Insofar as expected inflation reduces the demand for money, inflation will be higher since expenditure will be greater.

To complete this augmented version of the simple MG model, it remains to specify the expected price level. One possibility is that the expected price is some arbitrary extrapolation of previous prices, but we do not explore this possibility. Instead, we note that, as in equation (7-10), the model itself may be used to forecast prices, and REH under such circumstances would imply that the expected price was equal to its expected value, as implied by the model itself:

$$_tP^e_{t+1} = E_t(P_{t+1}/\Omega_t) \tag{7-25}$$

Following the solution procedure illustrated in equations (6-13)–(6-15) and substituting equation (7-25) into equation (7-22) implies the following equation in the price level

$$-bhcP_{t+1} + (1 + bk + cb(1+h))P_t - (1 + bk)P_{t-1} = -cbk\bar{Y}_t + cbM_t \tag{7-26}$$

i.e. a second order difference equation in the price level. The particular integral of equation (7-26) is $-k\bar{Y} + M$, assuming $\bar{Y}$ and M are constants.

At this juncture there are two alternative ways of proceeding. First, equation (7-26) may be used to solve for P_{t+1} in terms of $P_t, P_{t-1}, \bar{Y}_t$ and M_t, i.e. all the currently available information and the parameters of the model itself. It is precisely in this sense that the expected price level based on this solution is rational. These solutions may then be substituted into equation (7-22) and the entire model can be solved once more using these rational expectations. The expectations-augmented trajectories for prices and incomes[13] could then be calculated using the 'chain-rule' for forecasting. However, in the event that these forecasts were explosive, it would be necessary to apply a zero arbitrary constant to the unstable root as discussed at length in Chapter 6. This would be consistent with a boundary condition that precluded the possibility that the price level could in the long run be dominated by self-serving price expectations.

Secondly, the general solution for equation (7-26) may be obtained. Indeed, this was the procedure adopted in Chapter 6. P_{t+1} may then be derived from this general solution and the results substituted into equation (7-22). The two approaches are logically the same; the latter solves the difference equation while the former applies the chain-rule.[14]

The general solution for the expected price level from equation (7-26) is:

$$P^e(t) = A_1 \lambda_1^t + A_2 \lambda_2^t - k \bar{Y} + M \qquad (7\text{-}27)$$

where A_1 and A_2 are arbitrary constants and λ_1 and λ_2 are the roots of equation (7-26). If both of these roots are stable, equation (7-27) states that in the long term rational expectations imply that the price level will vary in strict proportion with the quantity of money and that it will vary inversely with the full-employment level of output. Since the underlying model implies these results, as discussed in Chapter 3, rational forecasters of the price level will take this information into consideration. They will also take into account the information contained in the model regarding short term or disequilibrium price developments, i.e. the information contained in the two roots and their arbitrary constants. A change in the quantity of money would generate a new profile of rational expectations for the price level via equation (7-27) based on the long term and disequilibrium properties of the model.

Note that in general, REH does not imply an immediate expected adjustment of the price level to its new equilibrium value since in practice the roots will be consistent with a protracted adjustment process. This is a formal statement of the earlier argument that REH, market efficiency and disequilibrium behavior are compatible and natural. However, at this juncture it is also worth noting what happens when h goes to infinity. Recalling the discussion in Chapter 6 (in relation to the parameter e in equation (6-22)), h will tend to infinity either as risk aversion disappears, or as economic agents become completely confident in their expectations. If, for either of these reasons, h were infinite, equation (7-22) would imply that the demand for money would be either zero (since it cannot be negative) or infinite, depending on whether expected inflation were negative or positive. If the supply of money is finite and positive the only possible solution is that the expected price level must equal its current value – i.e. the expected rate of inflation is zero. This can only happen when the macroeconomy is in general equilibrium; once P has fully adjusted to M, inflation will necessarily be zero. Therefore, when h is infinite, we may conclude that rational expectations will entirely eliminate disequilibria. This is, of course, a limiting and unrealistic case, yet it is worthy of mention if only to emphasize the point that risk aversion will imply disequilibrium behavior.

The same point may be made somewhat differently. Dividing the characteristic equation from equation (7-26) by h and taking its limit as h goes to infinity implies

$$-bc\lambda^2 + bc\lambda = 0 \tag{7-28}$$

Dividing this result by $bc\lambda$ implies that $\lambda = 1$, which in turn implies that $P_{t+1}^e = P_t$. If this condition is fulfilled, general equilibrium implies that the economy must never be in a disequilibrium situation, for otherwise inflation would not be zero.

So far we have been assuming that both roots in equation (7-27) are stable. If one of them happens to be unstable, the boundary condition that has previously been discussed implies that the arbitrary constant on the unstable root is zero, for otherwise we would have the implausible result that P can be plus or minus infinity. For example, if $|\lambda_2| > 1$ in equation (7-27), it would be necessary to set $A_2 = 0$ in order for P to satisfy the boundary condition that P cannot be infinite or zero.[15] In fact equation (7-27) is unstable since $-(1 + bk + cb(1 + h))(1 + bk) < 0$. In general both roots will be positive but one will be greater than unity and the other less than unity reflecting the reciprocal pairing problem discussed on p. 144. Under such circumstances[16] we may deduce that prices will be related through time by a first order rather than a second order process, i.e. via λ_1 rather than via λ_1 and λ_2. Rational expectations for the price level in period $t + 1$ will depend on the current price via λ_1 according to[17]

$$_tP_{t+1}^e = \lambda_1 (P_t + k\bar{Y} - M) - k\bar{Y} + M \tag{7-29}$$

This equation states that when the price level equals its long run equilibrium value of $M - k\bar{Y}$ the expected price in the next period will be unchanged since no further price adjustment will be forthcoming. However, if P does not equal $M - k\bar{Y}$, the rational expectation of the price level will adjust over time since the model suggests that it will do so.

Substituting equation (7-29) into equation (7-22) and solving the model on the basis of this rational expectation yields the following price equation:

$$[1 + bk + cb(1 - h\lambda_1 + h)]P_t - (1 + bk)P_{t-1} = cb(1 - h\lambda_1 + h)(M - k\bar{Y}) \tag{7-30}$$

Equation (7-30) represents the behavior of prices over time under the assumption that price expectations are formed rationally in terms of the simple MG model. The general solution for equation (7-30) is

$$P(t) = B\gamma^t + M - k\bar{Y} \tag{7-31}$$

where

$$\gamma = \frac{1 + bk}{1 + bk + cb(1 - h\lambda_1 + h)} = \lambda_1 \tag{7-32}$$

Equation (7-35) may be compared with equation (3-7), which was the general solution for $P(t)$ from the MG model in the absence of expectations. Because $\lambda_1 < 1$, γ will imply stability. Equation (7-31) states that in the long term the familiar quantity theory postulates will continue to hold whole $B\gamma^t$ indicates the optimal adjustment of price to its equilibrium value for given disequilibrating shocks.

Policy analysis

It may be concluded then that in the basic quantity theory model described by equations (7-22)-(7-25) the effects of random shocks to either prices, output or the money supply will tend to persist for some time although, as equation (7-31) implies, they will also tend to die out over time. Therefore, in this model monetary policy will not be superneutral. If, for example, the authorities expand the money supply in order to stimulate the economy, output will expand in the short run but not in the long run, where once again neutrality prevails. The stimulus will have two related origins. First, there will be the familiar real balance effect which has been discussed at length in Chapter 3. Secondly, agents will forecast that prices are expected to rise which, via equation (7-22), reduces the demand for money and, via equation (7-24), will result in an increase in aggregate demand. Therefore in general the model is amenable to demand management.

It has already been argued that if $h = \infty$ REH implies that the shocks will be fully absorbed and the economy will be in permanent equilibrium which leaves no room at all for effective demand management. For as soon as the authorities change the money supply, prices adjust instantaneously - real balances are unaltered and aggregate demand is unchanged. As it were, the expectation that money is neutral in the long run becomes fully discounted by the market, with the result that monetary policy is also neutral in the short run.

Superneutrality will also arise if $c = \infty$ in equation (7-23). If c is finite, a tâtonnement theory of price adjustment is implied; if demand is greater than the 'natural' level of output, entrepreneurs are assumed to respond by raising their prices in the current period but not necessarily by an amount which will entirely eliminate the excess demand. Such behavior may be rationalized (as discussed in Chapter 3) in terms of a search model of price formation where entrepreneurs do not want to jeopardize their market by overcharging when demand is high or undercharging when demand is low. As $c \to \infty$ it implies that entrepreneurs instantaneously set prices to eliminate excess demand or supply. Thus, when the authorities increase the money supply, prices immediately rise in proportion - there is no scope for demand management.

As $c \to \infty$ the root of the characteristic equation (7-26) becomes $b(1 + h) > 1$. Since (as the reader may check) there is only one root, and this root is unstable, the boundary condition implies that the price level and so the economy as a whole never can be disequilibrated.

Apart from these special cases, which may nonetheless be quite realistic, demand management will be feasible, but, as argued in Chapter 6, it is not self-evident that just because the authorities have the power and are sufficiently large to influence the economy that they should take advantage of that fact. We assume that the aggregate pricing equation (7-23) has been derived from optimal pricing behavior by all the agents in the economy. That is to say, for reasons best known to itself the market behaves according to equation (7-23). Moreover, since there are no reasons to believe the opposite, it is assumed that there is no divergence between optimal pricing behavior at the private and social levels. Clearly we cannot for the present enter into the microeconomics of optimal pricing behavior, so equation (7-23) is taken to illustrate the basic argument that follows. The same argument could naturally be founded on some contender for equation (7-23).

Likewise we assume that equations (7-22) and (7-24) reflect private portfolio optimization. In the former case agents decide for themselves how best to respond to expected inflation and in the latter case they work out how best to respond to portfolio imbalance. Once again these specifications are illustrative and, since there is no cause to believe otherwise, it is assumed that there is no divergence between the private and the social interest in relation to this behavior. In general the parameters h, c and b will reflect, inter alia, risk assessment and risk aversion, and, as in the case of the simple commodity model described in Chapter 6, risk will play an important role in the dynamics of market adjustment to random shocks.

If price expectations are formed rationally the response of the economy to a random shock will be Pareto-efficient, since all the behavioral responses are assumed to be optimal when risk and uncertainty are taken into consideration. For example a random shock that depressed output will persist for some time before dying away as already described. Ex post the resource loss is seen to be wasteful, but ex ante, if the economy is on its REH path as defined by equation (6-15), corrective action could not have been taken when risk and uncertainty are taken into consideration. It is of course easy to be wise after the event; the challenge is to out-perform the market before the event. Had this been possible, market forces would have taken advantage of profitable options, but, since by assumption this has not happened, no such options exist. They do not exist for the market, nor do they exist for the government, which has no better information about the economy, etc., than is generally available to the market.

We may conclude therefore, as in Chapter 6, that if there is no market failure there is no case for corrective action by the authorities. Alternatively, the case for macroeconomic stabilization policies under REH must be premised on the orthodox principle of market failure. If expectations are not formed rationally and the inequality condition of equation (6-38) is fulfilled, then market failure will be present and the authorities will have to consider the necessary corrective action. Alternatively, market failure may originate from several different sources. Therefore, under REH the lags that are inherent in economic adjustment must be respected by the authorities; they are certainly not to be regarded as a means for manipulating economic markets, although this may be conventional practice.

Clearly the market is far from perfect; nobody can claim otherwise. All that can be hoped for is that all avoidable imperfections are indeed avoided. As far as expectations are concerned this will be the case under REH, so that all avoidable errors in forecasting will indeed be avoided.

Discretionary policy and risk

In Chapter 6 it was shown how the intervention of a buffer-stock authority could be destabilizing, since it may have the effect of increasing the amount of risk to which the market has to be averse. The stochastic element in the intervention rule (assuming that it is not totally stochastic) is man-made risk and the market is constrained by it. Indeed, this risk may itself be regarded as an avoidable market imperfection. For example, in the case of a stabilization rule such as equation (7-15), $\sigma^2_{u_4}$ will have to be taken into consideration by the market. Just in the same way that e in equation (6-22) varied inversely with risk, so h in equation (7-22) varies inversely with risk. The lower is h the more persistent are the effects of shocks to the economy. Therefore, insofar as a stochastic stabilization rule generates man-made risk it will dampen the inherently stabilizing forces in the model.

The intuitive interpretation of this phenomenon is that the higher is $\sigma^2_{u_4}$ the more unsettled the market gets; it does not know what the authorities are going to do next. It cannot focus on what even at the best of times is a hazy notion of equilibrium because it is not sure how this equilibrium will be affected by subsequent government behavior. For example, under 'stop-go' policies and u-turns, $\sigma^2_{u_4}$ becomes large and government behavior clouds the underlying signals that the market is trying to decipher.

Augmenting the Phillips Curve under REH

We do not propose to explore all the models set out in Chapter 3 in terms of their dynamic structure when expectations are endogenous. Rather, our purpose is to illustrate the broad principles that are involved for macroeconomic policy formation under REH. Nevertheless, the Phillips Curve seems to be a sufficiently important issue in its own right to warrant separate investigation.

We therefore return to the *MGE* (money, goods and employment) model introduced in Chapter 3 (pages 68–72).

We begin by augmenting the Phillips Curve for wage inflation in equation (3–23) in terms of expected inflation:

$$W_t - W_{t-1} = n(Y - \bar{Y})_t + {}_tP^e_{t+1} - P_t \tag{7-33}$$

i.e. along with neoclassical assumptions we assume that there is no money illusion in the labor market. Equation (7–23) would have to be modified to

$$P_t - P_{t-1} = c(Y - \bar{Y})t + W_t - W_{t-1} \tag{7-34}$$

since it will now be necessary to take account of wage cost inflation. Equation (7–34) assumes that real profit margins are constant. The *MGE* model now comprises equations (7–22), (7–24), (7–33) and (7–34), while REH would also include equation (7–25). Notice that the expected price level appears twice in this specification, once in equation (7–22) and once in equation (7–33).

Solving this model for the price level, i.e. the analogue of equation (7–26), yields the following difference equation assuming REH:

$$-(1 + bk + bh(c + n))P_{t+1} + (2(1 + bk) + b(c + n)(1 + h))P_t - (1 + bk)P_{t-1}$$
$$= b(c + n)(M - k\bar{Y}) \tag{7-35}$$

This equation once more implies that the expected value for P_{t+1} can be solved in terms of currently available information regarding $P_t, P_{t-1}, M, \bar{Y}$ and the parameters of the model. Notice also that, as before, this expected value will depend on reactions to expected inflation itself via the parameter h and via the absence of money illusion in the Phillips Curve.

The general solution for equation (7–35) will be of exactly the same form as equation (7–27); λ_1 and λ_2 will obviously be defined in terms of a different set of structural parameters. However, as h approaches infinity the roots converge on the single value of unity, as before implying that rational expectations will tend to converge on long run equilibrium values.

Applying the boundary condition once again and taking (say) λ_1 as the stable root, the rational expectation of the price level will be determined according to equation (7–29). Substituting this result into the *MGE* model and solving for the price equation that reflects these rational expectations yields:

$$[(1 + bk)(2 - \lambda_1) + (c + n)(1 - \lambda_1) bh + (c + n)b]P_t - (1 + bk)P_{t-1}$$
$$= [(1 + bk + (c + n)bh)(1 - \lambda_1) + (c + n)b](M - k\bar{Y}) \tag{7-36}$$

The general solution for equation (7-36) will be of the same form as equation (7-31) since it is also a first order difference equation. However, the root will be

$$\gamma = \frac{1 + bk}{(1 + bk)(2 - \lambda_1) + (c + n)(1 - \lambda_1) bh + (c + n)b} < 1 \qquad (7\text{-}37)$$

This general solution indicates how price will vary over time, assuming optimal or rational expectations. Its principal property is that if the price level departs from its equilibrium value, it will tend to return to its equilibrium over time. In a stochastic world the macroeconomy will deviate from its long run equilibrium for many different reasons. However, each time this happens, REH implies that the tendency towards equilibration will occur in an optimal fashion. The authorities could not do better.

Fiscal policy

So far in this chapter the discussion has been almost exclusively concerned with monetary policy. This preoccupation has reflected the belief that, in neoclassical models of the economy, the stock of financial assets is the principal determinant of economy activity and especially the price level. In Chapter 5 the role of fiscal policy was reviewed in a neoclassical context but without any discussion of the influence of expectations. The main conclusions were that, if fiscal deficits are financed by increasing the money supply, the consequence will be inflationary, for the authorities have to allow the money supply to grow at an accelerating rate to maintain a given volume of public expenditure, as shown in equation (5-27). If finance is raised through taxation, the stock of financial assets is unchanged and private expenditure falls by an amount equal to the rise in public expenditure. However, the economy will be affected by disincentive effects. In the case of bond finance 'crowding out' takes place through higher rates of interest at which the private sector is prepared to hold the additional bonds in its portfolio. However, as indicated by equation (3-20), even this case could be inflationary.

Therefore, the influence of, say, an increase in government expenditure under REH depends critically on how the market expects the resultant deficit to be financed. In the case of money finance, inflation will be expected so that prices will tend to grow at a faster rate, which is bound to dampen the expansionary effects of fiscal policy. It is easy to see that in the limit an unbounded explosion of prices may be triggered. To show this we revert to the simple money-goods model presented on pages 123-4 where the government's budget deficit is financed entirely by printing money. Dropping the logarithmic presentation equation (5-23) becomes

$$\dot{M} = GP \tag{5-23'}$$

which determines the absolute change in the money supply. The demand for real money balances depends on output and varies inversely with expected inflation which in this perfect myopic foresight version is equal to the actual rate of inflation when expectations are rational. Assuming for simplicity that output is at its 'natural' level we may rewrite equation (3-2) as

$$M/P = kY - \beta\dot{P}/P \tag{3-2}$$

Equating the rate of growth of money supply and demand implies that equation (5-24) may be rewritten as

$$kY\dot{P} - \beta\ddot{P} = GP \tag{5-24'}$$

for which the general solution is

$$P(t) = A_1 e^{\lambda_1 t} + A_2 e^{\lambda_2 t} \tag{5-25'}$$

where

$$\lambda_1, \lambda_2 = \frac{-kY \pm \sqrt{(kY)^2 - 4\beta G}}{-2\beta} \tag{5-26'}$$

From equation (5-25') we may solve for the rate of inflation as

$$\frac{\dot{P}}{P} = \pi = \frac{\lambda_1 A_1 e^{\lambda_1 t} + \lambda_2 A_2 e^{\lambda_2 t}}{A_1 e^{\lambda_1 t} + A_2 e^{\lambda_2 t}} \tag{5-27'}$$

It follows that $\dot{\pi} > 0$ when $\Delta_1 \Delta_2 > 0$ in which case the tendency to hyperinflation depends on the strength of the initial inflationary shock as may be verified numerically. However, a boundary condition on A_1 and A_2 is $P(t) > 0$ as $t \to \infty$. If this is violated there will only be one root and thus a constant rate of inflation.

We thus arrive at the important conclusion that in RE models budget deficits may generate hyperinflation. The usual boundary conditions do not apply because monetary policy is endogenous and on the boundary monetary growth may be infinite if this is necessary to finance the deficit. Agents are aware of this possibility and build it into their expectations of inflation. Equation (3-2') that real balances in this case will tend to zero which in turn implies the destruction of the money-exchange economy; i.e. hyperinflation will destroy the economy.

The same general result applies when the budget deficit is financed by bonds in the context of the model presented in pages 66-8. The details differ but bond finance may generate hyperinflation as well as endlessly spiralling interest rates.

The role of built-in stabilizers

It is clear that as long as aggregate supply is determined according to equation (7-5) equilibrium macroeconomic models must imply that the level and distribution of output will be independent of policy feedback parameters. The same of course does not apply to disequilibrium models such as described by equations (7-22)-(7-32). But even in the equilibrium models there will be a role for fiscal and monetary policy provided it is not discretionary and does not rely on feedback terms. For example, certain changes in monetary and fiscal policy are automatic and do not rely on the discretion of the authorities. If output falls and unemployment rises built-in stabilizers will be triggered so that there will be an expansionary impetus to monetary and fiscal policy. Thus we may rewrite equation (7-15) as

$$M_t - M_{t-1} = \beta_1 (\bar{Y} - Y_{t-1}) + \beta_2 (\bar{Y} - Y_t) + u_4 t \qquad (7\text{-}15')$$

where β_1 reflects the discretionary component of government policy while β_2 reflects the presence of built-in stabilizers.

Under the assumptions of rational expectations (7-17) becomes

$$Y_t = \frac{u_t + \alpha u_4 t}{1 + \alpha \beta_2} + \bar{Y} \qquad (7\text{-}17')$$

where $\alpha = ba/jd$. As before, output is independent of β_1 but it is not independent of the built-in stabilizer since β_2 appears in equation (7-17'). The reason for this is that β_2 operates with respect to the current level of output so that current shocks affect current monetary and fiscal policy. It is this immediate response which prevents rational expectations from undermining their effectiveness. It is only when current policies respond to lagged output that rational expectations can frustrate their effects as previously discussed. The variance of output is

$$\sigma_2 = \frac{\alpha^2 \sigma_{u4}^2 + \sigma_u^2 + \alpha \sigma_{uu4}}{(1 + \alpha \beta_2)^2}$$

which implies that the variance of output varies inversely with the strength of the built-in stabilizer, a result which has also been noticed by McCallum and Whitaker [1979]. However, they emphasize that if the built-in stabilizers are not index-linked to the price level the variance of output might be increased by β_2. This is because the stabilizers under such circumstances are not real phenomena so that there can be no guarantee that the variance of output will be reduced in real terms.

Towards a general speculative model

For expositional purposes the models that have been explored so far in this chapter have entailed merely one expectational variable, namely the expected price level. In section III the expected exchange rate is considered alongside the expected price level. But even in closed-economy models it is reasonable to deploy expectational variables much more liberally than has been the case so far. Indeed, economic behavior is essentially speculative, since agents must always justify their behavior now in the light of what they think will happen in the future. This is clearly so in the case of financial assets, where expected capital gains are a major motivation of behavior; it also applies to real assets, where capital formation reflects expectations about future demand and prices.

In fact, as we shall see, it is both possible and sensible to design economic models where expectations play a major role in each of the behavioral relationships and with respect to a wide range of variables. We may refer to such a model as the 'general speculative model' (GSM).

The present purpose is not to explore the properties of GSM under REH (the zealous reader may of course do so) but to outline its basic structure in terms of expectational considerations. We begin with the real side of GSM before investigating its financial specification.

Real sector. Aggregate supply is assumed to be determined through a production function depending upon employment (L) and the capital stock (K)

$$Y_t^s = F_1(\overset{+}{L_t}, \overset{+}{K_{t-1}})\tag{7-38}$$

Equation (7-38) assumes that the capital stock at the end of the previous period will influence aggregate supply in the current period (the signs of the partial derivatives are indicated over the appropriate variables). In this case current investment (I) should depend upon the expected level of output in the next period relative to the current level of output. It will also depend upon the change in the expected real rate of interest (R) and K_{t-1} where the latter reflects replacement investment. Therefore the neoclassical theory of investment behavior suggested by Jorgenson [1963] may be recast in terms of expected values of future variables

$$I_t = F_2(\overset{+}{tY_{t+1}^e} - \overset{-}{Y_t}, \overset{-}{\Delta R_t}, \overset{+}{K_{t-1}})\tag{7-39}$$

where

$$R_t \equiv r_t - {}_tP_{t+1}^e + P_t\tag{7-40}$$

Equation (7-39) should be contrasted with naive accelerator models where investment is assumed to depend upon current and past changes in output. That is to say, entrepreneurs in these conventional models are assumed to be backward looking; it seems much more sensible to assume that entrepreneurs plan for the future as equation (7-39) implies than to assume that they base their decision on historical bygones.

Next we turn to a theory of employment in which expectations are explicitly considered. Neoclassical theory suggests that labor supply varies directly with real wages $(w \equiv W - P)$, since a higher wage rate will call forth a higher participation ratio. As discussed in Chapter 3, it also suggests that at a given level of output the demand for labor by firms varies inversely with the real wage rate. In a speculative model, however, prospective suppliers of labor may be hypothesized to hold back their labor today if they think they can get a better wage rate tomorrow. Strictly speaking, the expected real wage when discounted back to the present would have to be greater than the current real wage rate to justify the withholding of labor. This model is based on Lucas and Rapping [1969] and assumes that wages are fixed by contract for $C > 1$ time periods. If, instead, wage rates were completely flexible there would be nothing to speculate about since workers could work in the current time period without forfeiting their right to obtain a better wage in the next time period. Therefore the speculative labor supply schedule may be written as

$$L_t^s = F_3(\overset{+}{w}_t, {}_t\overset{}{w}_{t+1}^e - \overset{-}{w}_t - R_t)$$ (7-41)

In the steady-state, the term ${}_t w_{t+1}^e - w_t - R_t$ will vanish; the expected gains from witholding labor will be zero and the labor supply schedule reverts to a more recognizable form in terms of the real wage rate.

Likewise with the labor demand schedule, which may be written as

$$L_t^d = F_4(\overset{-}{w}_t, {}_t w_{t+1}^e - \overset{+}{w}_t - R_t, \overset{+}{Y}_t)$$ (7-42)

Entrepreneurs too may speculate on future wage prospects and will prefer to contract labor when it is relatively cheap in terms of their expectations of future wage rates.

Labor market equilibrium will be attained when

$$L_t^d = L_t^s$$ (7-43)

in which case the equilibrium real wage will depend positively on the discounted value of the expected wage rate and the level of economic activity

$$w_t^* = w^*({}_t\overset{+}{w}_{t+1}^e - R_t, \overset{+}{Y}_t)$$ (7-44)

Thus aggregate supply as determined by equation (7-38) depends on an interplay of speculative considerations since L_t is determined via equation (7-43). Current supply depends on ${}_{t-1}Y_t^e$, ${}_{t-1}P_t^e$ and ${}_{t-2}P_{t-1}^e$ via equation (7-39). It also depends on ${}_t W_{t+1}^e$ and ${}_t P_{t+1}^e$ via equations (7-41) and (7-42). Therefore, supply reflects numerous expectational considerations. Equation (7-43) assumes that labor market equilibrium is attained in the current period and should be contrasted with the tâtonnement process that is built into conventional Phillips Curve specifications such as equation (7-33). Alternatively, we may wish to replace equation (7-43) by

$$W_t - W_{t-1} = n(L^d - L^s)_t + {}_t P_{t+1}^e - P_t$$ (7-45)

so that wage rates adjust to their equilibrium value over time rather than instantaneously. In this case employment will be the smaller of labor supply

(L^s) and labor demand (L^d) since employers cannot be made to employ more than they wish if $L^s > L^d$ and since employers cannot employ more labor than is available if $L^d > L^s$.

Aggregate demand. So much for the supply side of GSM and its associated factor analysis. We now turn to the determination of aggregate demand. Investment has already been considered in equation (7-39). Consumption is assumed to be determined within the context of portfolio decision taking; either consumers expend or they accumulate financial assets. Therefore the consumption decision will depend on the stock of financial assets and their rate of return. We consequently modify equation (3-56) to allow for speculative factors. The demand for bonds will depend on the real expected return on bonds (R). However, it will also depend upon the expected capital gain on bond holdings. Since bond prices vary inversely with interest rates, the determinants of aggregate demand may be written as

$$Y_t^d = I_t + F_s(\overset{+}{M_t - P_t}, \overset{+}{B_t - r_t} - P_t, \overset{-}{R_t}, {}_t\overset{e}{r_{t+1}} \overset{+}{- r_t}) \tag{7-46}$$

Thus the higher the expected capital loss on bond holdings the more attractive will consumption be relative to saving. The expected rate of interest is therefore added to the list of expectational arguments that drive the model.

In equilibrium, aggregate demand and aggregate supply must be equal

$$Y_t^d = Y_t^s \tag{7-47}$$

in which case the price level (P) clears the goods market in each time period. Or analogously to equation (7-45) a tâtonnement process could be assumed in the goods market

$$P_t - P_{t-1} = c(Y_t^d - Y_t^s) + {}_tP_{t+1}^e - P_t \tag{7-48}$$

in which case the actual level of output will be equal to Y^s. If $Y^s > Y^d$ firms will be affected by unanticipated stockbuilding.

Monetary sector. To complete the GSM it is necessary to consider the portfolio decision between money and bonds, the allocation decision between financial assets and goods having been considered in equation (7-46). In terms of the variables in the model it remains to determine the rate of interest, which is determined by equation (7-49). Equation (7-49) is a money demand function based on equation (3-8) and extended to allow for speculative factors. The demand for real money balances is assumed as before to depend upon real income and the opportunity cost of holding money. The opportunity cost of holding money instead of bonds has two components. First, there is the expected real return on bonds (R). Secondly, however, the attractiveness of money holdings will vary inversely with the expected capital gain on bond holdings. Thus we may write

$$M_t - P_t = F_6 \left(\overset{+}{Y_t}, \overset{-}{R_t}, {}_t\overset{-}{P^e_{t+1}} - P_t, {}_t\overset{+}{r^e_{t+1}} - r_t \right) \qquad (7\text{-}49)$$

as the demand function for real balances.

Solution of GSM. This completes the model. M and B are exogenous variables reflecting the financing of the government's budget deficit. To derive the general solution of the model under rational expectations it will be necessary to apply either of the solution procedures described in Chapter 6. For example, the endogenous variables may be expressed as reduced form relationships based on equation (6-40) and rational expectations may then be calculated according to equations (6-44). Unstable roots would be eliminated according to equation (6-14) and the general solution of the model may be obtained.

The exercise is laborious although the principles are straightforward, and it is left to the zealous to try their hand. However, it should be clear that the distribution of output depends on monetary policy and that superneutrality is not a property of the GSM model. This may readily be seen by inspecting equations (7-41) and (7-42). Since employment does not depend upon a current error it follows from equation (7-38) that output does not depend upon a current error. In other words output is not determined on the basis of equation (7-5). Instead output will depend upon

$$Y^{s*}_t = Y^{s*} ({}_t W^e_{t+1} - W_t, W_t - P_t, r_t, \dots) \qquad (7\text{-}50)$$

all of which are nominal variables which are responsive to monetary policy. But, as argued before, the fact that the authorities can influence the level of economic activity does not mean to say that such behavior is desirable.

III The open economy

The principal objective in this section is to consider the implications of REH in the setting of an open economy. The basic principles of design have already been discussed in Chapter 3 so that they shall not be repeated here. Instead, the present focus will be on the role of exchange rate expectations in macroeconomic adjustment and their implications for the theory of macroeconomic policy in a neoclassical setting. In particular, exchange rate expectations are endogenized in the light of REH, i.e. the model itself is used to generate the exchange rate expectations that were previously regarded as exogenous to the system.

In Section II the role of employment stabilization policies was considered and it was argued that the criterion for government involvement is the principle of market failure. If the market has failed, neoclassical orthodoxy provides the authorities with a prima facie case for intervention in one form or another. In a dynamic context the market will have failed if its forecasts are suboptimal or irrational, therefore REH and the inequality condition given by equation (6-38) provide a normative basis for assessing the case for intervention in disequilibrium settings. These principles naturally lend themselves to the assessment of intervention in the foreign exchange market. To simplify the central argument we begin this section by exploring the dynamic behavior of the foreign exchange market in a partial equilibrium setting: i.e. we assume prices, output, etc., as given, while the exchange rate itself is taken as the principal endogenous variable. This simplification allows us to focus attention on the determination of the exchange rate in a dynamic setting and under REH.[18] Once more we use the REH solution as an efficiency benchmark for determining policy in the foreign exchange market. The REH solution for the exchange rate, $S(t)$, will be optimal in the sense that it will reflect all the currently available information, appropriately adjusted for risk aversion, that pertains to the exchange rate. Clearly if $S(t)$ does not follow an REH solution the authorities, in principle at least, will be able to design socially beneficial and activist policies in the foreign exchange market. But if the contrary holds, and $S(t)$ follows an REH solution the authorities could only make matters worse by intervening, either by excessive risk taking or by generating superfluous uncertainty in the exchange market itself. In other words, the guiding principles for foreign exchange policy should be essentially the same as for domestic policies.

Since we are by now already familiar with the principles of dynamic macroeconomic policy analysis in a closed economic setting, the chapter is completed by integrating the determination of exchange rates and the balance of payments with the rest of the economy. This amounts to a dynamic model of an open economy with endogenous expectations regarding both price and exchange rate developments. As such, it provides the most general and realistic framework for analyzing macroeconomic policy that will be developed in the present study. In such a setting, optimal disequilibrium time paths for output, prices, the exchange rate, etc., would be jointly determined. Therefore, optimality must be considered in terms of the system as a whole. Suboptimality in one part of the economy could contaminate the rest of the system. Say, for example, that price expectations were formed rationally while exchange rate expectations were not so formed.[19] Under such circumstances it would be perfectly rational for economic agents in the domestic economy to base their expected price levels on the irrational speculative behavior in the foreign exchange market since for them such irrational behavior is an integral part of the relevant model. However, rational price expectations will no longer be optimal for society as a whole under these circumstances, having been contaminated by irrational expectations in the foreign exchange market. The behavior of the individual will be optimal in an individual context, but rational behavior would be inefficient in a social context; the individual normally has no incentive to correct for antisocial distortions.

Clearly the converse could happen; i.e. with rational exchange rate expectations but irrational price expectations. The principles of policy intervention would, however, be the same. In a simultaneous system, market failure in one market will contaminate the efficiency status of all other markets. Principles of public finance formally recognize this issue; so should the principles of macroeconomic policy.

Exchange rate dynamics

Exchange rate expectations were introduced in Chapter 3 as a determinant of international portfolio decisions. In equation (3-51) it was hypothesized that foreigners' desired stock of domestic bond holdings depended, among other factors, on the expected rate of appreciation of domestic currency relative to foreign currency. Equation (3-52) hypothesized the corresponding relationship for residents' desired stock of bond holdings in foreign currency. In any period the balance of payments depends on the flow of international financial transactions on the capital account, i.e. on the net stock adjustments of residents' and foreigners' portfolios. This result was expressed in equation (3-53), and, since in this chapter we have adopted the idiom of discrete time rather than continuous time, this equation is appropriately rewritten as

$$K = (q_1 + q_3)(r_t - r_{t-1} - r_{wt} + r_{wt-1}) + (q_2 + q_4)(_tS^e_{t+1} - S_t$$
$$^-_{t-1}S^e_t + S_{t-1})$$

$(7-51)$

where $_tS^e_{t+1}$ is the exchange rate as of time t expected to prevail at time $t+1$, while $_{t-1}S^e_t$ is the exchange rate as of time $t-1$ expected to have prevailed at time t. In other words, net capital flows over the balance of payments depend on the change in the expected rate of exchange rate depreciation.

In the *MGEFB* model[20] it was assumed for expositional simplicity that the expected exchange rate was predetermined. In what follows, this unlikely assumption is modified and the expected spot rate is endogenized in terms of REH – that the expected spot rate will be the prediction of the *MGEFB* model itself. Thus the analogue of equation (7-10) for the exchange rate is

$$_tS^e_{t+1} = E_t(S_{t+1}/\Omega_t)$$

$(7-52)$

where $E_t(S_{t+1})$ is the expected value of the exchange rate at time $t + 1$ as determined at time t by the model. Since equation (7-52) would be an optimal and therefore efficient expectation, REH provides a benchmark for determining the socially efficient exchange rate path. Exchange rate policy may then be evaluated in the light of this benchmark. Clearly, alternative expectations-generating mechanisms would produce different results and it would only be by chance that the resultant exchange rate path, $S(t)$, would be optimal. The authorities could then intervene to equate $S(t)$ with its REH solution through the appropriate deployment of their foreign exchange reserves.

The REH path for the exchange rate is optimal in the sense that, when due allowance has been made for the risks in the foreign exchange market and agents' aversion to risk, it appropriately reflects the available information. Any other exchange rate would have implied that investors were taking positions which in the light of their expectations were causing them to incur too much risk or too little risk; either situation would be suboptimal. In other words the issue is exactly the same as that illustrated in fig. 6-4 except that instead of inventories of commodities we have inventories of financial assets of different currency denominations.

The exchange rate will reflect current account as well as capital account transactions and we may extract the partial equilibrium determinants of the exchange rate from the first row in equation (3-68) as modified by equation (7-51).[21]

$$\beta_5 \left({_t}S^e_{t+1} - S_t - {_{t-1}}S^e_t + S_{t-1} \right) - \beta_4 S_t = J \tag{7-53}$$

where J is a constant reflecting all the exogenous variables[22] (also assumed to be constant) that theoretically will affect the balance of payments and their parameters. Thus β_5[23] reflects the influence of the exchange rate on the capital account of the balance of payments while β_4 reflects the influence of the exchange rate on the current account. Notice the similarity between equation (6-13), which was derived from a simple model of commodity speculation, and equation (7-53). There we were talking of a stock–flow model of net commodity supply and speculation; here we are talking of a stock–flow model of net foreign exchange supply and speculation.

Equation (7-53) is dynamic; so it should be possible to forecast the expected value of tomorrow's exchange rate from what is known today about S, J, the parameters of the model and any random factors that happen to be current. We may now repeat the procedure that was applied in Chapter 6 and in the earlier part of the present chapter of

(i) solving for the rational exchange rate expectation in terms of the proposed model, and

(ii) substituting this rational expectation back into the model itself for the REH time path for the exchange rate, $S(t)$.

Under these previous assumptions equation (7-53) may be written as

$$\beta_5 S_{t+1} - (2\beta_5 + \beta_4)S_t + \beta_5 S_{t+1} = J \qquad (7\text{-}54)$$

and the general solution for the expected exchange rate will be

$$S^e(t) = A_1 \lambda_1^t + A_2 \lambda_2^t - J/\beta_4 \qquad (7\text{-}55)$$

Since these roots come in reciprocal pairs,[24] one of them (say λ_2) must violate the boundary condition that S cannot be zero or infinity. Setting the arbitrary constant A_2 to zero implies the following rational exchange rate expectation

$$_tS^e_{t+1} = \lambda_1 (S_t + J/\beta_4) - J/\beta_4 \qquad (7\text{-}56)$$

When the exchange rate equals its equilibrium value of $-J/\beta_4$, the expected exchange rate happens to be its equilibrium value. If the exchange rate is in disequilibrium, the rational exchange rate expectation will be based on its expected path in terms of the model which, in the present case, implies a geometric convergence to equilibrium.

Substituting this result into equation (7-53) for $_tS^e_{t+1}$ and $_{t-1}S^e_t$ yields the following result

$$\beta_5(\lambda_1 - 1) - \beta_4)S_t + \beta_5(1 - \lambda_1)S_{t-1} = J \qquad (7\text{-}57)$$

in which case the dynamic path for the exchange rate that reflects rational exchange rate expectations is

$$S(t) = B\gamma^t - J/\beta_4 \qquad (7\text{-}58)$$

where

$$\gamma = \frac{\beta_5(1 - \lambda_1)}{\beta_5(\lambda_1 - 1) - \beta_4} \qquad (7\text{-}59)$$

If the actual exchange rate path diverges from its REH path as calculated in terms of equation (7-58), it will be sub-optimal, in which case (at least in principle)[25] the monetary authorities should follow an activist policy of intervention in the foreign exchange market. The purpose of this intervention should be to restore the exchange rate to its REH path, since this is also a socially optimal path. The authorities would then be fulfilling their role as honest brokers with respect to market failure. In this respect stabilization policy would be both traditional and orthodox.

The reasons why REH models do not instantaneously revert to their initial equilibrium positions in the wake of random disturbances have been discussed at length in Chapter 6. The same reasons apply to the dynamic behavior of the foreign exchange market under REH. In the present model, equation (7-56) states that the market expects the exchange rate to converge at a geometric rate upon its initial equilibrium value, assuming the exchange rate has been disturbed from this value. Equation (7-58) states that if the market expects this to happen then indeed it will happen. Thus, although they will generally persist for some time, the effects of random shocks to the exchange rate will tend to die out over time. They do not die out straight away because speculators do not know what additional shocks the future holds in store. If there were no shocks or speculators were completely unaverse to risk the exchange rate would indeed be in permanent equilibrium.

This may be demonstrated by setting $\beta_5 = \infty$ which implies that as the expected rate of currency appreciation diverges from zero there is either an infinitely large inward or outward switch of speculative positions. That is to say investors in the foreign exchange market put all their money where their mouth is and back their expectations to the hilt. The determinants of c_5 are essentially the same as the determinants of e as given by equation (6-22) since a speculative currency position is exactly analogous to a speculative commodity position. Thus β_5 will tend to infinity as

(i) the variance of exchange rate expectations tends to zero, or as perfect certainty prevails; and

(ii) as investors become completely unaverse to risk.

If either of these unlikely conditions is fulfilled the roots of equation (7-54) converge on unity so that equation (7-56) states that the exchange rate expected to prevail in the next period is equal to the current exchange rate $(_tS^e_{t+1} = S_t)$. But this can only happen if the steady-state has been attained. We may therefore conclude that as β_5 tends to infinity the exchange rate will tend to be in permanent equilibrium.

The intuitive explanation for this is that speculators absorb all the shocks that bear upon the foreign exchange market. They do so since they are absolutely convinced that the exchange rate must revert to its equilibrium value and, since everybody wants to be on the right side of the market, speculative pressures force the exchange rate back into equilibrium straight away. But in general these conditions will not prevail since risk is always present and cannot be ignored. These arguments underline the importance of risk in disequilibrium behavior under REH, and it is risk and investors' aversion to it that will be largely responsible for deviations of exchange rates from their equilibrium values.

Indeed, it is quite possible that these factors may generate fairly regular cycles when the market is subject to random shocks. In general (as the next section shows) the response of the exchange rate to random disturbances will not be a first order process as it is in equation (7-59) but some higher order moving average process reflecting the complexity of lags in the model. If s is the deviation of S from its equilibrium value we may write

$$s_t = \sum_{i=1}^{K} \overline{w_i} s_{t-i} + \epsilon_t \qquad (7\text{-}60)$$

as the general time path of the exchange rate under REH where ϵ_t is a random disturbance which is serially independent. It is well known that random changes in ϵ will generate fairly regular cycles in s (see e.g. Slutsky [1937]). But such cyclical behavior does not imply that the market is inefficient or irrational since it is driven by factors that are entirely random and therefore unpredictable. The rationality condition merely requires that errors in expectations are serially independent which is quite a different matter to requiring that the exchange rate itself be serially independent. Fig. 7-1 illustrates how these cycles might arise under the simple assumption of a first order REH adjustment process. We begin our story at t_0 when a random shock causes the exchange rate to rise above its equilibrium value as indicated. The market responds by adjusting s back towards zero, but at t_1 a negative disturbance causes the exchange rate to fall below its equilibrium value. The market will tend to stabilize once more but at t_2 a positive shock carries the exchange beyond its equilibrium. This is followed by a negative shock at t_3 and a positive one at t_4. Thus it can be seen that random disturbances to REH models may generate cycles although quite obviously this will not always be the case.

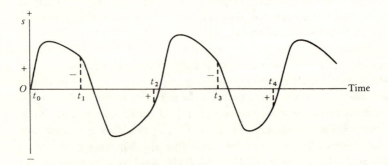

Fig. 7-1 Cyclicality and rational expectations

Foreign exchange intervention

These cycles or the deviation of the exchange rate from what seems to be its equilibrium value is of course not a self evident reason for the authorities to intervene in the foreign exchange market. It cannot be argued that the role of the authorities should be to set $s = 0$ because ex ante the authorities have no better view than the market of what future developments are likely to be. For example is the upward shift in the exchange rate a random factor or a movement in the equilibrium itself? Speculators are forced to ponder over such issues and to take risks and in so doing they have access to the same information as the authorities. Perhaps the only difference is that since they are risking their own resources speculators will pay more careful attention to the risks involved than would a bureaucrat who was intervening on the part of the authorities. But the proof of the pudding is in the eating and if the authorities can show that they can make profits on their intervention, it will have been justified. However, such profits must be earned fairly and not as a consequence of the authorities' ability to manipulate the market to its own advantage, which it can do on account of its size.

It is of course easy to be wise after the event. Rational exchange rate expectations are not necessarily correct. The best that can be hoped for is that exchange rate expectations are unbiased and efficient. As long as this hope is fulfilled and the inequality condition in equation (6–38) is not violated there will be no market failure and no case for exchange rate intervention. REH does not imply that the foreign exchange markets will not experience turbulence from time to time, nor does it imply that conditions will always be perfect. Mistakes, sometimes large ones, will happen but these errors will have been unavoidable under REH. This is as much as can be hoped for.

As in the case of buffer stock intervention, considered in Chapter 6 where it was argued that the stochastic element in intervention behavior could undermine the stabilizing tendencies of the market, so in the foreign exchange markets official intervention may be counter-productive. Instead of 'smoothing' the market the authorities run the risk of frightening off the speculators who would have undertaken this function under usual market incentives.

Distributed lags and the foreign exchange market

In section I it was noted that there are four principal sources of macro-dynamics. So far, in the interest of expositional simplicity, we have abstracted from the issue of distributed lags, although this was discussed in Chapter 6. Since the response of the current account to exchange rates may be distributed over a considerable period of time,[26] it would be appropriate enough to extend the analysis in the previous section by introducing such a distributed lag. A related issue is the so-called J-curve phenomenon[27] where, as the exchange rate depreciates, the current account might get worse before it eventually improves due to unfavorable valuation effects. This opens up the possibility for a floating exchange rate to be unstable.

β_4 denotes the long run response of the current account to the exchange rate. In what follows we assume that this response is distributed over $H + 1$ time periods with the weighting pattern

$$\sum_{h=0}^{H} w_h = 1 \tag{7-61}$$

Some earlier weights may be negative, reflecting J-curve effects. Equation (7-53) may therefore be rewritten as[28]

$$\beta_5 (_t S_{t+1}^e - S_t - _{t-1} S_t^e + S_{t-1}) - \beta_4 \sum_{h=0}^{H} w_h S_{t-h} = J \tag{7-62}$$

and the analogue to equation (7-54) is

$$\beta_5 S_{t+1} - (2\beta_5 + \beta_4 w_0) S_t + (\beta_5 - \beta_4 w_1) S_{t-1} - \beta_4 \sum_{h=2}^{H} w_h S_{t-h} = J$$

$$\tag{7-63}$$

Notice that, if this expression is divided by β_5, as β_5 approaches infinity the resulting $(H + 1)$th order characteristic equation converges onto a system with a single root $\lambda = 1$. In other words, when the speculative elasticity goes to infinity, all the lags in the model become fully anticipated and the expected exchange rate is equal to the current exchange rate. But this can only happen in equilibrium, for otherwise the exchange rate would rationally be expected to change. From this we may deduce that in this limiting case, where $\beta_5 = \infty$, rational expectations would be perfectly stabilizing regardless of J-curve effects and other lags.

More generally, β_5 will be finite on account of risk aversion. In this case equation (7-63) may be solved for S_{t+1}[29] and the solutions for $_t S_{t+1}^e$ and $_{t-1} S_t^e$ obtained. Substituting these two results into the underlying model, as expressed by equation (7-62), provides the following expression for the determination of the exchange rate under REH:

$$(\beta_5 + \beta_4 w_0) \Delta S_t - (\beta_5 - \beta_4 w_1) \Delta S_{t-1} - \beta_4 \sum_{h=0}^{H} w_h S_{t-h} = J \tag{7-64}$$

the general solution for which is

$$S(t) = \sum_{h=0}^{H} A_h \lambda_h^t - J/\beta_4 \tag{7-65}$$

where the A_h are arbitrary constants reflecting the initial and boundary conditions and λ_h are the roots.[30]

The time path for the exchange rate that is implied by equation (7-65) is optimal since it will reflect all the currently available information. Expectations will take into account the information that is contained in the knowledge that the current account responds with a distributed lag to previous exchange rate developments. However, it should be recalled that these expectations will be discounted as a result of risk aversion, otherwise the exchange rate would adjust immediately to its long run equilibrium solution.

If some of the roots are unstable they will not satisfy the boundary conditions and their arbitrary constants will be zero. Some of the remaining roots may imply oscillations of the exchange rate around its long term value,[31] the overshooting reflecting the risk aversion in the market as a whole. There is consequently nothing irrational in oscillating (but damped) exchange rate movements since oscillations reflect a natural human urge for caution. After the event it is easy to be clever; but before the event it may be the better part of valor to follow the underlying oscillations in the exchange rate (or prices, etc.) rather than to throw caution to the wind and to attempt to iron them out.

General equilibrium; internal and external balance

In the previous section the determination of the exchange rate was examined in a partial equilibrium setting. The only endogenous variable was the exchange rate itself; all other variables were held constant. In the case of a 'small' open economy the exogeneity of overseas variables such as import prices (P_m), world economic activity (Y_w), etc., is natural enough. But domestic income, prices, interest rates and so on are clearly endogenous and should interact closely with the exchange rate. This section therefore explores the simultaneous determination of these variables under the assumption that REH applies to the determination of the expected price level and the expected exchange rate. Thus the expected price level will reflect the rationality of the expected exchange rate and vice versa since both expectations generating processes are integral components of the model. As before, the optimality of such REH expectations provide a benchmark for gauging when policy intervention would be desirable.

We could 'augment' the *MGEFB* model described in equation (3-68) in terms of expectations. However, rather than do this we work with a simpler system based on the *MGEFB* model and the partial systems that have so far concerned us in the present chapter. In particular, we ignore the market for bonds since this does not affect the main thrust of the argument.

Equation (7-23) has to be modified to reflect import costs as well as wage costs:

$$P_t - P_{t-1} = c(Y - \bar{Y})_t + v(W_t - W_{t-1}) + (1 - v)(P_{mt} - P_{mt-1} - S_t + S_{t-1})$$

$$(7\text{-}66)$$

while equation (7-24) is modified to reflect the foreign resources balance[32] $(X_w^d - I)$:

$$Y_t = \text{constant} + b(M - M^d) - e_1^1(P + S - P_{xw})_t + e_2 Y_{wt} + (f_1^1 + f_2^1)(P_m - S - P)_t$$
$$- f_s Y_t$$

$$(7\text{-}67)$$

Thus aggregate demand depends on monetary adjustments, relative export and import prices and relative levels of economic activity at home and abroad.

We must also modify equation (7-53) regarding the determination of the exchange rate since domestic income and prices[33] will interact with the exchange rate. Thus from equation (3-68) we now have the following expression in S, S^e, Y and P:

$$\beta_s({}_tS^e_{t+1} - S_t - {}_{t-1}S^e_t + S_{t-1}) - \beta_4^1 S_t + f_s Y_t + \beta_1^1 P_t = J^1 \qquad (7\text{-}68)$$

where J^1 reflects the truly exogenous variables $(P_{xw}, P_m$ and $Y_w)$. The equations to be retained are (7-22), (7-25), (7-33) and (7-52), which combine to form the following 'augmented' simultaneous dynamic system

$$
\begin{bmatrix}
(-vB^{-1} + (1+v) - B) & -(c+vn) & (1-v)(1-B) \\
(bhB^{-1} - \alpha) & -\delta & -(\alpha - bh) \\
\beta_1^1 & f_s & (\beta_s B^{-1} - (2\beta_s + \beta_4^1) + \beta_s B)
\end{bmatrix}
\begin{bmatrix}
P \\
Y \\
S
\end{bmatrix}
$$
$$
=
\begin{bmatrix}
-(c+vn)\bar{Y} + (1-v)\Delta P_{mt} \\
-bM - e_1^1 P_{xw} - (f_1^1 + f_2^1)P_m - e_2 Y_w \\
\beta_3 P_{xw} + \beta_6 Y_w + \beta_7 P_m
\end{bmatrix}
\qquad (7\text{-}69)
$$

where

$$
\begin{aligned}
\alpha &= bh + e_1^1 + f_1^1 + f_2^1 & \text{(i)} \\
\beta &= 1 + bk + f_s & \text{(ii)} \\
B^i &= \text{backward/forward shift operator[34]} & \text{(iii)}
\end{aligned}
\qquad (7\text{-}70)
$$

The determinant of equation (7-69) is

$$\det = K_1 B^{-2} - K_2 B^{-1} + K_3 - K_4 B \tag{7-71}$$

where

$$K_1 = \beta_s (v\delta + (c + vn)bh) \tag{i}$$
$$K_2 = (2\beta_s + \beta_4^1)(v + (c + vn)bh) + \beta_s(\delta(1 + v) + \alpha(c + vn)) - f_s(1 - v)bh \tag{ii}$$
$$K_3 = (2\beta_s + \beta_4^1)(\delta(1 + v) + \alpha(c + vn)) + (c + vn)(bh\beta_s + \beta_1^1(\alpha - bh)$$
$$+ (1 - v)(\beta_1^1\delta - f_s(bh + \alpha)) + \delta\beta_s(1 + v) - vf_s(\alpha - bh) \tag{iii}$$
$$K_4 = \delta(1 + v)\beta_s + \delta(2\beta_s + \beta_4^1) + f_s(\alpha - bh) + \alpha(c + vn)\beta_s + (1 - v)(\beta_1^1\delta - \alpha f_s) \tag{iv}$$

$$\tag{7-72}$$

The general solutions for the rationally expected price level and exchange rate may subsequently be represented as

$$P^e(t) = A_1 \lambda_1^t + A_2 \lambda_2^t + A_3 \lambda_3^t + Q_1 \tag{7-73}$$
$$S^e(t) = A_4 \lambda_1^t + A_5 \lambda_2^t + A_6 \lambda_3^t + Q_2 \tag{7-74}$$

where the particular integrals are

$$Q_1 = \{-(c + vn)(\lambda\beta_4^1 + f_s(\alpha - bh))\bar{Y} + (c + vn)\beta_4^1 bM + (c + vn)(\beta_4^1 + \alpha - bh)$$
$$+ [(e_1^1 + \beta_3)P_{xw} + (f_1^1 + f_2^1 + \beta_3)P_m + (e_2 + \beta_6)Y_w]\} / \sum_{i=1}^{4} K_i \tag{i}$$

$$Q_2 = \{-(\delta\beta_1^1 - f_s(\alpha - bh))(c + vn)\bar{Y} + \beta_1^1(c + vn)bM - (c + vn)(\beta_1^1 + \alpha - bh)$$
$$\times [(e_1^1 + \beta_3)P_{xw} + (f_1^1 + f_2^1 + \beta_7)P_m + (e_2 + \beta_6)Y_w]\} / \sum_{i=1}^{4} K_i \tag{ii}$$

$$\tag{7-75}$$

under the assumptions that $\Delta P_m = 0$ and the exogenous variables are constants, and where the As are arbitrary constants.

Equations (7-73) and (7-74) will generate the rational expectations for P and S under the assumption that REH prevails in both the goods and the foreign exchange markets. This information will be contained in the λs and the As.[35] When these expectations are substituted back into equation (7-69) we may derive the 'augmented' solutions for price and the exchange rate over time. These solutions, $P(t)$ and $S(t)$, would be optimal in the sense that prices and quantities appropriately reflect all the information that is currently available.

We shall not perform this exercise here since the principles are identical (although, of course, the practice would be messier) to those already described with respect to the univariate models of expectations. Nevertheless, it is worth showing the limiting case when rational speculation in goods and foreign exchange markets become infinitely elastic, i.e. when both b and β_s go to infinity at the same time. In this case the determinant in equation (7–71) becomes:

$$B^{-2} - 3B^{-1} + 3 - B = \det \tag{7-76}$$

and the roots of the system converge on $\lambda = 1$.[36] This implies that ${}_tP^e_{t+1} = P_t$ and ${}_tS^e_{t+1} = S_t$, or, the expected price level is equal to its current value and the expected exchange rate is equal to its current value. But this can only happen if the economy is in equilibrium, for otherwise P and S would be changing and so would P^e and S^e. We may therefore conclude once more that REH under perfect certainty (i.e. where $b = \beta_s = \infty$) drives the macroeconomy immediately back to equilibrium.

Under such circumstances, the following events would take place when, e.g., the money supply is raised by 10% in an unconcealed fashion.[37]

(i) Goods prices would immediately be marked up by 10% since this is consistent with the new equilibrium price level.

(ii) The same would apply to wages; they would also go up by 10%.

(iii) Foreign exchange speculators immediately lower the exchange rate by 10% since this is consistent with its new equilibrium.

(iv) The net result is that no real effects take place; not only is there no long term money illusion, speculation makes sure there is no short term money illusion either.

In practice b and β_s will not equal infinity, in which case the macrodynamics will be considerably more complex. But the principles will be the same and the government should pursue activist intervention policies if in practice $S(t)$ and $P(t)$ do not adhere to their REH solutions. This would arise when P^e and S^e do not equal their rational expectations. It would also apply when P^e is equal to its rational expectation, but when S^e is not and vice versa. Under these latter circumstances there would be market failure since there would be a divergence between private and social optimality. It would be privately optimal for individuals to take account of irrational expectations in other markets since they would be an integral part of the appropriate model, but this clearly would not be socially desirable. The authorities should therefore act in the public interest by assuming their traditional role of compensating for breakdowns in the market mechanism.

CHAPTER 8

Theory and practice

Apart from summarizing the central thesis that has been proposed in this essay, this final chapter is designed to open a discussion on a number of practical issues concerned with the macroeconomic policy formation process that the study recommends. This conclusion is particularly appropriate since the discussion has been quite theoretical and for expositional purposes the models that have been proposed have been kept extremely simple. However, in view of 'the econometric problem' described in Chapter 1,[1] theoretical analysis per se assumes a special relevance in macroeconomic policy formation. Since empirical corroboration in economics is usually anything but clear-cut, we should understandably be tempted by the strengths of a priori argumentation in the selection of competing theoretical systems. Unsatisfactory though this may be, it is a fact of life, and it is precisely for this reason that the central thesis that has been proposed is hopefully more than mere theoretical abstraction. Nevertheless, it is necessary to ensure that the data do not reject the theory, and the econometric results reported in Chapter 4 indicate this to be the case in the United Kingdom as far as the neoclassical structure of the model is concerned. However, no attempt has been made to test REH although quite obviously this is an important area of research. In the meanwhile it seems sensible to presume that all men are rational until proven otherwise and that the burden of proof should be on those wishing to establish the contrary view. If assumptions have to be made at all, it seems sensible to assume that agents make the best possible forecasts that they can.

The central thesis

(i) We began in Chapter 1 by pointing out that, during the 1970s, macroeconomic policy formation seems to have gone through a significant sea change. Governments seem less prone to pursue 'Keynesian' macroeconomic fine-tuning and more inclined to leave the economy to resolve its own difficulties, especially in relation to employment.

(ii) It was also pointed out that roughly about the same time the theory of macroeconomic policy began to go through a similar change. The 'assign-

ment approach to policy had been challenged by approaches that focused on
the anticipatory and potentially nullifying effects of expectations in models
where long term money illusion is absent. The main purpose of this book is
to clarify the nature of this challenge.

(iii) The Keynesian revolution has clearly been a major influence on the
theory and practice of macroeconomic policy in the post-war era and has
provided the intellectual underpinnings for activist macroeconomic policies.
Yet REH implies that this should be unnecessary and even harmful. Chapter 2
therefore appraises the *General Theory* in the light of Keynes' treatment of
macroeconomic disequilibria and expectations.

(iv) The main findings are:

(a) The *General Theory* synthesized and rendered intellectually res-
pectable a series of notions that had been floated over the previous
fifty years or so.

(b) Keynes did not maintain that economies could have unemployment equilibrium in general equilibrium, only in partial equilibrium.
However, it was part of his style to overstate his case so that people
would take notice of his theory of effective demand.

(c) Despite their importance in the *General Theory*, Keynes' treatment
of expectations was inadequate (but entertaining). His judgment is
that in practice long term stabilizing expectations are dominated
by short term destabilizing speculation. There is consequently a
need to rework the theory of macroeconomic policy under REH
and where disequilibria reflect legitimate uncertainties and aversion
to risk.

(d) Nevertheless, Keynes was orthodox in the sense that he saw that
the principle of market failure was the fundamental criterion upon
which interventionist policies could be based. In the post-war
period this principle fell into neglect. Its resurrection forms an
important part of the remainder of the essay.

(v) Chapter 3 is concerned with deriving the long term properties of open
economies regarding unemployment, inflation, the balance of payments, and/
or the exchange rate, when wages and prices are flexible and respond to
excess demand and where there is no money illusion. It is shown that:

(a) Unemployment is self-correcting.

(b) When the exchange rate is flexible, inflation reflects the monetary
policies of the authorities.

(c) When the exchange rate is fixed, the balance of payments reflects
the monetary policies of the authorities.

(d) If, as much empirical evidence suggests, the demand for money is
interest elastic the price level in the long run will not simply
depend on the money supply. It will also depend upon the quantity

of government debt outstanding. In this context the fundamental cause of inflation is the budget deficit.

(a) implies that macroeconomic stabilization is not obviously required, while (b) and (c) imply that the authorities themselves can harm price and balance of payments developments. In such neoclassical macroeconomic models, the case for activist policies is considerably lessened as compared with economies where prices and wages are exogenous. This is because price and wage variability offer additional degrees of freedom for adjustment. (d) implies that fiscal policy may be inflationary too and that the setting of targets for the money supply does not on its own amount to a counter-inflationary strategy. The growth of the bond supply must also be constrained which in turn constrains the budget deficit of the authorities.

(vi) The basic model set out in Chapter 3 is extended in Chapter 4 to include an energy sector. The main results were:

(a) When the exchange rate is fixed, energy discoveries have no lasting balance of payments effects since the balance of payments is a monetary rather than a real phenomenon.

(b) When the exchange rate is flexible and the supply of money is fixed the price level will fall and the exchange rate will rise. Under such circumstances there is a risk of recession because of real balance constraints. In general the exchange rate will rise proportionately more than the fall in the price level since energy is a net contributor to the balance of payments.

(vii) In Chapter 4 some econometric results are reported for the UK which test the long run hypotheses developed in Chapter 3 regarding the determination of inflation, the exchange rate, the balance of payments, employment, wage rates and the level of economic activity. These preliminary results suggest that the UK data are consistent with the neoclassical approach to macroeconomic modeling, while Minford (1979) has gone on to show that the dynamics of such models may be understood in terms of REH.

(viii) Chapter 5 investigates the long term impact on the macroeconomy of fiscal policy, exchange and import controls, and prices and incomes policies in the light of the neoclassical model developed in Chapter 3. It is shown, for example, that because of the paramountcy of the relationship between the demand for money and nominal income:

(a) tariffs do not affect the balance of payments;

(b) nor do exchange controls;

(c) temporary prices and incomes policies do not affect the price level, and

(d) fiscal policy does not affect aggregate demand. If fiscal policy is financed through monetary expansion inflation will become endemic.

(ix) In Chapter 6 the positive and normative implications of the rational expectations hypothesis are analysed in the context of a simple market of supply and demand. REH may be regarded as neoclassical since rational expectations reflect all the information that is currently available.

(x) It is shown that under REH price and quantity movements will be optimal, despite the presence of disequilibria. Under such circumstances official intervention in the market would represent the undertaking of risk by the authorities on behalf of the people they are supposed to serve. Unless there is a divergence between private and social risk, such action by the authorities would not be justifiable. Moreover, since speculative elasticities vary inversely with risk, intervention would be destabilizing insofar as it generated additional uncertainties in the market.

(xi) It is emphasized that the criterion for government intervention at either the micro- or macroeconomic level is the neoclassical principle of market failure and the divergence between the private and social interest. This principle has fallen into neglect in macroeconomic analysis and REH provides a basis for its resurrection as a normative principle in economic policy evaluation.

(xii) In Chapter 7 exchange rate and price expectations are endogenized in terms of REH. It is argued that the behavior of economic aggregates under REH provides a benchmark for economic policy evaluation. If the economy diverges from its REH path the economy will be performing suboptimally and there will be a prima facie case for the authorities to take corrective action. This approach would put the theory of macroeconomic policy onto a radically different footing from its present one.

(xiii) A parallel concern is whether the authorities can influence the level of economic activity under REH. It is shown that in the limit they cannot – a 5% increase in the money supply leads immediately to a 5% increase in the price level and a 5% fall in the exchange rate so that real factors are left unchanged. In general, such superneutrality will not arise, although the REH has the effect of bringing forward in time responses in nominal variables so that the real responses are reduced.

The role of stabilization policy

In the previous chapter it was argued that activist stabilization policies would be required if macroeconomic aggregates did not follow their REH solutions. Indeed, this is the essence of a truly normative theory of macroeconomic policy. If employers are taking on too few employees, if consumers are demanding too few goods, if the net demand for foreign exchange is too high, etc., on account of irrational views about the future, it would be in the social interest for the authorities to intervene in these markets in a countervailing direction and to induce the economy to purchase the appropriate quantities. The authorities may call upon the usual array of macroeconomic policy instruments as appropriate, i.e. monetary, fiscal, exchange rate policies, etc., and in so doing would be assuming their traditional role of compensating for market failure.

But how in practice can the authorities determine whether or not there has been macroeconomic market failure in this sense and whether or not corrective action is required on their part? How can the authorities calculate the REH solutions that provide the benchmarks for macroeconomic stabilization policies? No detailed attempt will be made to provide full answers to the questions here. Rather, the objective has been to clarify the principles involved, although, quite obviously, principles without practical guidelines for their implementation are not too helpful. Nevertheless, we broach these questions even if somewhat tentatively.

In Chapter 6 (page 158) we discussed the important question of the 'appropriate' model. Throughout Chapters 3–7 we have been assuming that the appropriate model is known, albeit in an uncertain fashion. This means that the model's parameters will be estimated and, although in practice it is likely that the model will be more complicated than the ones that have been used here as illustrations, the authorities may solve for the REH solutions along the same lines that have been followed in the present study. To judge whether the macroeconomy has been performing optimally it will be necessary to identify two critical parameters in addition to those contained in the underlying model. First, it will be necessary to estimate the variance of the relevant set of expectations. If inflation is expected to be 10% per annum, or if the exchange rate is expected to depreciate by 10% what are the variances of these expectations? Clearly, for given states of risk aversion, the economy will react differently and less markedly to a 10% expected rate of inflation with a high variance than to a 10% expected rate of inflation with a low variance. These variances may be calculated from the estimated parameters of the model and will reflect its predictive powers and the randomness of the noise that the model and the data generate. Indeed, professional forecasters should be used to providing the estimated confidence limits for their forecasts.

Secondly, it will be necessary to estimate society's aversion to risk. Clearly, for given expectations and confidence limits, the economy will react differently and less markedly to a 10% expected rate of inflation when society is more risk averse than when society as a whole happens to be less risk averse. Unless there is a divergence between social and private risk, and assuming that all the necessary risk-reducing insurance schemes have been provided, the authorities would have no justification for being more or less risk averse than the market itself since it is the market that the authorities are appointed to serve.

In the hypothetical case that the correct expectation is for a 10% inflation rate but the economy as a whole expects 15%, the authorities would be duty bound to intervene (by contractionary policies) to correct for this bias. But when they do so they should apply the social risk aversion factor since this behavior would be consistent with the market's behavior had it acted on the correct expectation of 10%.[2]

Therefore, the authorities cannot judge current macroeconomic aggregates to be incorrect unless

(a) they have accounted for the variance of expectations;
(b) they have accounted for social risk aversion;
(c) they have combined these to determine the current REH solution.

This raises in turn the question of how to estimate social risk aversion. In principle this amounts to estimating the parameters of the social expected utility function based on equation (6-18), but how can this be done? One possibility is to draw on the work that financial economists have been doing on portfolio optimization under uncertainty, and as a starter to base social risk aversion on society's revealed preferences in these and related contexts, e.g. Summers [1967]. More importantly, economists will have to address themselves to the many conceptual issues that are involved in the context of macroeconomic expectations and this is posed as a challenge to the normative macroeconomic theoretician.

In the meanwhile it would be appropriate for the authorities to accustom themselves to considering social risk aversion. For example, they should reflect upon the expected capital losses on their interventions and taxpayers' reactions to the bill with which they will eventually be presented. Official foreign exchange intervention is also speculation and the central bank's losses have to be paid for by society as a whole. By what right should the authorities contemplate such possible losses?

Thus far we have been assuming that the appropriate model is known. In practice it is either not known, or there are conflicting views about the truth. Say the authorities' model differs from the market's model or models; what should the authorities do then? Economic aggregates may be appropriate in terms of the market's model but not in terms of the authorities'. As it were, the authorities could 'race' their model against that of the market and there is very little that can be said beyond the advice that each should act on the courage of his convictions. If say prevailing aggregates reflect a 'monetarist' view while the authorities have a 'Keynesian' model the REH solutions from the latter would be different from those of the former. This presents a genuine dilemma that has no obvious solution.

It was argued in Chapter 7 that, within the neoclassical models that were proposed, the authorities could influence real expenditure decisions by confusing the market under REH. Anticipated monetary expansions will not change the real course of the economy but unanticipated monetary expansions will be influencial in this regard.[3] Does this mean that the authorities should act covertly and steal upon the market in order to achieve its macroeconomic objectives? This clearly raises important questions of moral principle; even if these objectives were in the social interest can economic policy be regarded as defense policy that requires the veil of secrecy to be effective? Or should the principle of public conduct be that the authorities amply publicize the nature of their daily interventions in the various financial markets instead of relying on the temporary veil of secrecy that is extended by the inside lag between actions and their eventual publication in the official statistics? Even here it is often difficult to deduce the nature of government policy because of window-dressing in the official statistical publications. In practice these questions would require a review, e.g. of whether it was right that brokers acting on behalf of the authorities should be anonymous. On the face of it there are no obvious reasons why the authorities should act secretively or deceptively.

We should also bear in mind the prospects for 'government failure' as well as market failure, and in practice it would be appropriate to assess the possibly imperfect hidden hand of the market place against the perhaps heavy hand of the authorities. The desire to do better is natural enough, but the best should not be the enemy of the good. The temptation is for the authorities to be dissatisfied with disequilibrium situations, especially regarding unemployment, even if such disequilibria are consistent with REH. But apart from its unwarranted and even ineffectual nature, it has been argued that intervention could be destabilizing insofar as it adds to uncertainty. If REH is confirmed, the authorities must take a deep breath and let the macroeconomy come to terms with itself. We should not be too concerned whether REH is strictly confirmed since in practice the authorities will act inappropriately too. It is unavoidably a matter of judgment, but as long as behavior seems to be reasonable enough the authorities should sit back and focus on more microeconomic areas where their influence may be of more social use.

Appropriate macroeconomic policies

On the assumption that expectations are rational and the economy functions along neoclassical lines, what should the authorities in fact do? The analysis in the present essay suggests that they should minimize the risk and uncertainty that is generated by public sector operations. Since monetary growth is in part a consequence of government finance the authorities should adhere to pre-announced and fixed rules so that the economy at large does not have to worry about what the authorities are going to do next. The uncertainty that government operations needlessly create is a dead-weight welfare loss to the community as a whole. Thus in the case of a monetary growth rule of $x\%$ per annum society does not have to worry how fast the money supply is likely to grow. This frees creative decision taking for real rather than nominal purposes – for how much to invest rather than how to adapt to some unknown rate of inflation. Likewise with taxation policy and gilt edged or bond market policy. People should not be left in doubt about what tax rates are likely to be; fiscal variability will generate uncertainty which will reduce economic efficiency along the lines described. The fiscal weapon is quite unsuitable for short term stabilization purposes, although its use has been fairly common practice. Unnecessary uncertainty about official operations in the bond markets will also cause instability. Indeed, if, as argued in equation (3-20), the rate of inflation not only depends upon monetary growth but also upon the rate of growth of government liabilities, it will be essential for the authorities to adhere to some stable rate of growth of these assets too.

In this context it should be emphasized that the appropriate focus of a counter-inflation strategy is not necessarily upon the rate of inflation itself. In the light of REH the essential evil is with errors in expectations about the price level which lead to suboptimal decision taking and unnecessarily large rates of risk consumption by society at large. In terms of welfare analysis a perfectly anticipated inflation is an altogether different matter from an inflation that is unexpected. Apart from the X-efficiency costs (printing new price lists etc.) of inflation a society might be indifferent between alternative inflation rates provided that they are perfectly antici-pated. What matters is not whether inflation is 5 or 15 per cent but whether it can be relied upon to remain at 5 or 15 per cent. It is most probably the case that the inflation in the 1970s was unpopular because it was unexpected; and in certain countries the fear was that the authorities had either lost the will to control financial policy or had failed to appreciate the inflationary consequences of their behavior. It would have been an entirely different story had the inflation been correctly anticipated.

But this argument may be reversed; unexpected falls in the rate of inflation must also be penalized in the welfare calculus. The basic political objective of stopping inflation in its tracks would only be desirable if society expected it to happen. If they did not, or if inflation came down faster than expected, the welfare consequences would be reflected in excess unemploy-ment and uncertainty. An appropriately designed counter-inflation strategy is therefore one which minimizes the deviations between expected and actual inflation; the speed of the process is largely irrelevant. This requires the government to set out a medium term financial plan so that society can adapt in advance to future changes in the money supply and the size of the budget deficit.

These considerations suggest that the basic modus operandi of macro-economic policy should be for the government to set its cards out on the table for all to see. This will have the effect of minimizing uncertainty which will enable markets to function more efficiently. In the foreign exchange market official intervention would be inappropriate since if the foreign exchange market is already efficient further action by government could only be self-defeating and destabilizing.

Unemployment would converge on its 'natural' rate, but it may be argued that the 'natural' rate is too high. This clearly would be a contradiction in terms since in the absence of microeconomic distortions the 'natural' rate is what society wants it to be, and in this sense it cannot be too high. If the equilibrium level of unemployment is 7% or even higher, there is nothing wrong with this since prevailing unemployment benefits, spouse employ-ment, etc., imply that on average 7% of registered workers desire to be unemployed. Thus, just in the same way as under REH a floating exchange rate will find its appropriate level, so a freely floating labor market will find its own appropriate level of unemployment. Indeed, official attempts to stabilize unemployment at the wrong level would be positively harmful.

In practice, however, microeconomic distortions may prevent the 'natural' rate of unemployment from achieving its socially desirable level. But the appropriate policy response would seem to be to remove these distortions at the grass roots level rather than to rely on macroeconomic policies as the hammer that cracks the proverbial nut. Indeed, it seems worth considering two types of microeconomic constraint. The first concerns the equilibrium level of unemployment itself, while the second concerns the rate at which unemployment returns to its equilibrium level for given disequilibrium conditions. The former shifts the Phillips Curve, while the latter changes its short term slope. In practice, both situations may arise. The Phillips Curve will shift to the right if restrictive practices in labor markets generate mono-psonistic situations. For example, union closed shop agreements will prevent non-union workers from competing for employment so that real wages will stabilize at higher levels of unemployment. The slope of the Phillips Curve will reflect collective bargaining techniques. Ideally, the stronger the feed-back of unemployment onto wage rates, the faster the rate of macroeconomic equilibration. Since many if not most of these constraints are man-made, the authorities should take care that they do not legislate the Phillips Curve out of existence. The same applies to other areas where government controls may slow down adjustment processes or shift the equilibria to which these adjust-ments refer.

In other words, to improve macroeconomic performance, it is to micro-economics that policy makers should look; and all too often they may find that their own regulations have not been too helpful in relation to this objective.

Mathematical notes

The integration of monetary and income-expenditure theory that is a theme in the main text requires widespread application of stock-flow specifications for the structural equations that have been proposed. This means that equations may contain variables in terms of both levels and changes in levels. It is for this reason that it has been necessary to use differential and difference equations to carry the arguments forward.

Baumol's text (*Economic Dynamics* (3rd edition)) may serve as an ideal reference on the use of differential and difference equations in economics. The purpose of this appendix, however, is the limited one of setting out the rudiments that are required for understanding the mathematical dynamics that have been used in the present study. A working knowledge of linear and matrix algebra is assumed.

Differential equations

A static equation in a variable x only contains levels of x, e.g.

$$ax = k \tag{1}$$

A dynamic equation in x will contain both levels and changes in x. For example, if x is a function of time, a first order differential equation would include the first derivative of x with respect to time. In the text we denote this derivative as

$$\frac{dx}{dt} = \dot{x} = Dx \tag{2}$$

The dot denotes that the variable is a derivative with respect to time, while D is a differential operator that tells us to differentiate with respect to t the time dependent variable (or variables that are its multiplicands). The second derivative of x with respect to time would be written as:

$$\frac{d^2x}{dt^2} = \ddot{x} = D^2x \tag{3}$$

and so on.

An example of a first order differential equation is

$$ax + b\dot{x} = k \tag{4}$$

The solution for x from equation (1) is

$$x = k/a \tag{5}$$

but what is the solution for x from equation (4)? To answer this it is necessary to proceed through several stages.

(i) Begin by assuming that $k = 0$ and derive from equation (4) what is called the *auxiliary* or *characteristic* equation

$$a + b\lambda = 0 \tag{6}$$

where λ is the *root* of equation (4). This implies that

$$\lambda = -a/b \tag{7}$$

This root tells us how x varies over time in accordance with equation (4).

(ii) Had there been no constant term ($k = 0$), i.e. if the differential equation had been *homogeneous*, the solution for x would have been

$$x(t) = Ae^{\lambda t} \tag{8}$$

where A is an arbitrary constant. If $\lambda > 0$, x would grow over time. If $\lambda < 0$, x would fall over time until it eventually or asymptotically equalled zero. Figure A-1 illustrates these two possibilities. If $\lambda > 0$, the root is said to be *unstable* because it implies x will grow exponentially. If $\lambda < 0$, the root is said to be *stable* because it implies that x will approach zero exponentially.

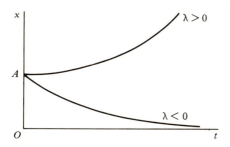

Fig. A-1 First order case: stable and unstable roots.

(iii) If $k \neq 0$, i.e. if the equation is non-homogeneous, it is necessary to find the *particular integral* which is the solution for x when $\dot{x}$ is assumed to be zero. This brings us back to equation (1) in which case the particular integral will be k/a.

(iv) The *general solution* for equation (4) is the sum of the particular integral and equation (8), or

$$x(t) = Ae^{\lambda t} + k/a \qquad (9)$$

If $\lambda < 0$, x will eventually equal k/a.

(v) If, when $t = 0$, $x = x_0$ we may use equation (9) to solve for the arbitrary constant

$$x_0 = A + k/a \qquad (10)$$

in which case equation (9) may be rewritten as

$$x(t) = (x_0 - k/a)e^{\lambda t} + k/a \qquad (11)$$

If k depends on time too the preceding steps would be inadequate. But since in the text we do not complicate the discussion in this way there is no need to describe such solutions here.

We now repeat these five stages for a second order differential equation

$$ax + b\dot{x} + c\ddot{x} = k \qquad (12)$$

(i) The auxiliary equation is

$$a + b\lambda + c\lambda^2 = 0 \qquad (13)$$

i.e. there are two roots. There are

$$\lambda_1 = \frac{-b + \sqrt{(b^2 - 4ac)}}{2c} \qquad (14)$$

$$\lambda_2 = \frac{-b - \sqrt{(b^2 - 4ac)}}{2c} \qquad (15)$$

(ii) In the homogeneous case the solution for x would be

$$x(t) = A_1 e^{\lambda_1 t} + A_2 e^{\lambda_2 t} \qquad (16)$$

The stability conditions are $b/c > 0$ and $ab/c^2 > 0$ in which case $\lambda_1, \lambda_2 < 0$. If $4ac > b^2$ the roots will be complex. Figure A-2 illustrates the four basic possibilities.

Case (a) Stable roots – not complex

Case (b) Unstable roots – not complex

Case (c) Stable roots – complex

Case (d) Unstable roots – complex

Complex roots are oscillatory.

(iii) The particular integral is k/a (setting $\dot{x}$ and $\ddot{x}$ to zero).

(iv) Therefore, the general solution for x is

$$x(t) = A_1 e^{\lambda_1 t} + A_2 e^{\lambda_2 t} + k/a \tag{17}$$

(v) If at $t = 0$ $x = x_0$ and at $t = 1$ $x = x_1$ we may solve for the arbitrary constants. Equation (17) may therefore be rewritten as

$$x(t) = \left[x_0 - (k/a) \frac{x_1 - (k/a)(1 - e^{\lambda_1}) - x_0 e^{\lambda_1}}{e^{\lambda_2} - e^{\lambda_1}} \right] e^{\lambda_1 t} \tag{18}$$

$$+ \left[\frac{x_1 - (k/a)(1 - e^{\lambda_1}) - x_0 e^{\lambda_1}}{e^{\lambda_2} - e^{\lambda_1}} \right] e^{\lambda_2 t} + k/a$$

Notice that if the auxiliary equation is

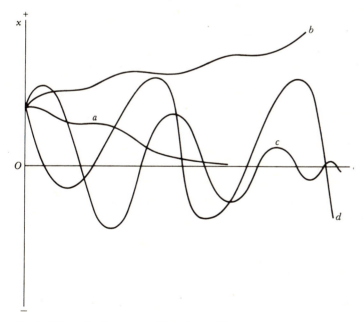

Fig. A–2 Second order case: stable and unstable roots.

$$1 - 2\lambda + \lambda^2 = 0 \tag{19}$$

λ_1 and λ_2 converge on unity.

If we have simultaneous differential equations of the form

$$\left. \begin{aligned} ax + b\dot{x} + cy &= k \qquad \text{(i)} \\ dy + e\dot{y} + fx &= m \qquad \text{(ii)} \end{aligned} \right\} \tag{20}$$

what are the general solutions for y and x? We may write equation (20) using differential operators as:

$$\begin{bmatrix} a + bD & c \\ f & d + eD \end{bmatrix} \begin{bmatrix} x \\ y \end{bmatrix} = \begin{bmatrix} k \\ m \end{bmatrix} \tag{21}$$

for which the determinant is

$$det = beD^2 + (ae + bd)D + ad - fc \tag{22}$$

The solutions for x and y are

$$\left. \begin{aligned} x &= \frac{dk - cm}{det} \qquad \text{(i)} \\ y &= \frac{am - fk}{det} \qquad \text{(ii)} \end{aligned} \right\} \tag{23}$$

or

$$\left. \begin{aligned} be\ddot{x} + (ae + bd)\dot{x} + (ad - fc)x &= dk - cm \qquad \text{(i)} \\ be\ddot{y} + (ae + bd)\dot{y} + (ad - fc)y &= am - fk \qquad \text{(ii)} \end{aligned} \right\} \tag{24}$$

Equations (24) are of the same form as equation (12) and their general solutions may be found as before.

Difference equations

Whereas differential equations are in continuous time, difference equations are in discrete time. Accordingly their solutions will be different but the principles involved are essentially the same. We begin with the case of the first order difference equation in x:

$$ax_t + bx_{t-1} = k \tag{25}$$

(i) The auxiliary equation is written as

$$a\lambda + b = 0 \tag{26}$$

which implies that

$$\lambda = -b/a \tag{27}$$

(ii) Had there been no constant term ($k = 0$), i.e. had the difference equation been homogeneous, the solution for x would have been

$$x(t) = A\lambda^t \tag{28}$$

where A is an arbitrary constant. If $|\lambda| > 1$, x would approach infinity with time. If $|\lambda| < 1$, x would approach zero with time. In this case, if $\lambda < 0$, x would oscillate from one period to the next. Therefore the stability condition is for $|\lambda| < 1$.

(iii) If $k \neq 0$, it is necessary to find the particular integral. In the case of difference equations this is found by dividing k by $a + b$

(iv) The general solution for x is therefore:

$$x(t) = A\lambda^t + k/(a + b) \tag{29}$$

The arbitrary constant may be evaluated as in equations (10) and (11).

The second order difference equation

$$ax_t + bx_{t-1} + cx_{t-2} = k \tag{30}$$

has

$$a\lambda^2 + b\lambda + c = 0 \tag{31}$$

as its auxiliary equation. The roots may be found as before. In this case the particular integral is $k/(a + b + c)$.

If we have simultaneous difference equations

$$\left.\begin{array}{ll} ax_t + bx_{t-1} + cy_t = k & \text{(i)} \\ dy_t + ey_{t-1} + fx_t = m & \text{(ii)} \end{array}\right\} \tag{32}$$

we may rewrite these as

$$\begin{bmatrix} a + bB & c \\ f & d + eB \end{bmatrix} \begin{bmatrix} x \\ y \end{bmatrix} = \begin{bmatrix} k \\ m \end{bmatrix} \tag{33}$$

where B is a backward operator, e.g. $B^i x = x_{t-i}$. Notice that in this case the auxiliary equation is

$$(ad - fc)\lambda^2 + (ae + bd)\lambda + be = 0 \tag{34}$$

Notes to Chapter 1

1   At the annual Labour Party Conference at Blackpool, 28 September 1976.
2   A useful discussion of some of these issues may be found in Budd [1975].
3   For some interesting empirical tests of these issues see Bronfenbrenner [1961].
4   The application of rational expectations to macroeconomics has been reviewed by Poole [1976] and Shiller [1978].
5   Or so we shall call the adaptive and extrapolative hypotheses since they are merely behavioral assertions without any foundations in economic theory itself.
6   See also Sargent and Wallace [1976]. Lucas [1976] discusses the built-in obsolescence in econometric models when policy changes.
7   See Stein (ed.) [1976] for a selection of essays on monetarism.
8   Especially Johnson [1958]. The monetary approach to the balance of payments is expounded in various essays in Frenkel and Johnson (eds.) [1976].
9   We take it for granted that they can when the behavioral theories hold good or when there is disequilibrium in the long term.
10 I have touched on this before in Beenstock [1978, Chapter 3].
11 Although to be fair their academic counterparts may consider this to be a debasement of intellectual standards and rightly or wrongly have refrained from seeking publicity for their views.
12 A fuller discussion may be found in Chapter 2.
13 This is reminiscent of the age-old debate about the measurement of capital. Legend has it that when Joan Robinson asked Bob Solow the time, he replied 'Time, now there's a difficult concept! But really it is 10.30.'
14 To some extent this overlaps with some previous efforts in Beenstock [1978, Chapter 3]. However, there our concern was essentially with the balance of payments to the virtual exclusion of domestic considerations.
15 The issues raised in this exposition will be of relevance to the current political debate about commodity price stabilization.

Notes to Chapter 2

1   See Kuhn [1962]. It is interesting to note that Mehta [1977] has reviewed the Keynesian revolution in the light of Kuhn's theories and identifies the *Treatise* rather than the *General Theory* as the critical turning of the tide.
2   Letter to George Bernard Shaw dated 1 January 1935.
3   I.e. that as consumption becomes saturated investment opportunities diminish.
4   Mehta [1977] cites other writers such as Foster and Catchings who wrote a series of books together, and Abbati. These authors did much to anticipate Keynes, especially regarding the dichotomy between savings and investment.

5   We use this term with caution. It does not imply any significant intellectual homo-
    geneity or any conscious effort by those concerned to revive pre-classical ideas,
    which in any case were not homogeneous. It refers to a trend in thought that ceased
    with the arrival of the classics.

6   House of Commons Debates 15 April 1929, p. 54.

7   It is ironical that the 'Treasury View' might have been right, at least in theory, after
    all, since it is consistent with the so-called crowding-out hypothesis that has been
    articulated in recent years.

8   Ohlin [1977] has argued that in Sweden macroeconomic theory was anticipating a
    number of Keynesian developments, some of which Keynes might have even known.

9   We abstract from the activist recommendation of the Macmillan Report (1931)
    since so much of it reflects the views of Keynes who was himself a very active
    member of the committee.

10 Howson and Winch [1977] provide a partial history of Keynes' operations during
    this period which underlines how determined and perhaps even unscrupulous
    Keynes could be in making his views felt.

11 In these respects the thesis that Patinkin [1976] has proposed is endorsed and
    developed further while the thesis proposed by Minsky [1975] is rejected.

12 Patinkin [1976, pp. 112-13] attributes this to 'a vestigial remnant of a view which
    Keynes actually held at an early stage of his work on the General Theory'. But his
    change of heart occurs within a space of no more than 26 pages.

13 To add to the confusion the real balance effect is explicitly recognized in the
    Treatise on Money.

14 The relationship between wealth and real balance effects is discussed in greater
    detail in the next chapter.

15 Moreover, recent research in the UK suggests that the real balance effect and wealth
    effects more generally exert a powerful influence on aggregate demand. See e.g.
    Minford, Brech and Matthews [1978] and Beenstock and Burns ([1979a].

16 Where indeed exchange rate expectations are assumed to be formed rationally in
    the light of the purchasing power parity model.

17 Keynes [1937] in response to Viner [1936].

18 *Collected Writings*, Vol. XIV.

19 See also the discussion on [1936, p. 150] and Keynes [1937].

20 Yet, Patinkin [1976, p. 110] does not consider that this would have changed
    Keynes' basic conclusions.

21 Patinkin [1966, pp. 643-4] has already commented on the looseness with which
    Keynes referred to 'equilibrium'. See also Patinkin [1976, pp. 100-1] for a dis-
    cussion of Marshall's influence on Keynes in this context.

22 Nevertheless, Minsky's arguments about the role of finance in the trade cycle add
    substantially to our knowledge of macrodynamics, but are an insufficient basis for
    rejecting the notion of stable equilibria altogether.

23 See Hirsch [1977].

24 Indeed, for much of the time Keynes unfairly personifies Pigou as the ogre of
    classical economics.

25 The *Collected Writings*, Vol. XIV, p. 2.

26 Samuelson [1947, p. 156] raises questions about Keynes' mathematical competence
    and ability.

27 The *Collected Writings*, Vol. XIV, p. 537. See also p. 555.

28 Incidentally, Harrod indicates in these letters that his perception of the Keynesian
    revolution was similar to Clower's, and he wanted Keynes to synthesize the income-

expenditure logic into the Walrasian market-clearing logic. His view was that Keynes was goint out of his way to polarize rather than to synthesize.

29   The *Collected Writings*, Vol. XIII, p. 634.
30   op. cit., p. 548.
31   The *Collected Writings*, Vol. XIV, p. 25.

Notes to Chapter 3

1   Recent years have witnessed considerable activity in this area, e.g. Grandmont and Younes [1973], Starr [1972] and Ostroy [1973].
2   In other words we disagree with Weintraub's [1977] judgment that sensible policy issues cannot be discussed until these micro problems have been more satisfactorily resolved.
3   This section reflects the discussion in Clower [1969, pp. 7-21].
4   Henceforth, variables are expressed as logarithms unless otherwise stated. This assists in the linear presentation of the models so that analytical solutions may be obtained. Parameters thus become elasticities.
5   Throughout this study $\bar{Y}$ is considered as the full-employment level of output.
6   Related issues are discussed in Blinder and Solow [1973, 1976] and Buiter (1977).
7   See e.g. Maki and Spindler [1975].
8   See e.g. Phelps (ed.) [1970].
9   In Chapter 7, where expectations are discussed explicitly, equation (3-22) is written as

$$\dot{W} = n(L - L^*) + P^e - P$$

where P^e is the expected price level. See equation (7-33).
10   Subject to the dynamic considerations discussed in Chapter 7.
11   A more detailed discussion of these issues which integrates forward exchange markets into the analysis may be found in Beenstock [1978, chapters 2 and 3].
12   For simplicity we abstract from interest payments and receipts across the balance of payments. These would be equal to $B_w r_w - B_f r$.
13   Substituting equations (3-58) and (3-40) into equation (3-41) and solving for P_x.
14   In what follows constant terms are ignored.
15   These results are linear approximations which reflect the linearization assumptions that have been made in the interests of expositional simplicity.

Notes to Chapter 4

1   I would like to thank Steven Bell, Heather Morley, Tony Gosling and Peter Warburton for their research assistance in preparing this section.
2   To obtain the steady-state solution, terms in first differences are set to zero and the result is solved for Log$P$. Thus we have

$$0 = 0.65537 - 0.0838761 \log \frac{P}{M} - 0.15671 \log GDP + 0.00069117 TIME$$

which solves for log$P$ as indicated in equation (4-3).
3   Work is in an advanced stage at the London Business School on this project. Preliminary results are reported in Beenstock and Burns [1979b].
4   A discussion of these issues may be found in Beenstock [1977].
5   More specifically, P_d is the price index for goods other than exportables and energy. In this sense it is an index of the domestic price level. Since P_x depends on P_d, P will be correlated with P_d.

6   Since $w > 0$. In practice e_1 will be insufficiently large to make β_1 negative in equation (3-66 (i)).
7   Recalling from equation (3-60 (i)) that $0 < \alpha_1 < 1$ and that $\beta_4 < 0$ from equation (3-66 (iv)).

Notes to Chapter 5

1   Assuming as before that $\beta_1 > 0$.
2   From equation (3-66 (i)) $f_1 + f_2 - \beta_1 = f_2(1 - \alpha_1) + \alpha_1 (1 - e_1)$. Since $0 \leqslant \alpha \leqslant 1$ it follows that the sign depends upon the relative values of the import (f_2) and export (e_1) price elasticities of demand.
3   For example Hutton and Minford [1975] estimate $e_1 = 1.6$ in the case of UK manufactured exports while Beenstock and Minford [1976] report comparable econometric estimates for a range of industrial countries.
4   Technically speaking this restriction does not apply to forward exchange policies which, however, we do not discuss here. A theoretical and empirical review of such policies may be found in Beenstock [1978].
5   Of course if public expenditure increases consumption, $\bar{Y}$ will fall since the capital stock will be lower and inflationary pressures will be greater. However, in this essay we do not explore the dynamic effects of consumption and investment on the macroeconomy. Bacon and Eltis [1978] have reviewed the effects of public expenditure on the UK economy.
6   A linear approximation of $yp(t + v)$ where y, p, etc., are antilogarithms of Y, P, etc.

Notes to Chapter 6

1   Although at the time, in the 1950s and early 1960s, the interactions between serially correlated errors, lagged endogenous variables and statistical efficiency were not as yet properly understood.
2   Useful but no doubt by now obsolescent surveys may be found in Poole [1976] and Shiller [1978]. No attempt is made at such a survey here.
3   See e.g. Sargent and Wallace [1976], Fischer [1977], McCallum [1977], Minford [1978].
4   See e.g. Sargent [1973] on inflationary expectations, Modigliani and Shiller [1973] on interest rates, McCallum [1977] and Beenstock [1978] on exchange rate expectations.
5   See Bhagwati (ed.) [1977].
6   In the present context P is expressed as a deviation from its long run equilibrium value $\bar{P}$. Thus

$$P = \frac{p - \bar{P}}{\bar{P}}$$

where p is the observed price and $\bar{P}$ reflects the intersection of D and S when $\Delta Z = 0$.
7   Since the product of the two roots is

$$\frac{(2e + a + b) + ((2e + a + b)^2 - 4e^2)^{1/2}}{2e} \times \frac{(2e + a + b) - ((2e + a + b)^2 - 4e^2)^{1/2}}{2e}$$

$$= \frac{4e^2}{4e^2} = 1$$

This issue is discussed more thoroughly below.

8   For expositional simplicity we abstract from storage, transactions costs, etc.

9   The intuitive explanation for this is that overshooting reflects speculators' uncertainty and risk aversion. Hesitation may result in over-shooting and e varies mainly with the degree of hesitation.

10 See e.g. Fama [1970].

11 Although in general the optimal control function would tend to depend on an entire history of prices.

Notes to Chapter 7

1   We shall return to this issue in the next chapter.

2   See Appendix 1.

3   Money and goods. See pages 56–63.

4   See the discussion in Chapter 1 for a critique of this approach. Ball et al. [1978] raise important practical objections to the formal optimization of macroeconomic policy.

5   As evidenced, for example, by equations (3–67) and (3–69).

6   See, for example, the discussion on page 60.

7   See the discussion on pages 83.

8   For example, equation (6–9).

9   An example of this is provided on page 152.

10 This, of course, is the theme in many standard references on microeconomic policy formation. See e.g. Musgrave and Musgrave [1976].

11 See the discussion associated with fig. 6–4.

12 See the appendix for details of these differences.

13 I.e. the analogue of fig. 3–3, but assuming rational expectations of inflation.

14 For example, Sargent and Wallace [1975] and Rutledge [1974] apply the chain-rule procedure.

15 Zero rather than -∞ since P cannot be negative.

16 For example if all the parameters in the model equal unity, $\lambda_1 = 0.585$ and $\lambda_2 = 3.415$.

17 Equation (7–29) is the analogue of equation (6–14).

18 I have discussed these issues elsewhere in Beenstock [1978, Chapter 4]. See also Dornbusch [1976] and Barro [1978].

19 Likewise, one may consider the case where in a single market one group of speculators were rational while the other group were extrapolators.

20 Described on pages 83–91.

21 In the interest of economy the detailed analysis is not repeated here. The reader is advised to refer to the discussion in Chapter 3.

22 I.e., $Y, P_d, r, P_{xw}, Y_w, P_m, r_w$.

23 Definitions of parameters are given in equations (3–66).

24 See the discussion on pages 144.

25 Practical issues will be discussed in Chapter 8.

26 See, e.g., the evidence cited in Beenstock and Minford [1976] and Junz and Rhomberg [1973].

27 A formal analysis of which may be found in Britton [1970].

28 A practical illustration of these principles based on an estimated econometric model of the foreign exchange market may be found in Bell and Beenstock [1979].

29 We adopt this procedure here since, in this more complicated case, $_t S_{t+1}^e$ cannot be expressed as a simple first order process as in equation (7–56).

30 There are $H + 1$ roots since equation (7-64) contains terms in $S_t, \ldots, S_{t - (H + 1)}$

31 This of course may happen only if $H > 0$.

32 See equation (3-64) for the determination of I and equation (3-40) for the determination of X_w^d. Primed coefficients are used to reflect the slight changes in the specification, i.e. P_d and P_x are not disaggregated.

33 Previously incorporated in J.

34 Thus $BP = P_{t-1}$, $B^{-1} P = P_{t+1}$.

35 As before, some of the arbitrary constants may be zero on account of boundary conditions for P and S.

36 The bivariate analogue of equation (7-28).

37 This case is also discussed in Calvo and Rodriguez [1977].

Notes to Chapter 8

1 Page 3.

2 In Chapter 6 it was explained how risk aversion and the variance of expectations related in terms of speculative elasticities. See pages 146–7.

3 Indeed, in RE models optimal policy is generally time-inconsistent in the sense that the optimal policy over the horizon $0, T = 0, K + K + 1, T$ is not the same as the optimal policy over the sub-horizons $0, K$ and $K + 1, T$. In other words, it generally pays the authorities to renege on their plans as argued by Holly and Zarrop (1979). On the other hand, the implied policy of persistent expectations frustration is hardly a viable form of political economy and would erode government credibility generally.

Almon, S. [1965], 'The Distributed Lag Between Capital Appropriations and Expenditures', *Econometrica*, 33 (January).

Bacon, R. and W. Eltis [1978], *Britain's Economic Problem: Too Few Producers*, 2nd edn, St Martin's Press, New York.

Ball, R. J. et al. [1978], *The Report of the Committee on Policy Optimization*, Her Majesty's Stationery Office, London, Cmnd 7148 (March).

–, T. Burns and P. Warburton [1980], 'An Exercise in International Monetarism' in Paul Ormerod (ed.) *Economic Modelling*, Heinemann, London.

Barro, R. J. [1976], 'Rational Expectations and the Role of Monetary Policy', *Journal of Monetary Economics*, 2 (January).

– [1978], 'A Stochastic Equilibrium Model of an Open Economy under Flexible Exchange Rates', *Quarterly Journal of Economics*, 92 (February).

– and S. Fischer [1976], 'Recent Developments in Monetary Theory', *Journal of Monetary Economics*, 2 (April).

– and H. Grossman [1976], *Money, Employment and Inflation*, Cambridge University Press.

Baumol, W. J. [1970], *Economic Dynamics*, 3rd edn, Macmillan, New York.

Beenstock, M. [1977], 'The Depletion of UK Oil Resources', *Energy: The International Journal* (September).

– [1978], *The Foreign Exchanges: Theory, Modelling and Policy*, Macmillan, London.

– and T. Burns [1979a]. 'Exchange Rate Objectives and Macroeconomic Adjustment in the UK', in R. Major (ed.) *Britain's Trade and Exchange Rate Policy*, Heinemann, London.

– and T. Burns [1979b]. 'An Aggregate Monetary Model of the UK Economy', London Business School mimeo.

– and J. A. Longbottom [1980], 'Inflation and Portfolio Balance in the UK', mimeo, London Business School.

– and A. P. L. Minford [1976], 'A Quarterly Econometric Model of World Trade and Prices, 1955-1971', in M. Parkin and G. Zis (eds.), *Inflation in Open Economies*, Manchester University Press and University of Toronto Press.

Bell, S. and M. Beenstock [1980], 'An Application of Rational Expectations to the UK Foreign Exchange Market', in D. Currie and W. Peters (eds.) *Studies in Contemporary Economic Analysis II*, Croom Helm.

Beveridge, W. H. [1909], *Unemployment, a Problem of Industry*, Longmans, Green and Company, London.

Bhagwati, J. N. (ed.) [1977], *The New International Economic Order: The North – South Debate*, The MIT Press, Cambridge, Mass. and London.

Blinder, A. S. and R. M. Solow [1973], 'Does Fiscal Policy Matter?', *Journal of Public Economics*, 2 (November).

– [1976], 'Does Fiscal Policy Still Matter?', *Journal of Monetary Economics*, 2 (November).

Box, G. E. P. and G. M. Jenkins [1970], *Time Series Analysis: Forecasting and Control*, Holden-Day, San Francisco.

Britton, A. J. C. [1970], 'The Dynamic Stability of the Foreign Exchange Market', *Economic Journal*, **80** (March).

Bronfenbrenner, M. [1961], 'Statistical Tests of Rival Monetary Rules', *Journal of Political Economy*, **69** (February).

Budd, A. P. [1975], 'The Debate on Fine-Tuning: The Basic Issues', *National Institute Economic Review* (November).

Buiter, W. H. [1977], 'Crowding Out and the Effectiveness of Fiscal Policy', *Journal of Public Economics*, 3 (July).

Calvo, G. A. and C. A. Rodriguez [1977], 'A Model of Exchange Rate Determination under Currency Substitution and Rational Expectations', *Journal of Political Economy*, **85** (June).

Clower, R. W. [1966], 'The Keynesian Counterrevolution: A Theoretical Appraisal', Chapter 5 in *The Theory of Interest Rates*, F. H. Hahn and F. P. R. Brechling (eds.), Macmillan, London.

– (ed.) [1969], *Monetary Theory: Selected Readings*, Penguin Books, England.

Davenport, H. J. [1906], *Outlines of Economic Theory*, Macmillan, New York.

– [1913], *Economics of Enterprise*, Macmillan, New York.

Davidson, J. E. H. et al. [1978], 'Econometric Modelling of Aggregate Time-Series Relationship between Consumers' Expenditure and Income in the United Kingdom', *Economic Journal*, **88** (December).

Dornbusch, R. [1976], 'Expectations and Exchange Rate Dynamics', *Journal of Political Economy*, **84** (December).

Eshag, E. [1963], *From Marshall to Keynes: An Essay on the Monetary Theory of the Cambridge School*, Blackwell, Oxford.

Fama, E. F. [1970], 'Efficient Capital Markets: A Review of Theory and Empirical Work', *Journal of Finance*, 25 (May).

Fischer, S. [1977], 'Long Term Contracts, Rational Expectations and the Optimal Money Supply Rule', *Journal of Political Economy*, **85** (February).

Foxwell, H. S. [1886], *Irregularities of Employment and Fluctuations of Prices*, Cooperative Printing House, Edinburgh.

Frenkel, J. and H. G. Johnson (eds.) [1976], *The Monetary Approach to the Balance of Payments*, George Allen and Unwin, London.

Friedman, M. [1959], *A Program for Monetary Stability*, Fordham University Press, New York.

– [1968], 'The Role of Monetary Policy', *American Economic Review* (March).

Grandmont, J. M. and Y. Younes [1973], 'On the Role of Money and the Existence of a Monetary Equilibrium', *Review of Economic Studies*, 39 (July).

Gurley, J. G. and E. S. Shaw [1960], *Money in a Theory of Finance*, Brookings Institute, Washington, DC.

Harris, J. and M. P. Todaro [1970], 'Migration, Unemployment and Development: A Two Sector Analysis', *American Economic Review*, **60** (March).

Harrod, R. F. [1951], *The Life of John Maynard Keynes*, Macmillan, London.

Hirsch, F. [1977], *The Social Limits to Growth*, Harvard University Press, Cambridge.

Holly, S and Zarrop M. [1979], 'On Optimality and Time Consistency when Expectations are Rational', mimeo, London Business School.

Howson, S. and D. Winch [1977], *The Economic Advisory Council, 1930–1939*, Cambridge University Press.

Hutchison, T. W. [1953], *A Review of Economic Doctrines, 1970–1979*, Clarendon Press, Oxford.

– [1968], *Economics and Economic Policy in Britain, 1946–1966*, George, Allen and Unwin, London.

Hutton, J. P. and A. P. L. Minford [1975], 'A Model of UK Manufactured Exports and Export Prices', Government Economic Service Occasional Papers, No. 11, HMSO, London.

Johannsen, N. [1908], *A Neglected Point in Connection with Crisis*, New York.

Johnson, E. [1977], 'Keynes as a Literary Craftsman' in D. Patinkin and J. Clark Leith (eds.), *Keynes, Cambridge and the General Theory*, Macmillan, London.

Johnson, H. G. [1958], 'Towards a General Theory of the Balance of Payments', in *International Trade and Economic Growth*; George Allen and Unwin, London.

— [1961], 'The General Theory after Twenty-Five Years', *American Economic Review*, 51 (May).

— [1972], 'The Monetary Approach to Balance of Payments Theory', Chapter 11 in *International Trade and Money*, M. B. Connolly and A. K. Swoboda (eds.), George Allen and Unwin, London.

— [1975], 'Keynes and British Economics', Chapter 12 in *Essays on John Maynard Keynes*, M. Keynes (ed.), Cambridge University Press.

Jorgenson, D. [1963], 'Capital Theory and Investment Behavior', American Economic Review, 53 (May).

Junz, H. and R. Rhomberg [1973], 'Price Competitiveness in Export Trade among Industrial Countries', *American Economic Review*, 63 (May).

Keynes, J. M. [1921], *A Treatise on Probability*, Macmillan, London.

— [1936], *The General Theory of Employment, Interest and Money*, Macmillan, London.

— [1937], 'The General Theory of Employment', *Quarterly Journal of Economics*, 51 (February).

— [1971], *Collected Writings*, Macmillan, London.

Kuhn, T. S. [1962], *The Structure of Scientific Revolutions*, University of Chicago Press.

Kyle, J. F. [1976], *The Balance of Payments in a Monetary Economy*, Princeton University Press, Princeton, NJ.

Leijonhufvud, A. [1968], *Keynesian Economics and the Economics of Keynes*, Oxford University Press.

Little, I. M. and J. Mirrlees [1977], *Project Appraisal and Planning in Developing Countries*, Heinemann, London.

Livesey, D. A. [1971], 'Optimizing Short-Term Economic Policy', *Economic Journal*, 81 (September).

Lucas, R. E. [1972], 'Econometric Testing of the Natural Rate Hypothesis' in O. Eckstein (ed.), *The Econometrics of Price Determination Conference*, Board of Governors of the Federal Reserve System, Washington DC.

— [1976], 'Econometric Policy Evaluation: A Critique', *Journal of Monetary Economics*, 1 (September).

— and L. A. Rapping [1969], 'Real Wages, Employment and Inflation', *Journal of Political Economy*, 77 (September/October).

McCallum, B. T. [1977], 'Price Level Stickiness and the Feasibility of Monetary Stabilization Policy with Rational Expectations', *Journal of Political Economy*, 85 (June).

— [1978a], 'Dating, Discounting and the Robustness of the Lucas-Sargent Proposition', *Journal of Monetary Economics*, 4 (January).

— [1978b], 'Price Level Adjustments and the Rational Expectations Approach to Macroeconomic Stabilization Policy', *Journal of Money Credit and Banking*, 10 (November).

— and J. K. Whitaker [1979], 'The Effectiveness of Fiscal Feedback Rules and Automatic Stabilizers under Rational Expectations', *Journal of Monetary Economics*, 5 (May).

McCracken, P. et al. [1977], *Towards Full Employment and Price Stability*, OECD, Paris.

Maki, D. and Z. A. Spindler [1975], 'The Effect of Unemployment Compensation on the Rate of Unemployment in Great Britain', *Oxford Economic Papers*, 27 (November).

Malinvaud, E. [1977], *The Theory of Unemployment Reconsidered*, Basil Blackwell, Oxford.

Mehta, G. [1977], *The Structure of the Keynesian Revolution*, Martin Robinson & Co., London.

Minford, A. P. L. [1978], *Substitution Effects, Speculation and Exchange Rate Stability*, North Holland, Amsterdam.

— [1979], 'A Rational Expectations Model of the UK under Fixed and Floating Exchange Rates', Dept of Economics, University of Liverpool.

— M. Brech and K. Matthews [1978], 'Speculation and Portfolio Balance – A Model of UK under Floating Exchange Rates', University of Liverpool.

— and D. Peel [1978], 'The Role of Monetary Stabilization Policy under Rational Expectations', University of Liverpool.

Minsky, H. P. [1975], *John Maynard Keynes*, Columbia University Press.

Modigliani, F. and R. J. Shiller [1973], 'Inflation, Rational Expectations and the Term Structure of Interest Rates', *Econometrica*, 40 (February).

— and R. Sutch [1966], 'Innovations in Interest Rate Policy', *American Economic Review*, 56 (May).

Mummery, A. F. and J. A. Hobson [1889], *The Physiology of Industry*, London.

Musgrave, R. A. and P. B. Musgrave [1976], *Public Finance in Theory and Practice* (2nd Edition), McGraw-Hill, New York.

Muth, J. F. [1961], 'Rational Expectations and the Theory of Price Movements', *Econometrica*, 29 (July).

Nerlove, M. [1958], 'Adaptive Expectations and Cobweb Phenomena', *Quarterly Journal of Economics*, 72 (May).

Ohlin, B. [1977], 'Some Comments on Keynesianism and the Swedish Theory of Expansion before 1935', in D. Patinkin and J. Clark Leith (eds.), *Keynes, Cambridge and the General Theory*, Macmillan, London.

Ostroy, J. [1973], 'The Informational Efficiency of Monetary Exchange', *American Economic Review*, 53 (September).

Patinkin, D. [1966], *Money, Interest and Prices* (second edition), Harper and Row, New York, Evanston and London.

— [1976], *Keynes' Monetary Thought: A Study of its Development*, Duke University Press, Durham, NC.

— and J. Clark Leith (eds.) [1977], *Keynes, Cambridge and the General Theory*, Macmillan, London.

Pesek, B. P. and T. R. Saving [1967], *Money, Wealth, and Economic Theory*, The Macmillan Company, New York.

Phelps, E. S. (ed.) [1970], *Microfoundations of Employment and Inflation Theory*, Norton, New York.

— and J. B. Taylor [1977], 'Stabilizing Powers of Monetary Policy under Rational Expectations', *Journal of Political Economy*, 85 (February).

Pigou, A. C. [1908], 'Economic Science in Relation to Practice', Inaugural Lecture, Cambridge University.

Pindyck, R. S. [1973], *Optimal Planning for Economic Stabilization: The Application of Control Theory to Stabilization Policy*, North Holland Publishing Company, Amsterdam.

Poole, W. [1976], 'Rational Expectations in the Macro Model', *Brookings Papers on Economic Activity*, No. 2.

Robertson, J. M. [1892] *The Fallacy of Saving: A Study in Economics*, London.

Robinson, J. [1975], 'What has become of the Keynesian Revolution?', Chapter 13 in *Essays on John Maynard Keynes*, M. Keynes (ed.), Cambridge University Press.

Rutledge, J. [1974], *A Monetarist Theory of Inflationary Expectations*, Lexington Books, Lexington.

Samuelson, P. A. [1946], 'Lord Keynes and the General Theory', *Econometrica*, 14 (July).

— [1947], 'The General Theory', Chapter 13 in S. E. Harris (ed.), *The New Economics*, Alfred A. Knopf, New York.

Sargent, T. J. [1973], 'Rational Expectations, the Real Rate of Interest and the Natural Rate of Unemployment', *Brookings Papers on Economic Activity*, No. 2.

Sargent, T. J. and N. Wallace [1975], 'Rational Expectations, the Optimal Monetary Instrument and the Optimal Money Supply Rate', *Journal of Political Economy*, 83 (April).

— [1976], 'Rational Expectations and the Theory of Economic Policy', *Journal of Monetary Economics*, 2 (April).

Shiller, R. J. [1978], 'Rational Expectations and the Dynamic Structure of Macroeconomic Models', *Journal of Monetary Economics*, 4 (January).

Slutsky, E. [1937], 'The Summation of Random Causes as the Source of Cyclical Processes', *Econometrica*, 5 (April).

Starr, R. [1972], 'Exchange in Barter and Monetary Economies', *Quarterly Journal of Economics*, 86 (May).

Stein, J. (ed.) [1976], *Monetarism*, North Holland, Amsterdam.

Summers, R. [1967], 'A Peek at the Trade-off Relationship between Expected Return and Risk', *Quarterly Journal of Economics*, 81 (August).

Tinbergen, J. [1956], *Economic Policy: Principles and Design*, North Holland Publishing Company, Amsterdam.

Tobin, J. [1958], 'Liquidity Preference as Behaviour Towards Risk', *Review of Economic Studies* (February).

Viner, J. [1936], 'Mr. Keynes on the Causes of Unemployment', *Quarterly Journal of Economics*, 51 (November).

Weintraub, E. R. [1977], 'The Microfoundations of Macroeconomics: A Critical Survey', *Journal of Economic Literature*, 15 (March).

— [1979], *Microfoundations: The Compatibility of Microeconomics and Macroeconomics*. Cambridge University Press.

Wicksteed, P. H. [1910], *The Common Sense of Political Economy*, London.

INDEX